CRIMINAL JUSTICE, LAW ENFORCEMENT AND CORRECTIONS

CRIMINAL JUSTICE ISSUES IN THE UNITED STATES

CRIMINAL JUSTICE, LAW ENFORCEMENT AND CORRECTIONS

Additional books in this series can be found on Nova's website under the Series tab.

Additional e-books in this series can be found on Nova's website under the e-books tab.

CRIMINAL JUSTICE, LAW ENFORCEMENT AND CORRECTIONS

CRIMINAL JUSTICE ISSUES IN THE UNITED STATES

JAVIER PLAISANCE

New York

Library of Congress Cataloging-in-Publication Data

ISBN: 978-1-53613-819-1

Published by Nova Science Publishers, Inc. † New York

Contents

PREFACE

The CRS Reports that comprise this book examines criminal justice issues we are currently facing in the United States. The first chapter examines mental incompetency and firearms ineligibility, and amendments to acts such as the Restoring Americans' Healthcare Freedom Reconciliation Act, which were initiated after the mass shootings in San Bernardino in December 2015 and in Orlando in June 2016. The next report examines how domestic terrorism, hate crime and homegrown violent extremism relate (and differ) from one another and current trends. Additional reports include an overview on human trafficking trends, background, federal programs and issues for Congress on missing adults (age 18 and older). The Federal Bureau of Investigation (FBI) reported that as of December 31, 2016, approximately 54,000 cases were pending. Finally, as a general rule, federal judges must impose a minimum term of imprisonment upon defendants convicted of various controlled substance (drug) offenses and drug-related offenses. The severity of those sentences depends primarily upon the nature and amount of drugs involved, the defendant's prior criminal record, any resulting injuries or death, and in the case of the related firearms offenses, the manner in which the firearm was used. This last chapter revisits the mandatory minimum sentencing of federal drug offenses and offenders in the United States.

Chapter 1

GUN CONTROL, MENTAL INCOMPETENCY, AND SOCIAL SECURITY ADMINISTRATION FINAL RULE*

William J. Krouse[1], Scott D. Szymendera[2] and William R. Morton[3]
[1]Specialist in Domestic Security and Crime Policy
[2]Analyst in Disability Policy
[3]Analyst in Income Security

SUMMARY

On February 2, 2017, the House of Representatives passed a Congressional Review Act disapproval resolution (H.J.Res. 40) to overturn a final rule promulgated by the Social Security Administration (SSA) regarding implementation of firearms restrictions for certain persons. The SSA final rule is to implement provisions of the NICS Improvement Amendments Act of 2007 (NIAA; P.L. 110-180) on

* This is an edited, reformatted and augmented version of "Gun Control, Mental Incompetency, and Social Security Administration Final Rule" by William J. Krouse, Scott D. Szymendera and William R. Morton that was originally published by the Congressional Research Service on February 13, 2017.

reporting requirements for any federal agency holding records on persons prohibited from possessing firearms. NIAA mandates that agencies must share those records with the Federal Bureau of Investigation (FBI) for inclusion in a computer index accessible to the National Instant Criminal Background Check System (NICS). As described in this report, some of these prohibiting records are based upon findings of "mental incompetency" made during certain federal benefits claims processes administered by the Department of Veterans Affairs (VA) since 1998 and the SSA beginning in December 2017.

If enacted, the disapproval joint resolution would not allow the SSA final rule to take effect. The joint resolution would also bar the SSA from promulgating any rule in the future that would be "substantially the same" as the disapproved rule unless the agency received a new statutory authorization to do so. On January 30, 2017, Senator Charles Grassley introduced a similar disapproval resolution (S.J.Res. 14). The matter awaits Senate consideration.

Activated by the FBI, NICS is a national computer network that allows federally licensed gun dealers to initiate a background check through either the FBI or a state or local authority, before transferring a firearm to an unlicensed, private person. Under federal law, persons who are "adjudicated as a mental defective" are ineligible to ship, transport, receive, or possess firearms or ammunition. In 1998, the Bureau of Alcohol, Tobacco, Firearms and Explosives promulgated a rule that defined this term to include any individual that a court, board, commission, or other lawful authority has made a determination that—as a result of marked subnormal intelligence, mental illness, incompetency, condition or disease—he or she is a person who:

- is a danger to himself or others;
- lacks the mental capacity to contract or manage his affairs;
- is found insane by a court in a criminal case; or
- is found incompetent to stand trial, or not guilty by reason of lack of moral responsibility.

Since 1998, the Department of Veterans Affairs has referred the name of any beneficiary determined to be incompetent—because he or she lacks the mental capacity to contract or manage their own affairs due to injury or disease—to the FBI for inclusion in the NICS index pursuant to the Brady Handgun Violence Prevention Act, 1993 (Brady Act; P.L. 103-159). Under NIAA, since 2007, the VA must inform any benefits claimant that such determinations could lead to a loss of his or her firearms rights and privileges. But, NIAA also requires any federal authority that provides prohibiting mental health records to the FBI for inclusion in the NICS index to establish an administrative process, by which prohibited beneficiaries may petition to have those rights and privileges restored.

Pursuant to both the Brady Act and NIAA, the SSA final rule specifies the conditions under which individuals are to be reported for inclusion in the NICS index as Social Security or SSI disability beneficiaries who are too mentally incompetent to be trusted with firearms or ammunition. The rule also outlines SSA's process for notifying affected individuals as well as an administrative appeals process under which such individuals may request relief from the federal firearms prohibitions. The final rule became effective on January 18, 2017; however, compliance is not required until December 19, 2017.

INTRODUCTION

On February 2, 2017, the House of Representatives passed a Congressional Review Act disapproval resolution (H.J.Res. 40) to overturn a final rule promulgated by the Social Security Administration (SSA) regarding implementation of firearms restrictions for certain persons.[1] The House joint resolution passed by recorded vote: 235-180 (Roll no. 77). If enacted, this disapproval resolution would not allow the SSA final rule to take effect. The joint resolution would also bar the SSA from promulgating any rule in the future that would be "substantially the same" as the disapproved rule unless the agency received a new statutory authorization to do so. On January 30, 2017, Senator Charles Grassley introduced a similar disapproval resolution (S.J.Res. 14). Both disapproval resolutions await Senate consideration.

The SSA final rule is to implement provisions of the NICS Improvement Amendments Act of 2007 (NIAA) on reporting requirements for any federal agency holding records on persons prohibited from possessing firearms.[2] NIAA mandates that agencies must share those records with the Federal Bureau of Investigation (FBI) for inclusion in a

[1] For further information, see CRS Report R43992, *The Congressional Review Act (CRA): Frequently Asked Questions*, by Maeve P. Carey and Christopher M. Davis. Also, see Social Security Administration, "Implementation of the NICS Improvement Amendments Act of 2007," 81 *Federal Register* 91702-91715, December 19, 2016.

[2] P.L. 110-180, January 8, 2008; 121 Stat. 2559.

computer index accessible to the National Instant Criminal Background Check System (NICS). As described below, some of these prohibiting records are based upon findings of "mental incompetency" made during certain federal benefits claims processes administered by the Department of Veterans Affairs (VA) since 1998 and the SSA beginning in December 2017.[3]

BRADY ACT, NICS, AND FIREARMS INELIGIBILITY

As amended by the Brady Handgun Violence Prevention Act, 1993 (Brady Act), the Gun Control Act of 1968 (GCA) requires background checks to be completed for all unlicensed persons seeking to obtain firearms from federally licensed gun dealers (otherwise referred to as federal firearms licensees, or FFLs).[4]

Pursuant to the Brady Act, the FBI activated NICS on November 30, 1998. This national computer network allows FFLs to initiate a

---

[3] The SSA final rule reflects gun control initiatives pursued by President Barack Obama in January 2013 in response to the December 2012 Newtown mass shooting. The SSA rule took several years to develop. Alan Zarembro, "Move Would Extend Gun Checks: Obama Administration Pushes to Include Certain Beneficiaries of Social Security in National Database," *Los Angeles Times*, July 18, 2015, p. A1. See also White House, *FACT SHEET: New Executive Actions to Reduce Gun Violence and Make Our Communities Safer*, January 4, 2016, https://obamawhitehouse.archives.gov/the-press-office/2016/01/04/fact-sheet-new-executiveactions-reduce-gun-violence-and-make-our; White House, *Memorandum for Heads of Executive Departments and Agencies on Improving Availability of Relevant Executive Brand Records to the National Instant Criminal Background Check System*, January 16, 2013, https://obamawhitehouse.archives.gov/the-press-office/2013/01/16/presidentialmemorandum-improving-availability-relevant-executive-branch; and White House, *Now Is the Time: The President's Plan to Protect Our Children and Our Communities by Reducing Gun Violence*, January 16, 2013, http://www.wh.gov/now-is-the-time.

[4] P.L. 103-159, November 30, 1993, 107 Stat. 1536. Congress passed the Brady Act after nearly six years of sometimes contentious debate. As originally introduced in the 100th Congress, the Brady bill (H.R. 975 and S. 466) called for a seven-day waiting period on handgun transfers. Supporters deemed this waiting period necessary to give law enforcement officials the time necessary to conduct a thorough background check. Later versions of the bill would have implemented a five-business-day waiting period. Opponents of the waiting period called for an "instant" computerized criminal history background check systems as had been implemented in four states (VA, FL, MD, and DE).

background check through either the FBI or a state point of contact (POC),[5] before transferring a firearm to an unlicensed, private person.[6]

Under the GCA, there are nine classes of persons prohibited from shipping, transporting, receiving, or possessing firearms or ammunition:

- persons convicted in any court of a crime punishable by imprisonment for a term exceeding one year;
- fugitives from justice;
- unlawful users or addicts of any controlled substance as defined in Section 102 of the Controlled Substances Act (21 U.S.C. §802);
- persons adjudicated as "mental defective" or committed to mental institutions;
- unauthorized immigrants and nonimmigrant visitors (with exceptions in the latter case);[7]
- persons dishonorably discharged from the U.S. Armed Forces;
- persons who have renounced their U.S. citizenship;
- persons under court-order restraints related to harassing, stalking, or threatening an intimate partner or child of such intimate partner; and

---

[5] The FBI handles background checks entirely for most states, while other states serve as full or partial points of contact (POCs) for state and local firearms background check purposes. In POC states, federally licensed gun dealers contact a state agency, and the state agency contacts the FBI for background checks.

[6] Under federal law, persons who are not "engaged in the business" of dealing in firearms are not required to be licensed to ship, transport, receive, or possess firearms. Intrastate, firearms transactions between unlicensed persons are not covered by the recordkeeping or the background check provisions of the GCA. However, these transactions and other matters such as possession, registration, and the issuance of licenses to firearms owners may be covered by state laws or local ordinances.

[7] Until 2011, ATF interpreted this provision to apply to any noncitizen whose immigration status was "nonimmigrant alien," regardless of whether the alien had been required to obtain a visa prior to arrival at a U.S. port of entry. In 2011, ATF was informed by the DOJ Office of Legal Counsel (OLC) that its interpretation was too broad and that the prohibition "applies only to nonimmigrant aliens who must have visas to be admitted, not to all aliens with nonimmigrant status." See 2011 WL 6260326 (O.L.C) (Oct. 28, 2011). As such, nonimmigrants who enter the country validly without a visa (e.g., under the Visa Waiver Program) are eligible to purchase firearms and ammunition; however, those individuals must meet a residency requirement, which requires them to demonstrate that they have "the intention of making a home" in the state where they wish to purchase the firearm. See 77 *Federal Register* 33625- 33634 (June 7, 2012).

- persons convicted of a misdemeanor crime of domestic violence.[8]

In addition, there is a 10th class of persons prohibited from shipping, transporting, or receiving (but not possessing) firearms or ammunition:

- persons under indictment in any court of a crime punishable by imprisonment for a term exceeding one year.[9]

It is also unlawful for any person to sell or otherwise dispose of a firearm or ammunition to any of the prohibited persons enumerated above, if the transferor (seller) has reasonable cause to believe that the transferee (buyer) is prohibited from receiving those items.[10]

MENTAL INCOMPETENCY AND FIREARMS INELIGIBILITY

To implement the Brady Act, inter-agency discussions were held in 1996/1997 about who should be considered "adjudicated as a mental defective" for the purposes of gun control.[11] These discussions were largely led by the Bureau of Alcohol, Tobacco, Firearms and Explosives (ATF), the agency principally responsible for administering and enforcing federal gun control laws. On June 27, 1997, the ATF promulgated a final rule defining the following terms:

> "Adjudicated as a mental defective" includes a determination by a court, board, commission, or other lawful authority that a person, as a result of marked subnormal intelligence or a mental illness, incompetency, condition, or disease, (1) is a danger to himself or others, or (2) lacks the mental capacity to manage his own affairs. The term also includes (1) a finding of insanity by a court in a criminal case and (2)

---

[8] 18 U.S.C. §922(g).
[9] 18 U.S.C. §922(n).
[10] 18 U.S.C. §922(d).
[11] To reflect terms currently utilized in discussing this issue, to the extent possible, the term, "mentally incompetent" will be used in place of "mental defective."

those persons found incompetent to stand trial or found not guilty by reason of lack of mental responsibility pursuant to articles 50a and 72b of the Uniform Code of Military Justice, 10 U.S.C. Sections 850a, 876(b).

"Committed to a mental institution" means a formal commitment of a person to a mental institution by a court, board, commission, or other lawful authority. The term includes commitments: (1) to a mental institution involuntarily; (2) for mental defectiveness or mental illness; or (3) for other reasons, such as drug use. The term does not include a person who is admitted to a mental institution for observation or who is voluntarily admitted.

"Mental institution" includes mental health facilities, mental hospitals, sanitariums, psychiatric facilities, and other facilities that provide diagnoses by licensed professionals of mental retardation or mental illness, including psychiatric wards in general hospitals.[12]

In its final rule, ATF noted that the Department of Veterans Affairs had commented on the proposed rulemaking and had "correctly interpreted" the proposed definition of "adjudicated as a mental defective" to include persons who have been determined to be "mentally incompetent" by the Veterans Benefits Administration (VBA).[13] Under current VA procedures, an individual is considered "mentally incompetent" if he or she lacks the mental capacity to contract or manage his or her own affairs for reasons related to injury or disease (under 38 C.F.R. §3.353).[14] In a proposed rulemaking, the ATF opined that the inclusion of "mentally incompetent" in the definition of "mental defective" was wholly consistent with the legislative history of the 1968 Gun Control Act.[15]

In the wake of the December 2012, Newtown, CT, mass shooting,[16] the ATF issued proposed regulations to clarify further individuals who might

---

[12] *Federal Register*, vol. 62, no. 124, June 27, 1997, p. 34634.

[13] Ibid., p. 34637.

[14] *Federal Register*, vol. 61, no. 174, September 6, 1996, p. 47095.

[15] Ibid.

[16] On December 14, 2012, in Newtown, CT, a 20-year-old male entered Sandy Hook Elementary School and shot 20 1st graders and 6 adult staff members to death. He also shot his mother to death. For further information, see *Report of the State's Attorney for the Judicial District*

fall under this definition. This proposed regulation has not been made final.[17] It is significant to note that the NICS index is not intended to be a registry of all individuals diagnosed with a mental illness. Nonetheless, the subsequent legislative history shows that some Members of Congress have long taken issue with the ATF interpretation of the term "adjudicated as a mental defective."[18]

NICS Improvement Amendments Act of 2007

In April 2007, an offender armed with two pistols shot to death 32 individuals and nonfatally wounded another 17, before shooting himself to death at the Virginia Polytechnic Institute and State University (Virginia Tech) in Blacksburg, Virginia. Due to his disturbing on-campus behavior, the offender had previously been evaluated by health care professionals and ordered by a judge to undergo "outpatient" mental health treatment, because he was deemed to be a threat to himself or others.[19] At that time, however, Virginia state law only referred the subjects of "inpatient" court orders for such treatment to the FBI for inclusion in the NICS index.[20] Following this massacre, the Virginia governor, now-Senator Timothy Kaine, reviewed the state statute and determined that henceforward

---

of Danbury on the Shootings at Sandy Hook Elementary School and 36 Yogananda Street, Newtown, Connecticut on December 14, 2012, November 25, 2013, 116 pp.

[17] U.S. Department of Justice, Bureau of Alcohol, Tobacco, Firearms, and Explosives, "Amended Definition of 'Adjudicated as a Mental Defective' and 'Committed to a Mental Institution' (2010R-21P)," 79 *Federal Register* 774, January 7, 2014.

[18] In the 110th, 111th, 112th, and 113th Congresses, either the Senate or House, or both, acted on bills that would have prohibited the VA from finding a veteran or other beneficiary to be "mentally incompetent" and thus a "mental defective" for the purposes of gun control, unless such a finding were made by a judge, magistrate, or other judicial authority based upon a finding that the beneficiary posed a danger to himself or others. None of these bills were enacted. For further information, see CRS Report R42987, *Gun Control Legislation in the 113th Congress*, by William J. Krouse.

[19] For further information, see *Mass Shootings at Virginia Tech, April 16, 2007: Report of the Virginia Tech Review Panel Presented to Timothy M. Kaine, Governor, Commonwealth of Virginia*, August 2007, 147 pp.

[20] Ibid.

subjects of either court-ordered inpatient or outpatient mental health care under such circumstances would be referred to the FBI for inclusion in the NICS index.[21]

In response to the Virginia Tech mass shooting, Congress passed the NICS Improvement Amendments Act of 2007 (NIAA).[22] This act includes provisions designed to encourage states to make available to the Attorney General certain records related to persons who are disqualified from acquiring firearms, particularly disqualifying records related to mental health adjudications, as well as domestic violence misdemeanor convictions and restraining orders. To accomplish this, the act establishes a framework of incentives and disincentives whereby the Attorney General is authorized to either waive a grant match requirement or reduce a law enforcement assistance grant depending upon a state's compliance with the act's goals of bringing such firearms-related disqualifying records online.

During congressional debate, however, some Members expressed opposition to the NIAA based on the assertion that, under these amendments, any veteran who was or had been diagnosed with Post Traumatic Stress Disorder (PTSD)[23] and was found to be a "danger to himself or others would have his gun rights taken away ... forever."[24] Members of Congress included a provision in NIAA that required agencies to inform a claimant beforehand that they could lose their gun rights and privileges if they are found to be mentally incompetent as a condition of a benefit program's administration and eligibility. In addition, as under the state grant provisions, NIAA required those referring agencies to establish a firearms disabilities relief program, whereby any individual referred to the NICS index for reasons related to mental incompetency would be able

---

[21] Ibid.

[22] P.L. 110-180, January 8, 2008; 121 Stat. 2559.

[23] PTSD is a disorder that can occur after one has been through a traumatic event. Symptoms may manifest soon after the trauma, or may be delayed. For further information, see U.S. Department of Veterans Affairs, National Center for Posttraumatic Stress Disorder, Fact Sheet, http://www.ncptsd.va.gov/ncmain/ncdocs/fact_shts/fs_what_is_ptsd.html.

[24] Larry Pratt, "Veterans Disarmament Act to Bar Vets from Owning Guns," September 23, 2007, http://www.prisonplanet.com/articles/september2007/230907Disarmament.htm.

to petition to have his or her gun rights and privileges restored, if and when he or she had overcome the incapacities that led to the initial finding.

Thirty-two states and the VA have established disability relief programs under NIAA. The Bureau of Justice Statistics (BJS) has awarded $94.9 million in NICS improvement grants to state, local, and tribal governments from FY2009 through FY2015. According to the BJS, there were 298,571 prohibiting records related to mental incompetency in the NICS index as of January 1, 2007. Of those records, state and local authorities had contributed 159,418 records (53.4%). According to the FBI, there were 4,658,573 active prohibiting records related to mental incompetency in the NICS index as December 31, 2016. Of those records, state and local authorities had contributed 4,487,573 records (96.3%). From the beginning of 2007 to the end of 2016, the number of those records contributed by state and local authorities to the NICS index had increased by 2,715%.

Federal agencies had contributed 171,083 such records to the NICS index, of which the VA had contributed 167,815 (98.1%), as of December 31, 2016. By comparison, federal agencies had contributed 139,153 records to the NICS index as of January 1, 2007, the bulk of which were contributed by the VA. The December 2016 SSA final rule established a similar program to the VA's; however, the SSA has not referred any disqualifying records to the FBI for inclusion in NICS.

Federal Department and Agency Requirements Under NIAA

NIAA included several provisions that address the submission of disqualifying records by federal departments and agencies to the FBI for inclusion in NICS.

Attorney General's Authority to Secure Records

P.L. 110-180 amends the Brady Handgun Violence Prevention Act[25] to strengthen the Attorney General's authority to secure from any department or agency of the U.S. government information on persons who are prohibited from possessing or receiving a firearm under federal or state law.[26] The act requires those departments or agencies to (1) "furnish electronic versions" of that information quarterly; (2) update, correct, modify, or remove those records as required to maintain their timeliness, if those records are stored in any databases that are maintained or made available to the Attorney General, and (3) inform the Attorney General of any record changes so NICS could also be updated to reflect those changes. Furthermore, the act requires the Attorney General to submit to Congress an annual report on the compliance of each U.S. department or agency that possesses such disqualifying records.

Record Accuracy and Confidentiality

Regarding any information submitted or maintained in NICS, the act requires the Attorney General to ensure that information be kept accurate and confidential and that obsolete and erroneous names be removed from NICS and destroyed in a timely manner.[27] The act also requires the Attorney General to work with the states to develop computer systems that would electronically notify the Attorney General when a court order has been issued, lifted, or otherwise removed, or when a person has been adjudicated as mentally defective or committed to a mental institution.

Records Prohibited from Inclusion in NICS

Effective at date of enactment, the act prohibits any department or agency of the U.S. government from providing the Attorney General with any record regarding the mental health of a person, or any commitment of a person to a mental institution, if (1) the adjudication or commitment has

---

[25] P.L. 103-159, Section 103(e).
[26] Section 101(a) of P.L. 110-180.
[27] Section 101(b)(2) of P.L. 110-180.

been set aside or expunged, or the person has otherwise been fully released or discharged from all mandatory treatment, supervision, or monitoring; (2) the person in question has been found by a court, board, commission or other lawful authority to no longer suffer from a mental health condition; or (3) the adjudication or commitment is based solely on a medical finding of disability, without an opportunity for hearing by a court, board, or other lawful authority, and the person has not been adjudicated as a mental defective.[28]

Relief from Mental Defective Disability

Within 120 days of the date of enactment (i.e., March 7, 2008), the act requires further that each department or agency of the U.S. government that makes adjudications related to the mental health of a person that impinges upon eligibility to possess or receive firearms to establish a process by which a person who is the subject of such an adjudication or determination could apply for relief from that disability.[29] (In this sense, the disability is the person's ineligibility to transfer or possess a firearm under 18 U.S.C. §922(d)(4) or (g)(4).) The act requires further that applications for disability relief be processed not later than 365 days after receipt, and if the agency fails to resolve an application within 365 days for any reason (including a lack of appropriated funds), the application is deemed to have been resolved, triggering de novo judicial review.

In addition, "relief and review" provided under the act (subparagraph 101(c)(2)(B)) is required to be made available according to standards outlined in 18 U.S.C. section 925(c).[30] For persons who are granted relief from disability under the act, or who are the subject of mental health records that the act prohibits from being turned over to the Attorney

---

[28] Section 101(c)(1) of P.L. 110-180.

[29] Subparagraph 101(c)(2)(A) of P.L. 110-180.

[30] Subparagraph 101(c)(2)(B) of P.L. 110-180. Under 18 U.S.C. §925(c), the Attorney General (previously, the Secretary of the Treasury) is allowed to consider petitions from a prohibited person for "relief from disabilities" and have his firearms transfer and possession eligibility restored. Since FY1993, however, a rider on the ATF annual appropriations for salaries and expenses has prohibited the expenditure of any funding provided under that account on processing such petitions. For FY1993, see P.L. 102-393; 106 Stat. 1732 (1992). For FY2015, see P.L. 113-235, 128 Stat. 2187 (2014).

General, the underlying events that were the basis for those records are deemed not to have occurred for the purposes of determining firearms transfer and possession eligibility under federal law.

Notice of Firearms Eligibility Loss and Disability Relief

Effective 30 days after the date of enactment, the act requires any federal department or agency that conducts proceedings to adjudicate a person as a mental defective to provide both oral and written notice to that person at the beginning of the adjudication process (1) that persons adjudicated as a mental defective are prohibited from purchasing, possessing, receiving, shipping or transporting a firearm or ammunition under federal law; (2) what the penalties are for violating related federal firearms provisions; and (3) what relief from such disability with respect to firearms is available under federal law.[31]

SENATE ACTION IN THE 114TH CONGRESS

In the 114th Congress, the Senate considered several amendments following the December 2015 San Bernardino, CA, and June 2016 Orlando, FL, mass shootings. In addition, Congress included a provision in an enacted bill that addresses VA procedures.

Manchin-Toomey Amendment

On December 3, 2015, for example, during Senate consideration of the Restoring Americans' Healthcare Freedom Reconciliation Act (H.R. 3762), Senators Joe Manchin and Patrick Toomey offered an amendment (S.Amdt. 2908) that would have amended veterans law to prohibit the VA

---

[31] Paragraph 101(c)(3) of P.L. 110-180.

from turning records on veterans or other beneficiaries who had been determined mentally incompetent over to the FBI for inclusion in NICS index unless certain notification and review conditions had been met.[32] Under the amendment, the Secretary of Veterans Affairs first would have been required to provide to a beneficiary, who had been deemed mentally incompetent for VA purposes, notification that included (a) the determination made by the Secretary; (b) a description of the implications of such a determination upon one's firearms eligibility under federal law; and (c) the right to request review by the board that would have been established by the VA or a court of competent jurisdiction.

Within 180 days of enactment, the Manchin-Toomey amendment would have required the Secretary of Veterans Affairs to establish a board that would have reviewed, upon request by a VA beneficiary, whether the individual's status as mentally incompetent for the purpose of receiving benefits prevented him from possessing firearms under the GCA. As mentioned above, a VA beneficiary would have had the option to request such a review from this board or from a court of competent jurisdiction. Under the Manchin-Toomey provision, the board would have been able to consider the individual's honorable discharge or decoration in determining whether he or she "cannot safely use, carry, possess, or store firearms due to mental incompetency." A beneficiary who received a determination from the board also would have been permitted to seek judicial review in federal court of the board's decision. It appears that until this review process was complete, a person would not have been considered "adjudicated as a mental defective" for purposes of firearms eligibility. As

---

[32] On June 15, 2016, Senator Manchin submitted a nearly identical amendment (S.Amdt. 4716) during consideration of the FY2017 Departments of Commerce and Justice, Science, and Related Agencies (CJS) Appropriations bill (H.R. 2578, the expected vehicle for S. 2837); however, the amendment was not brought to a vote. Also, in the 114th Congress, Representatives Peter King and Mike Thompson introduced a measure, the Public Safety and Second Amendment Rights Protection Act of 2015 (H.R. 1217), which was nearly identical to the Manchin-Toomey amendment. For further information, see CRS Report R44655, *Gun Control: Federal Law and Legislative Action in the 114th Congress*, by William J. Krouse. In addition, the Senate previously considered the Manchin-Toomey amendment (S.Amdt. 715 to S. 649, 113th Congress) following the Newtown, CT, mass public shooting in April 2013. For further information, see CRS Report R42987, *Gun Control Legislation in the 113th Congress*, by William J. Krouse.

such, it appears that the Secretary, by implication, would not have been permitted to make a NICS referral during this period of time.

If a beneficiary did not request review by a board or court of competent jurisdiction within 30 days after receiving the initial notification from the Secretary, then the beneficiary who was to be determined mentally incompetent would have been considered "adjudicated as a mental defective" for purposes of the GCA. This suggests that the Secretary would not have been able to make a NICS referral until the 30-day period had passed.

For VA beneficiaries who had already been considered "adjudicated as a mental defective" after being determined mentally incompetent by the VA, the Manchin-Toomey amendment would have required the Secretary to provide, within 90 days of enactment, written notice to these individuals of the opportunity for administrative review and appeal, as would have been established by the amendment. Furthermore, the amendment would have also required the Secretary to review and revise all policies and procedures whereby beneficiaries are determined to be mentally incompetent, so that any individual "who is competent to manage his own financial affairs, including receipt of Federal benefits, but who voluntarily turns over the management thereof to a fiduciary is not" considered "adjudicated mentally defective" for purposes of the GCA. Within 30 days of conducting this review, the Secretary would have been required to submit to Congress a report detailing the results of the review and any resulting policy and procedural changes.

Murphy Amendment

On June 16, 2016, by comparison, during Senate consideration of the Departments of Commerce and Justice, Science, and Related Agencies Appropriations Bill, 2017 (H.R. 2578, the expected vehicle for S. 2837), Senator Christopher Murphy offered an amendment (S.Amdt. 4750) that would have codified the ATF current regulatory definition of "adjudicated as a mental defective."[33]

Grassley Amendments

In the 114th Congress, Senator Charles Grassley offered amendments (S.Amdt. 2914 and S.Amdt. 4751), during consideration of H.R. 3762 and H.R. 2578, respectively. These Grassley amendments would have also amended the GCA and replaced the term "adjudicated as a mental defective" with the term "mentally incompetent" in both 18 U.S.C. Section 922(d) and (g). In addition, these amendments would have also amended the GCA to define the terms, "has been adjudicated mentally incompetent or has been committed to a psychiatric hospital," "order or finding," and "psychiatric hospital." These definitions and other language would have narrowed the scope of whose records, and under what circumstances, a federal or state agency could refer to the FBI for inclusion in the NICS mental defective file. The Senate blocked all of the Manchin-Toomey, Murphy, and Grassley amendments described above on procedural grounds.[34]

In addition, during the 114th Congress, Senator Grassley submitted an amendment (S.Amdt. 4120), during consideration of the National Defense Authorization Act for Fiscal Year 2017 (S. 2943). This amendment would have prohibited the VA Secretary from making a NICS referral to the FBI on any person as "adjudicated as a mental defective," "without the order or finding of a judge, magistrate, or other judicial authority of competent jurisdiction that such person is a danger to himself or herself or others." This amendment was not brought to a vote.

---

[33] The Murphy amendment reflects language previously included in a proposal introduced by Senator Chuck Schumer and Representative Jackie Speier, the Fix Gun Checks Act (S. 2934 and H.R. 3411) in the 114th Congress.

[34] For further information, see CRS Report R44655, *Gun Control: Federal Law and Legislative Action in the 114th Congress*, by William J. Krouse.

P.L. 114-255 Provision

In December 2016, Congress included a provision in the 21st Century Cures Act that codified VA implementation of NIAA.[35] This provision is discussed in greater detail below.

VA IMPLEMENTATION OF NIAA

As noted above, the VA has contributed the bulk of the federal records in the NICS index related to individuals who have been "adjudicated as a mental defective." Hence, the VA and its policies are one example of federal implementation of the Brady Act and NIAA. Under current VA regulations, the VA has the authority to determine the competency status of a person receiving VA benefits.[36] The VA may appoint a fiduciary to receive benefits on behalf of a beneficiary determined to be incompetent. In addition, the VA is to refer the name of any beneficiary determined to be incompetent to the FBI for inclusion in the NICS.[37]

Individuals Who Have Their Names Reported to NICS

The VA is to report the names of all beneficiaries determined to be incompetent to the FBI for inclusion in the NICS. The VA's regulations define a "mentally incompetent person" as:

---

[35] P.L. 114-255, December 13, 2016; 130 Stat. 1307; codified at 38 U.S.C. §5501A.

[36] 38 C.F.R. §3.353.

[37] The authority for the VA to refer the names of beneficiaries determined to be incompetent to the FBI for inclusion in the NICS is not explicitly provided for in the VA regulations. However, it is described in Department of Veterans Affairs, *M21-1 Adjudication Procedures Manual*, Section III.v.9.B.4.a., http://www.knowva.ebenefits.va.gov/system/templates/selfservice/va_ss/#!portal/554400000001018/topic/554400000004049/M21-1-Adjudication-ProceduresManual.

> one who because of injury or disease lacks the mental capacity to contract or to manage his or her own affairs, including disbursement of funds without limitation.[38]
>
> When making a determination as to the competency of a beneficiary, the regulations require that VA only make a determination of incompetency if either:
>
> - the medical evidence is clear, convincing, and leaves no doubt as to the beneficiary's incompetency; or
> - there is a definite expression regarding the beneficiary's incompetency by responsible medical authorities.[39]

In addition, the regulations provide that if there is reasonable doubt as to the incompetency of the beneficiary, the beneficiary will be determined to be competent.[40]

How Are Affected Individuals Notified by the VA and What Information Is Provided?

Federal regulations require that a beneficiary be notified by the VA about the agency's proposed determination of incompetency.[41] It is the policy of the VA that both this notice, as well as the notice of the final determination of incompetency, include information on the impact of an incompetency decision on the beneficiary's right to purchase, possess, receive, or transport a firearm or ammunition.[42]

---

[38] 38 C.F.R. §3.353(a)

[39] 38 C.F.R. §3.353(c).

[40] 38 C.F.R. §3.353(d).

[41] 38 C.F.R. §3.353(e).

[42] Department of Veterans Affairs, *M21-1 Adjudication Procedures Manual*, Section III.v.9.B.4.b.

How Do Affected Individuals Have Their Records Removed from the NICS?

Beneficiaries who have had their names submitted by the VA to the FBI for inclusion in the NICS due to determinations of incompetency may contest both the determination and the inclusion of their names on the NICS. The VA's determination of incompetency is subject to the same due process and appeals procedures as other VA decisions.[43] For the purposes of a determination of incompetency, this includes the following procedures provided in regulation and codified in statute pursuant to Section 14017 of the 21st Century Cures Act:[44]

- notice by the VA to the beneficiary of the proposed determination and supporting evidence;
- the opportunity for the beneficiary to request a hearing;
- the opportunity for the beneficiary to present evidence, including the opinion of a medical professional or other person, as to the beneficiary's capacity to manage his or her benefits; and
- the opportunity to be represented by counsel, at no cost to the federal government, and bring a medical professional or other person to provide testimony at any hearing.

A beneficiary dissatisfied by the decision of the VA regarding his or her competency has the right to a hearing before the Board of Veterans Appeals (BVA) and the right of judicial review of the BVA's decision by the U.S. Court of Appeals for Veterans Claims. Decisions of the U.S. Court of Appeals for Veterans Claims may be appealed to the U.S. Court of Appeals for the Federal Circuit.

In addition to contesting or appealing the determination of incompetency, a beneficiary may separately seek relief from the VA's decision to report his or her name to the FBI for inclusion in the NICS. Because the decision of the VA to report a beneficiary to the FBI for

---

[43] 38 C.F.R. §§3.103 and 3.353(e).

[44] P.L. 114-255, December 13, 2016; 130 Stat. 1307; codified at 38 U.S.C. §5501A

inclusion in the NICS is not considered a decision by the agency on a benefit provided by law, the VA does not have a duty to assist the beneficiary with the request for relief, burden of proof is on the beneficiary requesting relief, and failure to meet the burden of proof is sufficient cause for the request for relief to be denied.[45]

When deciding whether or not to grant a veteran's request for relief, the VA must consider the following types of evidence:

- a current statement from the beneficiary's primary mental health physician that assesses the beneficiary's current and past mental health status; and
- evidence concerning the beneficiary's reputation.[46]

The VA must deny a request for relief if there is clear and convincing evidence that the beneficiary would be a danger to himself/herself or others if the relief was granted.[47] If such evidence does not exist, the VA must consider granting the request for relief.[48] In order to grant relief, there must be clear and convincing evidence that affirmatively, substantially, and specifically, shows that:

- the beneficiary is not likely to act in a manner that is dangerous to the public; and
- granting relief will not be contrary to the public interest.[49]

A decision of the VA to deny relief cannot be appealed to the BVA or U.S. Court of Appeals for Veterans Claims, but is subject to judicial review by a U.S. District Court.[50]

---

[45] Department of Veterans Affairs, *M21-1 Adjudication Procedures Manual*, Section III.v.9.B.4.c. Federal law at 38 U.S.C. §5103A requires the VA to assist claimants in obtaining evidence necessary to substantiate their claims for benefits.

[46] Department of Veterans Affairs, *M21-1 Adjudication Procedures Manual*, Section III.v.9.B.4.h.

[47] Ibid., Section III.v.9.B.4.i.

[48] Ibid., Section III.v.9.B.4.j.

[49] Ibid.

[50] Ibid., Section III.v.9.B.4.g.

SSA IMPLEMENTATION OF NIAA

In March 2013, the Department of Justice (DOJ) issued guidance to agencies regarding the identification and sharing of relevant federal records and their submission to the NICS. DOJ later determined that SSA must report to the Attorney General information about certain Social Security and Supplemental Security Income (SSI) beneficiaries for whom a representative payee (fiduciary) is appointed because they are determined by SSA to be unable to manage their benefits due to a mental impairment.

SSA issued a notice of proposed rulemaking concerning its implementation of the NIAA on May 5, 2016,[51] and published its final rule on December 19, 2016.[52] The new rule specifies the conditions under which SSA will report for inclusion in the NICS a Social Security or SSI disability beneficiary's disqualifying records. The rule also outlines SSA's process for notifying affected individuals as well as the administrative appeals process under which such individuals may request relief from the federal firearms prohibitions. The final rule became effective on January 18, 2017; however, compliance is not required until December 19, 2017.[53]

Individuals Who Would Have Their Records Reported to the NICS

Under the new rule, an individual is to be considered to be "adjudicated as a mental defective" by SSA if the individual meets all of the following requirements:

- has filed a claim for Social Security or SSI benefits based on a disability;

---

[51] Social Security Administration (SSA), "Implementation of the NICS Improvement Amendments Act of 2007," 81 *Federal Register* 27059, May 5, 2016.

[52] SSA, "Implementation of the NICS Improvement Amendments Act of 2007," 81 *Federal Register* 91702, December 19, 2016.

[53] See 20 C.F.R. §§421.100-421.170.

- has been determined to have an impairment (or combination of impairments) that meets or medically equals the criteria of one of the mental disorders specified in SSA's *Listing of Impairments* (Step 3 of the disability determination process);[54]
- has a primary diagnosis code based on a mental impairment;
- has attained age 18 but not yet attained Social Security's full retirement age (currently 66); and
- has had a representative payee appointed because he or she has been determined by SSA to be mentally incapable of managing benefit payments.

In general, adult Social Security and SSI disability beneficiaries are presumed to be capable of managing or directing the management of their benefits. However, if legal, medical, or lay evidence exists to the contrary, SSA will make a capability determination. If the agency determines that it is clearly in the best interest of the beneficiary to do so, it will certify benefit payments to another person as a representative payee. In this case, the appointment of a representative payee for a beneficiary with a listing-level mental impairment demonstrates that the individual "lacks the mental capacity to manage his own affairs."

According to the new rule, SSA will identify individuals who meet the aforementioned requirements on a *prospective* basis, meaning that the final rule will largely affect certain new disability beneficiaries. However, the agency is to report existing disability beneficiaries to the NICS who currently do not meet all five requirements but who later demonstrate a

---

[54] Section 12.00 of appendix 1 to subpart P of 20 C.F.R §404. SSA employs a five-step sequential evaluation process for determining whether an adult is disabled for Social Security and SSI purposes. According to the agency, claimants determined to meet the criteria at Step 3 of the process are the most severely disabled because they are awarded benefits based solely on medical evidence, whereas claimants awarded at the later steps are awarded benefits based on a combination of medical and vocational evidence. Because SSA will not report to the NICS individuals whom the agency finds disabled at Step 5 of the process, the new rule will affect a subsample of the disability beneficiary population who have a representative payee and whose primary impairment is a mental disorder. For more information on the sequential evaluation process, see CRS Report RL32279, *Primer on Disability Benefits: Social Security Disability Insurance (SSDI) and Supplemental Security Income (SSI)*, by William R. Morton.

change in status that satisfies all five requirements. The Obama Administration estimated that the new rule will affect about 75,000 individuals annually.[55] A report by SSA's Office of the Inspector General found that about 81,000 Social Security and SSI disability awardees in FY2015 met all five requirements for reporting to the NICS, which was about 9% of the total disability awardee population.[56]

How Would Affected Individuals be Notified by SSA and What Information Would be Provided?

Under the rule, SSA plans to provide both oral and written notice to the affected individual that he or she meets all five criteria for reporting to the NICS and that when final, such reporting will prohibit the individual from possessing firearms. In addition, SSA plans to inform the affected individual of his or her ability to request relief from the federal firearms prohibitions at any time after SSA's adjudication has become final.

How Would Affected Individuals Have Their Records Removed from the NICS?

SSA plans to notify the Attorney General that an affected individual's record should be removed if (1) the individual is now capable of managing his or her benefit payments, (2) the individual died, (3) SSA receives information that it reported the record to the NICS in error, or (4) the agency grants the individual's request for relief under the new rule.[57] In

---

[55] Obama Administration, "FACT SHEET: New Executive Actions to Reduce Gun Violence and Make Our Communities Safer," https://obamawhitehouse.archives.gov/the-press-office/2016/01/04/fact-sheet-new-executiveactions-reduce-gun-violence-and-make-our.

[56] SSA, Office of the Inspector General, *The Social Security Administration's Implementation of Reporting Information to the National Instant Criminal Background Check System*, A-01-16-50218, September 2016, http://oig.ssa.gov/auditsand-investigations/audit-reports/A-01-16-50218. Figure includes awards issued only at the initial and reconsideration stages of the adjudicative process. The total disability awardee population includes children under age 18.

[57] The decision to appoint a representative payee is subject to SSA's formal appeals process with certain exceptions.

requesting relief, an affected individual must prove that he or she is not likely to act in a manner dangerous to public safety and such relief will not be contrary to the public interest. Affected individuals denied relief by SSA may file a petition seeking judicial review in U.S. district court.

CONCLUSION

As discussed above, Congress has passed legislation to encourage state, local, tribal, and territorial governments to submit prohibiting records to the FBI for inclusion in the NICS index for individuals who have been "adjudicated as a mental defective" and, therefore, deemed too mentally incompetent to be trusted with firearms or ammunition. The legislative record suggests that some Members of Congress have taken issue with the current regulatory definition of "adjudicated as a mental defective," while other Members would prefer to have it codified.

The VA has complied with the Brady Act and NIAA and submitted prohibiting records on beneficiaries "who because of injury or disease lack the mental capacity to contract or to manage his or her own affairs." After the December 2012 Newtown, CT, tragedy, the Obama Administration directed the SSA to administer the Brady Act and NIAA in a similar manner.

The SSA adopted a final rule that does not completely parallel the VA's administration of these laws, in that it would result in a narrower set of prohibiting records of beneficiaries being submitted to the FBI for inclusion in the NICS index. As described above, the SSA tied such "adjudications" to "mental impairments," in addition to a beneficiary's ability to handle his or her day-to-day affairs, whereas the VA only ties it to the beneficiary's ability to manage his or her day-to-day affairs.

As the legislative record shows, some Members of Congress oppose NICS referrals based upon the grounds that an individual "lacks the mental capacity to manage his [or her] own affairs."[58]

Opponents of the SSA final rule argue further that a mental impairment, even when tied to incapacity to manage one's own affairs, is not sufficient grounds to make such NICS referrals to the FBI, without an "order or finding of a judge, magistrate, or other judicial authority of competent jurisdiction that such person is a danger to himself or herself or others."[59] They also point to the position taken by mental health advocates that reporting the incapacitated or mentally disabled under current VA procedures and the SSA final rule, without any regard to their propensity to be violent, reinforces ingrained stereotypes about the disabled.[60]

Proponents maintain that the VA and SSA are faithfully addressing public safety by implementing provisions of the Brady Act and NIAA.[61] They argue that measures to prevent mentally incompetent persons from acquiring firearms are justified because firearms in their view are dangerous instruments that amplify violence in the United States to unacceptable levels.[62] They underscore that issues related to notification of loss and restoration of gun rights and privileges were addressed in NIAA and incorporated into the current VA procedures and the SSA final rule.[63]

---

58 American Civil Liberties Union, *Vote YES on the Resolution of Disapproval, H.J. Res. 40 (Social Security Administration NICS Final Rule)*, by Faiz Shakir and Vania Leveille (February 1, 2017), https://waysandmeans.house.gov/wp-content/uploads/2017/01/ACLU.pdf.

59 Senator Richard Burr, "S.Amdt. 720, Sec. 114. Conditions for Treatment of Certain Persons as Adjudicated Mentally Incompetent for Certain Purposes," Senate Debate on Safe Communities, Safe Schools Act of 2013, *Congressional Record*, vol. 159 (April 17, 2013), pp. S2719-S2720.

60 Consortium for Citizens with Disabilities, *CCD Rights TF Letter of Support for the House CRA on the SSA NICS Rule*, January 26, 2017, http://www.c-c-d.org/fichiers/CCD-Rights-TF-House-Letter-of-Support-for-CRA-on-SSANICS-Jan-2017.pdf.

61 Everytown for Gun Safety, *January 2016 Executive Actions*, January 5, 2016, https://everytownresearch.org/january2016-executive-actions/.

62 Americans for Responsible Solutions, "ARS Denounces House GOP Vote to Weaken the National Instant Criminal Background Check System," February 2, 2017, http://americansforresponsiblesolutions.org/2017/02/02/ssarule/.

63 Ibid.

Chapter 2

SIFTING DOMESTIC TERRORISM FROM HATE CRIME AND HOMEGROWN VIOLENT EXTREMISM*

Jerome P. Bjelopera
Specialist in Organized Crime and Terrorism

In light of the violence related to protests in Charlottesville, VA, on August 12, 2017, policymakers may be interested in how the concepts of domestic terrorism, hate crime, and homegrown violent extremism compare with one another. They are fairly distinct ideas that federal law enforcement agencies use to categorize key types of criminals whose illegal activities are at least partly ideologically motivated. Specifically, these terms may be part of public discussion regarding a widely reported incident involving James Alex Fields, who according to witnesses drove his car into a group of people protesting a rally featuring white supremacists in Charlottesville on August 12. Fields allegedly killed 1 person and

---

* This is an edited, reformatted and augmented version of "Sifting Domestic Terrorism from Hate Crime and Homegrown Violent Extremism" by Jerome P. Bjelopera that was originally published by CRS Insight on August 14, 2017. (IN10299)

injured 19 others. The Department of Justice has opened a civil rights investigation into the incident, presumably pursuing possible hate crime charges. Additionally, Attorney General Jeff Sessions has publicly stated that terrorism investigators are involved in investigating the incident, ostensibly exploring the possibility of characterizing it as an act of domestic terrorism rather than a hate crime.

DOMESTIC TERRORISM

Domestic terrorism cases differ from ordinary criminal activity in key ways. Most importantly, unlike ordinary criminals—who are often driven by self-centered motives such as profit and tend to opportunistically seek easy prey— domestic terrorists are driven by a cause or ideology. If the motives involved eventually align with the definition laid out in *18 U.S.C. §2331(5),* presumably the case becomes a domestic terrorist investigation.

The Federal Bureau of Investigation (FBI) has *defined domestic terrorism* as "acts of violence that [violate] the criminal laws of the United States or any state, committed by individuals or groups without any foreign direction, and appear to be intended to intimidate or coerce a civilian population, or influence the policy of a government by intimidation or coercion, and occur primarily within the territorial jurisdiction of the United States."

Domestic terrorists are a widely divergent lot, drawing from *many philosophies and worldviews* to justify their illegal acts. They can be motivated to commit crimes in the name of ideas such as *animal rights, environmental rights, white supremacy, anti-government beliefs,* and *anarchism,* for example. Importantly, the expression of these world-views— minus the commission of crimes—involves constitutionally protected activity. As such, individuals and movements openly and *legally* espousing such beliefs distance themselves from terrorists who use the ideas to justify their own criminal actions.

The FBI safeguards against cases focused *solely on constitutionally protected activities.* All FBI investigations have to be conducted for an authorized national security, criminal, or foreign intelligence collection purpose. Investigations may not solely monitor the exercise of First Amendment rights. Finally, the Department of Justice and the FBI conceptualize domestic terrorism in terms of threats, not named or designated groups or actors.

HATE CRIME

Current federal law defines hate crimes to include any crime against either person or property in which the offender intentionally selects the victim because of the victim's actual or perceived race, color, religion, national origin, gender, gender identity, disability, or sexual orientation. Hate crimes may appear to involve ideological issues. However, as described by one FBI official, a "hate crime" "generally involve[s] acts of personal malice directed at individuals" and is missing the broader motivations driving acts of domestic terrorism. For investigators, distinguishing between "personal malice" and ideologically motivated actions may be difficult in specific cases. This suggests that sorting domestic terrorism from hate crimes depends on the degree of a suspect's intent. Did the suspect articulate an ideology, belong to a domestic terrorist group, or follow an extremist movement? The grey area between domestic terrorism and hate crime suggests that in some instances, suspects with links to domestic terrorist movements or ideologies supporting domestic terrorism may be charged with hate crimes. It is unclear to what extent this influences how the government understands the threat posed by extremist movements that hold racist beliefs. If some individuals of this ilk commit crimes against police or judges, for example, is the government more apt to label this activity as terrorism while individuals sharing these same racist motivations but targeting ordinary citizens based on race, religion, disability, ethnic origin, or sexual orientation are charged with hate crimes?

The Harpham Case

The FBI's public description of the case of confessed would-be bomber Kevin Harpham exemplifies how difficult it may be to characterize acts as domestic terrorism. Initially the FBI viewed the case as domestic terrorism. In 2011, Harpham, allegedly motivated by white supremacist ideology, left a bomb—which never detonated—along the route of a parade in Spokane, WA, honoring Dr. Martin Luther King Jr. The FBI's Northwest Joint Terrorism Task Force *led the investigation. In prepared public remarks* framing the "current state of the terrorism threat" from April 2011, the then-FBI assistant director for the Counterterrorism Division noted that Harpham's case was one of "several recent domestic terrorism incidents [that] demonstrate the scope of the threat." Harpham eventually pled guilty to committing a federal hate crime and attempting to use a weapon of mass destruction. Thereafter, the *bureau described the case* as the successful prevention of a "horrific hate crime."

Homegrown Violent Extremism

The FBI and DHS have *popularized the phrase* "homegrown violent extremist" (HVE). It divides domestic terrorists from U.S.-based terrorists motivated by the ideologies of foreign terrorist organizations. Reportedly, according to DHS and the FBI, *an HVE is* "a person of any citizenship who has lived and/or operated primarily in the United States or its territories who advocates, is engaged in, or is preparing to engage in ideologically-motivated terrorist activities (including providing support to terrorism) in furtherance of political or social objectives promoted by a foreign terrorist organization, but is acting independently of direction by a foreign terrorist organization." They also assert that an HVE is not a domestic terrorist—these are two distinct categories of terrorist actors.

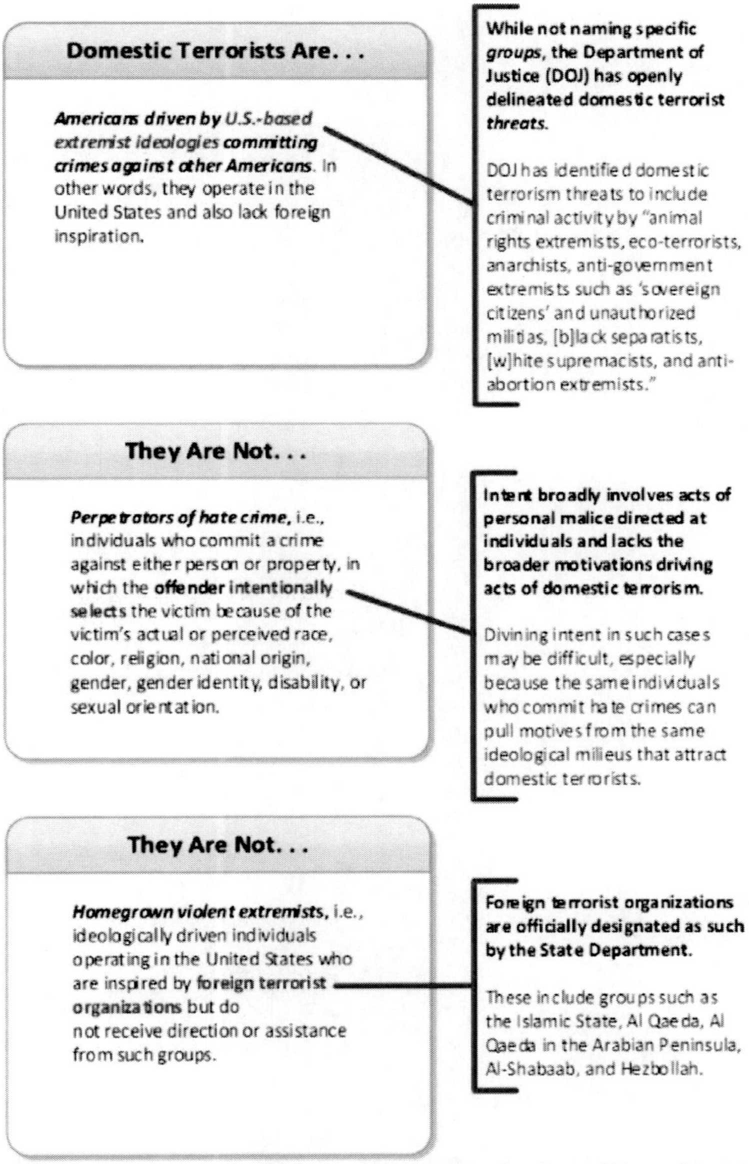

Source: CRS graphic derived from information in https://www.fbi.gov/about-us/investigate/civilrights/hate_crimes/overview; https://www.fbi.gov/news/testimony/animal-rights-extremism-andecoterrorism; Department of Justice, Counter-terrorism White Paper; https://www.fbi.gov/news/stories/2009/september/domterror_090709.

Figure 1. Who Are Domestic Terrorists?

Chapter 3

THE STATE DEPARTMENT'S *TRAFFICKING IN PERSONS* REPORT: SCOPE, AID RESTRICTIONS, AND METHODOLOGY*

Liana W. Rosen
Specialist in International Crime and Narcotics

SUMMARY

The State Department's annual release of the *Trafficking in Persons* report (commonly referred to as the TIP Report) has been closely monitored by Congress, foreign governments, the media, advocacy groups, and other foreign policy observers. The 109th Congress first mandated the report's publication in the Trafficking Victims Protection Act of 2000 (TVPA; Div. A of the Victims of Trafficking and Violence Protection Act of 2000, P.L. 106-386).

Over time, the number of countries covered by the TIP Report has grown, peaking at 188 countries, including the United States. In the 2017 TIP Report, the State Department categorized 187 countries. Countries

* This is an edited, reformatted and augmented version of "The State Department's *Trafficking in Persons* Report: Scope, Aid Restrictions, and Methodology" by Liana W. Rosen that was originally published by the Congressional Research Service on September 19, 2017.

were placed into one of several lists (or *tiers*) based on their respective governments' level of effort to address human trafficking between April 1, 2016, and March 31, 2017. An additional category of special cases included three countries that were not assigned a tier ranking because of ongoing political instability (Libya, Somalia, and Yemen).

Its champions describe the TIP Report as a keystone measure of government efforts to address and ultimately eliminate human trafficking. Some U.S. officials refer to the report as a crucial tool of diplomatic engagement that has encouraged foreign governments to elevate their own antitrafficking efforts. Its detractors question the TIP Report's credibility as a true measure of antitrafficking efforts, suggesting at times that political factors distort its country assessments. Some foreign governments perceive the report as a form of U.S. interference in their domestic affairs.

Continued congressional interest in the TIP Report and its country rankings has resulted in several key modifications to the process. Such modifications have included the creation of the special watch list, limiting the length of time a country may remain on a subset of the special watch list, expanding the list of criteria for determining whether countries are taking *serious and sustained efforts* to eliminate trafficking, establishing a list of governments that recruit and use child soldiers, and prohibiting the least cooperative countries on antitrafficking matters from participating in authorized trade negotiations. These modifications were often included as part of broader legislative efforts to reauthorize the TVPA, whose current authorization for appropriations expires at the end of FY2017.

Recent Developments: On June 27, 2017, the U.S. Department of State released the 17th edition of the TIP Report—the first for the Administration of President Donald J. Trump. In spite of State Department efforts to alleviate congressional concerns that the report's methodology is susceptible to political pressure, several Members in the 115th Congress have introduced legislation to further modify key aspects of the annual country ranking and reporting process.

The most significant changes to the TIP Report methodology are contained in H.R. 2200, the Frederick Douglass Trafficking Victims Prevention and Protection Reauthorization Act of 2017, which passed the House on July 12, 2017. If enacted, the changes could reduce State Department flexibility and discretion in assigning tier rankings to countries and increase the number of countries that would fall into the worst category (Tier 3)—while also making it potentially more difficult for countries to attain the best category (Tier 1). Other proposed changes to the TIP Report methodology are contained in S. 377, S. 952, H.R. 436, H.R. 1191, and H.R. 2219.

While some observers may anticipate that changes to the TIP Report's methodology will improve its overall credibility and country ranking process, others may question whether such changes will confuse foreign governments and be perceived as too complex. The reputational harm of a poor ranking in the TIP Report has motivated some countries to improve their antitrafficking efforts. It is not clear, however, if this scenario will hold true indefinitely. If the prospect of achieving a top ranking in the TIP Report begins to appear unattainable, could the TIP Report's ability to motivate countries to improve their antitrafficking efforts—and thus its value as a policy tool for international engagement to combat human trafficking—diminish?

INTRODUCTION

Congress has led both U.S. and international efforts to eliminate severe forms of trafficking in persons, particularly with its enactment of the Victims of Trafficking and Violence Protection Act of 2000 (P.L. 106-386). Division A of that act, the Trafficking Victims Protection Act of 2000 (TVPA), established U.S. antitrafficking policy to (1) *prevent* trafficking, (2) *protect* trafficking victims, and (3) *prosecute* and punish traffickers (known as the three Ps).

A key element of the TVPA's foreign policy objectives involved a new requirement for the Secretary of State to produce an annual report on human trafficking and to rank foreign governments based on their antitrafficking efforts. In the ensuing reports, which the State Department titled as *Trafficking in Persons* (TIP) reports, the department developed a ranking system in which the best countries were identified as Tier 1 and the worst Tier 3. Moreover, the TVPA stipulated that the worst performers (Tier 3 countries) in the TIP Report could be subject to potential restrictions on certain types of U.S. foreign aid and other U.S. and multilateral funds—a policy that is intended to motivate countries to avoid Tier 3 by prioritizing antitrafficking efforts.

The TIP Report's annual release remains a topic of widespread interest among international and domestic stakeholders, including Congress. Since the TVPA's enactment 17 years ago, Congress has continued to adjust the requirements associated with how countries are ranked in the TIP Report, as well as the policy consequences of such rankings. (See *Figure 1* below.)

These changes were often the result of congressional dissatisfaction with some aspect of the TIP Report:

- Due to difficulty discerning differences among Tier 2 countries, Congress modified the TVPA in 2003 to create a special watch list, composed of countries that deserve enhanced scrutiny.[1]
- Out of concern that countries were listed for too many consecutive years on the special watch list, Congress modified the TVPA in 2008 to limit the number of years a country may remain on it.[2]
- In response to the plight of children exploited in armed conflict, Congress modified the TVPA in 2008 to require the State Department to identify countries whose governments recruit and use child soldiers.[3]
- With the objective of linking U.S. trade policy to antitrafficking outcomes, Congress in 2015 prohibited Tier 3 countries from participating in authorized trade negotiations.[4]
- As a result of greater awareness of antitrafficking best practices, Congress has incrementally expanded its expectations for governments to conduct serious and sustained efforts to address human trafficking.

In light of ongoing congressional scrutiny of the State Department's TIP Report and its country ranking process, several bills in the 115th Congress have been introduced to further modify requirements associated with the TIP Report. Some of these proposed changes could significantly change—and at least temporarily complicate—the current TIP Report's

---

[1] §6 of the Trafficking Victims Protection Reauthorization Act of 2003 (2003 TVPRA; P.L. 108-193) amended §110 of the Trafficking Victims Protection Act of 2000 (TVPA); 22 U.S.C. 7107.

[2] §107 of the William Wilberforce Trafficking Victims Protection Reauthorization Act of 2008 (2008 TVPRA; P.L. 110-457) amended §110 of the TVPA; 22 U.S.C. 7107.

[3] See Title IV of P.L. 110-457, the Child Soldiers Prevention Act of 2008 (CSPA); 22 U.S.C. 2370c et seq.

[4] §106 of the Bipartisan Congressional Trade Priorities and Accountability Act of 2015 (TPA; Title I of P.L. 114-26) added this statutory restriction; it was subsequently amended to allow for a waiver by §914 of the Trade Facilitation and Trade Enforcement Act of 2015 (P.L. 114-125); 19 U.S.C. 4205.

methodology.[5] A critical question is whether further changes to the TIP Report's methodology will incentivize countries to boost their antitrafficking efforts or, in contrast, may erode the legitimacy of the TIP Report as a credible tool to advocate for human trafficking concerns.

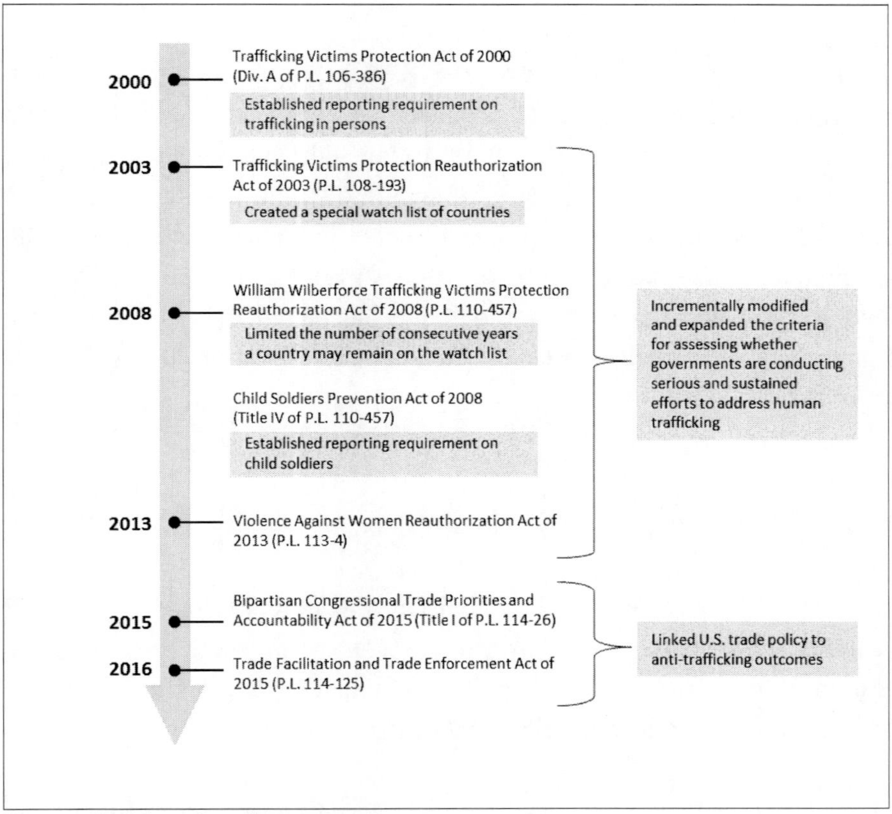

Source: CRS, based on Congress.gov.

Figure 1. Key Legislative Changes to the TIP Report, 2000-2016.

This CRS report describes the legislative provisions that govern the U.S. Department of State's production of the annual TIP Report, reviews country ranking trends in the TIP Report, and identifies recent congressional oversight of and legislative activity to modify the TIP

[5] For further discussion, see "Legislative Oversight and Outlook" section, below.

Report. Answers to selected frequently asked questions (FAQs) are included throughout the report.

TIP Report Scope

The contents of each annual TIP Report are governed by two provisions, one in the TVPA, as amended, and a second in the Child Soldiers Prevention Act of 2008 (CSPA).[6] In addition, current law requires the President and the Secretary of State to prepare related follow-on documentation for certain categories of countries. These include reporting requirements that were added to the TVPA as part of TVPA re-authorization acts, as well as requirements contained in the Bipartisan Congressional Trade Priorities and Accountability Act of 2015 (TPA), as amended.

Reporting Requirements in the TVPA

The TVPA, as amended, establishes the core contents of the TIP Report. Specifically, it requires the Secretary of State to submit to appropriate congressional committees an annual report, due not later than June 1 each year, which describes, on a country-by-country basis:[7]

- government efforts to eliminate severe forms of trafficking in persons;
- the nature and scope of trafficking in persons in each country; and
- trends in each government's efforts to combat trafficking.

---

[6] §110 of the TVPA (22 U.S.C. 7107) and §404 of the CSPA (22 U.S.C. 2370c-1).

[7] *Appropriate congressional committees* in the TVPA refer to the Senate Foreign Relations Committee (SFRC), the Senate Judiciary Committee (SJUD), the House Foreign Affairs Committee (HFAC), and the House Judiciary Committee (HJUD). See §103 of the TVPA; 22 U.S.C. 7102.

FAQ: What Are Severe Forms of Trafficking in Persons?

The TVPA defines severe forms of trafficking in persons to mean:

A. sex trafficking in which a commercial sex act is induced by force, fraud, or coercion, or in which the person induced to perform such act has not attained 18 years of age; or
B. the recruitment, harboring, transportation, provision, or obtaining of a person for labor or services, through the use of force, fraud, or coercion for the purpose of subjection to involuntary servitude, peonage, debt bondage, or slavery.[8]

This definition is largely consistent with the definition of trafficking in persons contained in the United Nations Protocol to Prevent, Suppress and Punish Trafficking in Persons, Especially Women and Children[9] (adopted by the U.N. in 2000)—and TIP Reports use the terms trafficking in persons, severe forms of trafficking in persons, and human trafficking interchangeably. TIP Reports have also described human trafficking as *modern slavery*.[10]

The 2017 TIP Report illustratively describes common manifestations of human trafficking to include sex trafficking, child sex trafficking, forced labor, bonded labor (also known as debt bondage), domestic servitude, forced child labor, and unlawful recruitment and use of child soldiers.[11] Some government and nongovernmental entities may apply different definitions to refer to human trafficking, sometimes conflating human trafficking with human smuggling, illegal adoptions, international trade in human organs, child pornography, and prostitution.

---

[8] §103 of the TVPA; 22 U.S.C. 7102.

[9] For the treaty's current status, see United Nations Treaty Collection, *Protocol to Prevent, Suppress and Punish Trafficking in Persons, Especially Women and Children, supplementing the United Nations Convention against Transnational Organized Crime*, https://treaties.un.org/Pages/ViewDetails.aspx?src=IND&mtdsg_no=XVIII-12-a&chapter=18&lang=en.

[10] See U.S. Department of State, *Trafficking in Persons*, report (TIP Report), June 28, 2017.

[11] Ibid.

Required Country Lists in the TIP Report

Central to the TVPA's reporting requirements is a set of country lists, based on whether governments are achieving four minimum standards that the law prescribes for the elimination of severe forms of trafficking in persons. Specifically, the TVPA requires the report to include[12]

- a list of countries whose governments fully comply with the minimum standards for the elimination of severe forms of trafficking in persons; although the TVPA does not use the tier nomenclature, TIP Reports describe this list as Tier 1. (See Table 1 below.)
- a list of countries whose governments do not fully comply with the minimum standards but are making significant efforts to become compliant; TIP Reports describe this list as Tier 2. (See Table 2 below.)
- a list of countries whose governments do not fully comply and are not making significant efforts to become compliant; TIP Reports describe this list as Tier 3. (See Table 3 below.)

In accordance with the 2003 amendments to the TVPA, which required the creation of a new "special watch list," the 2004 TIP Report introduced a new category of country ranking, called the Tier 2 Watch List.[13] For further discussion, see section on "Reporting Requirements Related to the Special Watch List."

---

[12] §110 of the TVPA; 22 U.S.C. 7107.

[13] §6 of the 2003 TVPRA amended §110 of the TVPA; 22 U.S.C. 7107

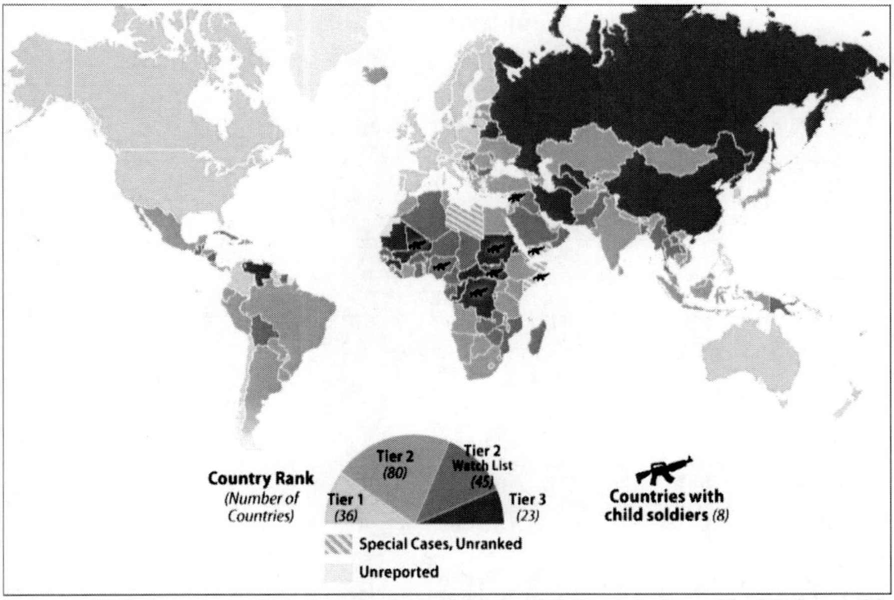

Source: CRS, based on U.S. Department of State, TIP Report, June 28, 2017, pp. 20, 46.

Figure 2. 2017 TIP Report: Country Rankings.

Table 1. Tier 1 Countries in the 2017 TIP Report

Armenia	Denmark	Korea, South	St. Maarten
Australia	Finland	Lithuania	Slovakia
Austria	France	Luxembourg	Slovenia
The Bahamas	Georgia	Netherlands	Spain
Belgium	Germany	New Zealand	Sweden
Canada	Guyana	Norway	Switzerland
Chile	Ireland	Philippines	Taiwan
Colombia	Israel	Poland	United Kingdom
Czechia	Italy	Portugal	United States

Source: U.S. Department of State, TIP Report, June 28, 2017, p. 46.

Table 2. Tier 2 Countries in the 2017 TIP Report

Afghanistan	Ecuador	Lesotho	St. Vincent and the Grenadines
Albania	Egypt	Macedonia	Seychelles
Angola	El Salvador	Malawi	Sierra Leone
Argentina	Estonia	Malaysia	Singapore
Aruba	Ethiopia	Maldives	Solomon Islands
Afghanistan	Ecuador	Lesotho	St. Vincent and the Grenadines
Azerbaijan	Fiji	Malta	South Africa
Bahrain	Greece	Mauritius	Sri Lanka
Barbados	Honduras	Mexico	Tajikistan
Bhutan	Iceland	Micronesia	Tanzania
Bosnia and Herzegovina	India	Mongolia	Timor-Leste
Botswana	Indonesia	Morocco	Togo
Brazil	Jamaica	Namibia	Tonga
Brunei	Japan	Nepal	Trinidad and Tobago
Cambodia	Jordan	Palau	Tunisia
Costa Rica	Kazakhstan	Panama	Turkey
Cote D’Ivoire	Kenya	Paraguay	Uganda
Croatia	Kosovo	Peru	Ukraine
Curaçao	Kyrgyz Republic	Qatar	United Arab Emirates
Cyprus	Latvia	Romania	Uruguay
Dominican Republic	Lebanon	St. Lucia	Vietnam

Source: U.S. Department of State, TIP Report, June 28, 2017, p. 46.

Table 3. Tier 3 Countries in the 2017 TIP Report

Belarus	Congo, Democratic Republic of	Iran	Sudan
Belize	Congo, Republic of	Korea, North	Syria
Burundi	Equatorial Guinea	Mali	Turkmenistan
Central African Republic	Eritrea	Mauritania	Uzbekistan
China	Guinea	Russia	Venezuela
Comoros	Guinea-Bissau	South Sudan	

Source: U.S. Department of State, TIP Report, June 28, 2017, p. 46.

Other Required Information in the TIP Report

In addition to the required country lists, the TVPA requires the State Department to include other information in the annual TIP Report. This includes[14]

- information on what the United Nations, Organization for Security and Cooperation in Europe, North Atlantic Treaty Organization, and other multilateral organizations, as appropriate, are doing to prevent their employees, contractors, and peacekeeping forces from engaging in human trafficking or exploiting victims of trafficking;
- information on changes in the global patterns of human trafficking, including prevalence data, disaggregated by source, transit, and destination countries, as well as nationality, gender, and age;
- information on emerging human trafficking issues; and
- information on "promising practices in the eradication of trafficking in persons."[15]

---

[14] §110 of the TVPA, as amended; 22 U.S.C. 7107.

[15] §1205 of the Violence Against Women Reauthorization Act of 2013 (2013 VAWRA; P.L. 113-4) added this requirement to §110 of the TVPA; 22 U.S.C. 7107. The 2014 TIP Report contained a section entitled "Promising Practices in the Eradication of Trafficking in Persons." Although the phrase *promising practices* is used in the 2015 Report, subsequent TIP Reports do not contain a section on "Promising Practices in the Eradication of

Reporting Requirements in the CSPA

Congress enacted the Child Soldiers Prevention Act of 2008 (CSPA) as part of its 2008 reauthorization of the TVPA.[16] A key element of the CSPA is the requirement to include in the annual TIP Report an additional list of foreign governments that recruit and use child soldiers in their armed forces or in government-supported armed groups. Government-supported armed groups include paramilitaries, militias, and civil defense forces. The 2017 TIP Report identified eight countries on the CSPA list: the Democratic Republic of Congo, Mali, Nigeria, Somalia, South Sudan, Sudan, Syria, and Yemen.

FAQ: Who is a *child soldier?*

The CSPA of 2008 defines child solider (including those "serving in any capacity, including in a support role such as a cook, porter, messenger, medic, guard, or sex slave") to mean children:

(i) under 18 years who take direct part in hostilities as a member of government armed forces;
(ii) under 18 years who are compulsorily recruited into governmental armed forces;
(iii) under 15 years who are voluntarily recruited into governmental armed forces; or
(iv) under 18 years who are recruited or used in hostilities by non-state armed forces.

Trafficking in Persons." Moreover, the 2016 and 2017 TIP Reports do not contain the phrase *promising practices*.

[16] Title IV of the 2008 TVPRA; 22 U.S.C. 2370c et seq.

Reporting Requirements Related to the Special Watch List

Apart from the TIP Report, the TVPA, as amended, requires the Secretary of State to submit to appropriate congressional committees a special watch list composed of countries determined by the Secretary of State to require special scrutiny during the following year. This requirement to develop a special watch list was first enacted in the TVPA reauthorization of 2003.[17]

The TVPA mandates that this list be composed of three types of countries: (1) countries upgraded in most recent TIP Report and now assessed to be fully compliant with the minimum standards (from Tier 2 to Tier 1); (2) countries upgraded in the most recent TIP Report and now assessed to be making significant efforts toward compliance with the minimum standards (from Tier 3 to Tier 2); and (3) a subset of Tier 2 countries in which

- the absolute number of victims is very significant or significantly increasing;
- there is a failure to provide evidence of increasing efforts to combat severe forms of trafficking in persons, compared to the previous year; or
- the determination that significant efforts are being made to become compliant is based on government commitments to take additional future steps over the next year.

Relationship to the Tier 2 Watch List

Although the TVPA, as amended, authorizes the special watch list to be submitted separately from the TIP Report, the State Department introduced it as a feature in the 2004 TIP Report.[18] Beginning with the

---

[17] This criterion was added by §6 of the 2003 TVPRA and amended by §1205 of the 2013 VAWRA; 22 U.S.C. 7107. The 2004 TIP Report was the first TIP Report to include the "special watch list." Beginning with the 2005 TIP Report, the State Department termed the special watch list countries that were not upgraded as "Tier 2 Watch List." For further discussion, see subsection on "Relationship to the Tier 2 Watch List."

[18] §110 of the TVPA, as amended, specifically requires the special watch list to be submitted to appropriate congressional committees no later than the date when the President submits a

2004 TIP Report, the department included a fourth list of countries in its annual TIP Report, called the Tier 2 Watch List. This Tier 2 Watch List is composed of the special watch list countries whose governments would otherwise be listed on Tier 2, except that the absolute number of victims is large or growing, or antitrafficking efforts appear to have stalled or have yet to be implemented. (See *Table 4* below.)

Table 4. Tier 2 Watch List Countries in the 2017 TIP Report

Algeria	Djibouti	Macau	Rwanda
Bangladesh	The Gambia	Marshall Islands	Senegal
Benin	Ghana	Moldova	Serbia
Bolivia	Guatemala	Montenegro	Suriname
Bulgaria	Haiti	Mozambique	Swaziland
Burkina Faso	Hong Kong	Nicaragua	Thailand
Burma	Hungary	Niger	Zambia
Cabo Verde	Iraq	Nigeria	Zimbabwe
Cameroon	Kuwait	Oman	
Chad	Laos	Pakistan	
Cuba	Liberia	Papua New Guinea	

Source: U.S. Department of State, TIP Report, June 28, 2017, p. 46.

Mid-Year Interim Assessment

Due on February 1 each year, the TVPA, as amended, requires the Secretary of State to submit to appropriate congressional committees an interim assessment of the progress made by each special watch list country since the last TIP Report.[19] These mid-year assessments are typically brief, stating both positive and negative developments in each special watch list country. Readers are unable to predict, based solely on these reports,

notification and determination regarding which countries will be barred or waived from certain categories of foreign assistance due to their failure to comply with the minimum standards and make significant efforts toward compliance. The latter notification and determination is required to be made not less than 45 days or more than 90 days after submission of the TIP Report (due June 1) or an "Interim Report" pursuant to §110(b)(2) of the TVPA, which may be referring to a provision that was struck by §1205(2) of the 2013 VAWRA.

[19] §110 of the TVPA, as amended by §6 of the 2003 TVPRA; 22 U.S.C. 7107.

whether a country's ranking will improve, remain the same, or decline in the next TIP Report.

Watch List Downgrades

The TVPA, as amended, requires that a country on the special watch list (in practice, the Tier 2 Watch List) for two consecutive years be subsequently listed among those whose governments do not fully comply and are not making significant efforts to become compliant (Tier 3). The requirement to limit the length of time a country may remain on the watch list was enacted in the TVPA reauthorization of 2008.[20] The first year in which it came into effect was 2009 and the first year in which a Tier 2 Watch List country was downgraded for its duration in this tier category was 2013.

In the 2017 TIP Report, a total of five countries were downgraded to Tier 3 after two or more consecutive years on the Tier 2 Watch List:

- *China* (downgraded after three consecutive years on the Tier 2 Watch List);
- *Democratic Republic of Congo* (downgraded after two consecutive years);
- *Republic of Congo* (downgraded after two consecutive years);
- *Guinea* (downgraded after four consecutive years); and
- *Mali* (downgraded after four consecutive years).

Watch List Downgrade Waivers

Pursuant to the TVPA, as amended, the President may waive downgrades for up to two years if the President determines and reports credible evidence justifying a waiver because

- the country has a written plan to begin making significant efforts to become compliant with the minimum standards for the elimination of trafficking in persons;

---

[20] §110 of the TPVA, as amended by §107 of the 2008 TVPRA; 22 U.S.C. 7107.

- the written plan, if implemented, would constitute significant efforts to become compliant with the minimum standards; and
- the country is devoting sufficient resources to implement the plan.[21]

In the 2017 TIP Report, a total of nine countries received waivers to stay on Tier 2 Watch List for more than two consecutive years. (See Table 5 below.)

FAQ: How Is Congress Notified of Watch List Downgrade Waivers?

Credible evidence in support of downgrade waivers is to be submitted to the Senate Foreign Relations and the House Foreign Affairs Committees. Within 30 days after such congressional notification, the TVPA, as amended, also requires the Secretary of State to provide a detailed description of such evidence on a publicly available website maintained by the State Department.[22]

Reporting Requirements in the TPA

The President is required to submit to appropriate congressional committees additional information on countries upgraded from Tier 3 in the prior year's TIP Report. Pursuant to the Bipartisan Congressional Trade Priorities and Accountability Act of 2015 (TPA), as amended, the President must submit detailed descriptions of credible evidence

[21] Ibid. The President delegated this waiver authority to the Secretary of State. See 75 FR 67023.

[22] §110 of the TPVA, as amended by §107 of the 2008 TVPRA and §1205 of the 2013 VAWRA; 22 U.S.C. 7107. The 2013 VAWRA added the public notice provision. A December 2016 U.S. Government Accountability Office (GAO) report found that the State Department had not posted the requisite detailed description online until September 2016. See GAO, *Human Trafficking: State Has Made Improvements in Its Annual Report but Does Not Explicitly Explain Certain Tier Rankings or Changes*, GAO-17-56, December 2016. For the 2017 public notification, see State Department, Office to Monitor and Combat Trafficking in Persons, "Memorandum of Justification Consistent with Section 110(B)(2)(D) of the Trafficking Victims Protection Act of 2000," webpage, July 18, 2017, https://www.state.gov/j/tip/rls/reports/2017/272651.htm.

supporting these upgrades.[23] The detailed descriptions may be accompanied by copies of documents providing such evidence.

In the 2017 TIP Report, nine countries were upgraded from Tier 3 in the 2016 TIP Report: Algeria, Burma, Djibouti, The Gambia, Haiti, Marshall Islands, Papua New Guinea, Suriname, and Zimbabwe.

Table 5. Tier 2 Watch List Countries for More than Two Consecutive Years

Country	2014 TIP Report	2015 TIP Report	2016 TIP Report	2017 TIP Report
Antigua and Barbuda	Tier 2 Watch List	Tier 2 Watch List	Tier 2 Watch List	Tier 2 Watch List
Bolivia	Tier 2 Watch List	Tier 2 Watch List	Tier 2 Watch List	Tier 2 Watch List
Bulgaria	Tier 2	Tier 2 Watch List	Tier 2 Watch List	Tier 2 Watch List
Cuba	Tier 3	Tier 2 Watch List	Tier 2 Watch List	Tier 2 Watch List
Gabon	Tier 2	Tier 2 Watch List	Tier 2 Watch List	Tier 2 Watch List
Ghana	Tier 2	Tier 2 Watch List	Tier 2 Watch List	Tier 2 Watch List
Laos	Tier 2 Watch List	Tier 2 Watch List	Tier 2 Watch List	Tier 2 Watch List
Pakistan	Tier 2 Watch List	Tier 2 Watch List	Tier 2 Watch List	Tier 2 Watch List
Saudi Arabia	Tier 3	Tier 2 Watch List	Tier 2 Watch List	Tier 2 Watch List

Source: U.S. Department of State, TIP Reports, 2014-2017, pp. 58, 54, 56, and 46, respectfully.

Note: Country Rank Outcomes in the 2014-2017 TIP Reports

[23] The TPA is Title I of P.L. 114-26, the Defending Public Safety Employees' Retirement Act. The TIP Report-related provision in the TPA was amended by §914 of the Trade Facilitation and Trade Enforcement Act of 2015. See 19 U.S.C. 4205. The President delegated this reporting requirement to the Secretary of State. See 81 FR 35579.

EXPECTATIONS FOR THE ELIMINATION OF TRAFFICKING

As discussed above, a central and required element of each TIP Report is the evaluation of each government's commitment to eliminating severe forms of trafficking in persons. Countries are assessed on the basis of four *minimum standards* and 12 *criteria* prescribed by the TVPA, as amended.[24] While the four minimum standards have not been amended since the TVPA was first enacted, the criteria for evaluating what constitutes *serious and sustained efforts* to eliminate trafficking have been modified and expanded through multiple reauthorizations of the TVPA since 2000.[25] Although these provisions prescribe the means through which the State Department evaluates the efforts of foreign governments, country-specific considerations often leave State Department officials considerable discretion in categorizing countries (for further discussion, see section on "Ranking Dispute Resolution" below).

Four Minimum Standards

The TVPA identifies four minimum standards for the elimination of trafficking, which governments are expected to achieve:[26]

1. Governments should prohibit severe forms of trafficking in persons and punish such acts.
2. Governments should prescribe punishment commensurate with that of grave crimes for the knowing commission of any act

---

[24] §108 of the TVPA, as amended; 22 U.S.C. 7106.

[25] Although the four minimum standards have not been amended since the TVPA was first enacted, §106 of the 2008 TVPRA revised a prefatory provision that specified the types of countries, which would be evaluated in TIP Reports for compliance with the minimum standards. Originally, §108 of the TVPA stated that the minimum standards were "applicable to the government of a country of origin, transit, or destination for a significant number of victims of severe forms of trafficking." §106 of the 2008 TVPRA removed from §108 of the TVPA the phrase *a significant number of*— a phrase that the State Department had previously used to limit the number of countries subject to rankings in the TIP Report.

[26] §108 of the TVPA; 22 U.S.C. 7106.

involving sex trafficking induced by force, fraud, or coercion; sex trafficking involving a child; or any act that includes rape, kidnapping, or which causes death.

3. Governments should prescribe punishment for the knowing commission of any severe form of trafficking in persons that is sufficiently stringent to deter future acts and adequately reflect the heinous nature of the offense.
4. Governments should make *serious and sustained efforts* to eliminate severe forms of trafficking in persons.

Twelve Criteria for *Serious and Sustained Efforts*

In assessing whether governments are achieving the fourth minimum standard, that of making *serious and sustained efforts* to eliminate severe forms of trafficking in persons, the TVPA initially included seven criteria, or indicative factors.[27] Subsequent TVPA reauthorizations amended the TVPA to modify some of the original criteria and expand the list. There are currently 12 criteria:

1. Enforcement and prosecution—whether governments vigorously investigate and prosecute acts of severe forms of trafficking in persons, including convicting and sentencing those responsible for such acts.[28]
2. Victim protection—whether governments protect victims of severe forms of trafficking in persons, encourage their assistance in the investigation and prosecution of such trafficking, and ensure that victims are not inappropriately incarcerated, filed, or otherwise

[27] The Conference Report accompanying the TVPA clarified that countries are not required to meet all the listed criteria. Specifically it states: "The conferees do not expect that a government would be required to fulfill all the criteria... in order to be making 'serious and sustained efforts' to eliminate severe forms of trafficking in persons. Rather, the subsection requires only that the Secretary consider these factors in determining whether the government is making such efforts." See Conference Report to Accompany H.R. 3244, Victims of Trafficking and Violence Protection Act of 2000, H.Rept. 106-939, October 5, 2000, p. 96.

[28] This criterion was amended by §6 of the 2003 TVPRA and §106 of the 2008 TVPRA.

penalized for unlawful acts resulting directly from having been trafficked.[29]

3. Trafficking prevention—whether governments have adopted measures to prevent severe forms of trafficking in persons.[30]
4. International cooperation—whether governments cooperate with other governments in the investigation and prosecution of severe forms of trafficking in persons and whether governments have entered into bilateral, multilateral, or regional law enforcement cooperation and coordination arrangements with others.[31]
5. Extradition—whether governments extradite those charged with acts of severe forms of trafficking in persons on terms and to an extent similar to those charged with other serious crimes.
6. Trafficking patterns and human rights protections—whether governments monitor migration patterns for evidence of severe forms of trafficking in persons and whether law enforcement responses to such evidence are both consistent with the vigorous investigation and prosecution of acts of such trafficking and with the protection of a victim's human rights.
7. Enforcement and prosecution of public officials—whether governments vigorously investigate, prosecute, convict, and sentence public officials who participate in or facilitate severe forms of trafficking in persons, as well as whether governments take all appropriate measures against officials who condone such trafficking.[32]
8. Foreign victims—whether noncitizen victims of severe forms of trafficking in persons are insignificant as a percentage of all victims in a country.[33]
9. Partnerships—whether governments have entered into effective and transparent partnerships, cooperative arrangements, or

[29] This criterion was amended by §106 of the 2008 TVPRA.

[30] This criterion was amended by §104 of the 2005 TVPRA (P.L. 109-164), §106 of the 2008 TVPRA, and §1204 of the VAWRA of 2013.

[31] This criterion was amended by §1204 of the 2013 VAWRA.

[32] This criterion was amended by §6 of the 2003 TVPRA, §104 of the 2005 TVPRA, and §1204 of the 2013 VAWRA.

[33] This criterion was added by §6 of the 2003 TVPRA.

agreements that have resulted in concrete and measurable outcomes with the United States or other external partners.[34]

10. Self-monitoring—whether governments systematically monitor their efforts to satisfy certain above-listed criteria and publicly share periodic assessments of such efforts.[35]
11. Progress—whether governments achieve appreciable progress in eliminating severe forms of trafficking in persons, compared to the previous year's assessment.[36]
12. Demand reduction—whether governments have made serious and sustained efforts to reduce demand for commercial sex acts and international sex tourism.[37]

ACTIONS AGAINST GOVERNMENTS FAILING TO MEET MINIMUM STANDARDS

The TVPA established that certain types of foreign assistance may not be provided to governments that are not committed to meeting the minimum standards for the elimination of severe forms of trafficking in persons (Tier 3 countries).

> It is the policy of the United States not to provide nonhumanitarian, non-trade-related foreign assistance to any government that—
>
> (i) does not comply with minimum standards for the elimination of trafficking; and
> (ii) is not making significant efforts to bring itself into compliance with such standards.[38]

---

[34] This criterion was added by §1204 of the 2013 VAWRA.

[35] This criterion was added by §6 of the 2003 TVPRA (and moved by §1204 of the 2013 VAWRA).

[36] Ibid.

[37] Key elements of this criterion had previously been included in the third criterion, as added by §104 of the 2005 TVPRA. It was later moved and modified by §106 of the 2008 TVPRA and then moved again by §1204 of the 2013 VAWRA.

FAQ: What constitutes *significant efforts*?

In determining whether a government is making significant efforts to become compliant with the four minimum standards for the elimination of trafficking, the TVPA requires the Secretary of State to consider three factors:

- the extent to which a country is a source, transit, or destination for severe forms of trafficking in persons;
- the extent of noncompliance with the minimum standards by the countries, including in particular whether public officials are involved in severe forms of trafficking in persons; and
- what measures are reasonable, due to resource and capability constraints, to bring the government into compliance with the minimum standards.[39]

Aid Restrictions in the TVPA

The TVPA's provisions to restrict certain types of U.S. aid and certain other categories of U.S. and multilateral funding to Tier 3 countries began with the 2003 TIP Report. Funding subject to potential restriction includes *nonhumanitarian, non-trade-related foreign assistance* authorized pursuant to the Foreign Assistance Act of 1961, sales and financing authorized by the Arms Export Control Act (AECA), and educational and cultural exchange funding, as well as loans and other funding provided by multilateral development banks and the International Monetary Fund.

---

[38] §110 of the TVPA; 22 U.S.C. 7107.
[39] Ibid.

Aid Authorized by the Foreign Assistance Act of 1961

Nonhumanitarian, non-trade-related foreign assistance is defined in the TVPA[40] as assistance authorized pursuant to the Foreign Assistance Act of 1961 (FAA) except for the following:

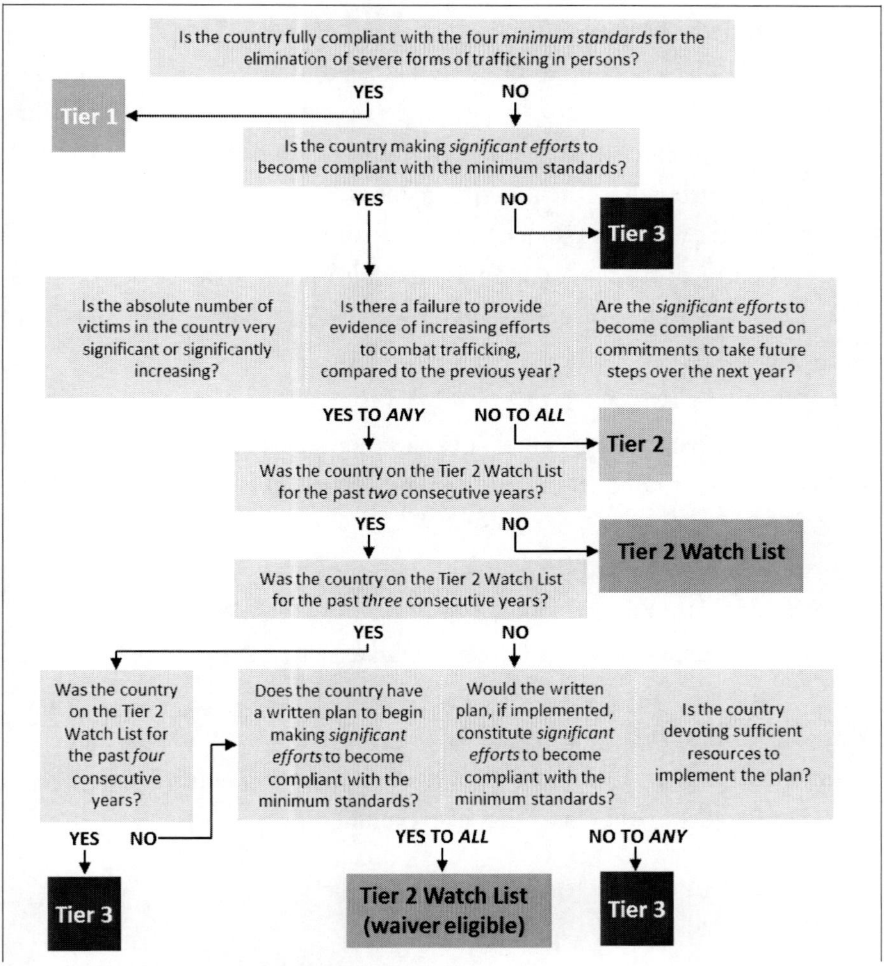

Source: CRS, based on the TVPA, as amended.

Figure 3. Country Ranking Decisions: Which Tier in the TIP Report?

---

[40] §103 of the TVPA; 22 U.S.C. 7102.

- Assistance authorized under Chapter 4 of part II of the FAA in support of programs, projects, or activities conducted by nongovernmental organizations and eligible for Development Assistance under Chapter 1 of part I of the FAA;
- International Narcotics Control assistance authorized under chapter 8 of part I of the FAA;
- Any other counternarcotics assistance authorized under Chapters 4 or 5 of part II of the FAA (Economic Support Fund and International Military Education and Training), subject to certain congressional notification procedures;[41]
- Disaster relief assistance, including any assistance under Chapter 9 of part I of the FAA (International Disaster Assistance);
- Antiterrorism assistance authorized under Chapter 8 of part II of the FAA;
- Refugee assistance;
- Humanitarian and other development assistance in support of programs conducted by nongovernmental organizations under Chapters 1 and 10 of the FAA;[42]
- Overseas Private Investment Corporation programs authorized under Title IV of Chapter 2 of part I of the FAA; and
- Other trade-related or humanitarian assistance programs.

Sales and Financing Authorized by the Arms Export Control Act

Pursuant to the TVPA, *nonhumanitarian, non-trade-related foreign assistance* subject to aid restriction also includes

[41] For the notification procedures, see Section 634 of the FAA, as amended (22 U.S.C. 2394-1).

[42] Pursuant to notes in the U.S. Code, the TVPA's reference to Chapters 1 and 10 of the FAA probably refers to Chapters 1 and 10 of part I of the FAA, which authorize development assistance and the Development Fund for Africa.

- Sales or financing on any terms authorized by the AECA—with the exception of sales or financing provided for narcotics-related purposes if congressionally notified.[43]

Funding for Educational and Cultural Exchanges

In the case of countries that do not receive such *nonhumanitarian, non-trade-related foreign assistance*, the TVPA authorizes the President to withhold funding for participation by officials or employees of Tier 3 in educational and cultural exchange programs.[44]

Loans and Other Funds Provided by Multilateral Development Banks and the International Monetary Fund

The TVPA authorizes the President to instruct the U.S. Executive Directors of each multilateral development bank and of the International Monetary Fund to vote against and otherwise attempt to deny loans or other uses of funds to Tier 3 countries.[45]

Presidential Determinations, Waivers, and Certifications

Between 45 and 90 days after submission of the annual TIP Report (due June 1), the TVPA[46] requires the President to make a determination regarding whether and to what extent antitrafficking aid restrictions are to be imposed on Tier 3 countries during the following fiscal year. (See *Table 6* below.) Typically issued near the beginning of the fiscal year and published in the *Federal Register*, the presidential determinations address the following:

---

[43] For the notification procedures, see Section 634 of the FAA, as amended (22 U.S.C. 2394-1).

[44] §110 of the TVPA; 22 U.S.C. 7107.

[45] Pursuant to §110 of the TVPA (22 U.S.C. 7107), the U.S. Executive Directors of each multilateral development bank and the International Monetary Fund may support loans and other uses of funds to Tier 3 countries for humanitarian assistance; trade-related assistance; or development assistance that directly addresses basic human needs, is not administered by the government of the Tier 3 country, and confers no benefit to that government.

[46] The TVPA specifies that Presidential determinations are to be made between 45 and 90 days after submission of the annual TIP Report or an "Interim Report" pursuant to §110(b)(2) of the TVPA. The Interim Report may be in reference to provision that was struck by §1205(2) of the 2013 VAWRA.

- *Applicability of aid restrictions*—whether to withhold *nonhumanitarian, nontrade-related assistance* authorized by the FAA and the AECA, including whether to withhold funding for education and cultural exchanges and loans and other funds provided by multilateral development banks and the International Monetary Fund;
- *Duplication of aid restrictions*—whether ongoing, multiple, broad-based restrictions, comparable to those specified by the TVPA, on assistance in response to human rights violations are already in place;
- *Subsequent compliance*—whether the Secretary of State has found that the government of a Tier 3 country is now compliant with the minimum standards or is making significant efforts to become compliant; and
- *National interest concerns*—whether to continue assistance, in part or in whole, because it would promote the purposes of the TVPA or is otherwise in the national interest of the United States—including when the continuation of assistance is necessary to avoid significant adverse effects on vulnerable populations, such as women and children.

Pursuant to the TVPA, the President may selectively waive aid restrictions for national interest concerns, including exercise of the waiver for one or more specific programs, projects, or activities. Following the initial presidential determination required by the TVPA, as amended, the President may make additional determinations to waive, in part or in whole, aid restrictions on Tier 3 countries.[47]

---

[47] §110 of the TVPA, as added by §6 of the 2003 TVPRA; 22 U.S.C. 7107.

Table 6. Aid Restrictions and Waivers for Tier 3 Countries, Pursuant to the TVPA, FY2004-FY2017

<table>
<tr><th>Fiscal Year</th><th>Aid Restricted</th><th>Full National Interest Waivers</th><th>Partial National Interest Waivers</th><th>Waivers Due to Subsequent Compliance</th></tr>
<tr><td>FY2004</td><td rowspan="4">Burma, Cuba, North Korea</td><td rowspan="2">None</td><td>Liberia, Sudan</td><td>Belize, Bosnia and Herzegovina, Dominican Republic, Georgia, Greece, Haiti, Kazakhstan, Suriname, Turkey, Uzbekistan</td></tr>
<tr><td>FY2005</td><td>Equatorial Guinea, Sudan, Venezuela</td><td>Bangladesh, Ecuador, Guyana, Sierra Leone</td></tr>
<tr><td>FY2006</td><td>Ecuador, Kuwait, Saudi Arabia</td><td>Cambodia, Venezuela</td><td>Bolivia, Jamaica, Qatar, Sudan, Togo, United Arab Emirates</td></tr>
<tr><td>FY2007</td><td>Saudi Arabia, Sudan, Uzbekistan</td><td>Iran, Syria, Venezuela, Zimbabwe</td><td>Belize, Laos</td></tr>
<tr><td>FY2008</td><td>Burma, Cuba</td><td>Algeria, Bahrain, Malaysia, Oman, Qatar, Saudi Arabia, Sudan, Uzbekistan</td><td>Iran, North Korea, Syria, Venezuela</td><td>Equatorial Guinea, Kuwait</td></tr>
<tr><td>FY2009</td><td>Burma, Cuba, Syria</td><td>Algeria, Fiji, Kuwait, Papua New Guinea, Qatar, Saudi Arabia, Sudan</td><td>Iran, North Korea</td><td>Moldova, Oman</td></tr>
<tr><td>FY2010</td><td>Cuba, North Korea</td><td>Chad, Kuwait, Malaysia, Mauritania, Niger, Papua New Guinea, Saudi Arabia, Sudan</td><td>Burma, Eritrea, Fiji, Iran, Syria, Zimbabwe</td><td>Swaziland</td></tr>
</table>

Table 6. (Continued)

FY2011	Eritrea, North Korea	Democratic Republic of Congo, Dominican Republic, Kuwait, Mauritania, Papua New Guinea, Saudi Arabia, Sudan	Burma, Cuba, Iran, Zimbabwe	None
FY2012	Eritrea, Madagascar, North Korea	Algeria, Central African Republic, Guinea-Bissau, Kuwait, Lebanon, Libya, Mauritania, Micronesia, Papua New Guinea, Saudi Arabia, Sudan, Turkmenistan, Yemen	Burma*, Cuba, Democratic Republic of Congo, Equatorial Guinea, Iran, Venezuela, Zimbabwe	
FY2013	Cuba, Eritrea, Madagascar, North Korea	Algeria, Central African Republic, Kuwait, Libya, Papua New Guinea, Saudi Arabia, Yemen	Democratic Republic of Congo, Equatorial Guinea, Iran, Sudan, Syria, Zimbabwe	
FY2014	Cuba, Iran, North Korea	Algeria, Central African Republic, China, Guinea-Bissau, Kuwait, Libya, Mauritania, Papua New Guinea, Russia, Saudi Arabia, Uzbekistan, Yemen	Democratic Republic of Congo, Sudan, Equatorial Guinea, Eritrea, Syria, Zimbabwe	
FY2015	Iran, North Korea, Russia	Algeria, Central African Republic, The Gambia, Guinea-Bissau, Kuwait, Libya, Malaysia, Mauritania, Papua New Guinea, Saudi Arabia, Thailand, Uzbekistan, Yemen	Cuba, Democratic Republic of Congo, Equatorial Guinea, Eritrea, Syria, Venezuela, Zimbabwe	

FY2016	Iran, North Korea	Algeria, Belarus, Belize, Burundi, Central African Republic, Comoros, The Gambia, Guinea-Bissau, Kuwait, Libya, Marshall Islands, Mauritania, Thailand	Equatorial Guinea, Eritrea, Russia, South Sudan, Syria, Venezuela, Yemen, Zimbabwe	None
FY2017		Algeria, Belarus, Belize, Burma, Burundi, Central African Republic, Comoros, Djibouti, The Gambia, Guinea-Bissau, Haiti, Marshall Islands, Mauritania, Papua New Guinea, Suriname, Turkmenistan, Uzbekistan	Equatorial Guinea, Eritrea, Russia, South Sudan, Sudan, Syria, Venezuela, Zimbabwe	

Sources: Determination of the President of the United States, Nos. 2003-35 (68 FR 53871), 2004-46 (69 FR 56155), 2005-37 (70 FR 57481), 2006-25 (71 FR 64431), 2008-4 (72 FR 61037), 2009-5 (73 FR 63839), 2009-29 (74 FR 48365), 2010-15 (75 FR 67017, 68411), 2011-18 (76 FR 62599), 2012-16 (77 FR 58921, as amended by 77 FR 61046), 2013-16 (78 FR 58861), 2014-16 (79 FR 57699), 2016-01 (80 FR 62435), 2016-12 (81 FR 70311).

Notes: Following the President's delegation of authority on February 3, 2012 (see 77 FR 11375), the Secretary of State revised Presidential Determination No. 2011-18 on February 6, 2012, to waive prohibitions on U.S. support for assistance to Burma through international financial institutions. See U.S. Department of State Public Notice No. 7799 (77 FR 9295). Other presidential delegations of authority were issued on July 29, 2013, for Syria (78 FR 48027) and on October 5, 2015, for Yemen (78 FR 6505).

As part of the President's determinations, the TVPA also requires the President to include a certification by the Secretary of State that no counternarcotics or counterterrorism assistance authorized by the FAA or arms sales and financing authorized by the AECA is intended to be received or used by any agency or official who has participated in, facilitated, or condoned a severe form of trafficking in persons.[48]

Security Assistance Restrictions in the CSPA

Countries listed in the current TIP Report as having recruited and used child soldiers are prohibited from receiving certain types of security assistance, including

- excess defense articles;[49]
- international military education and training;[50]
- peacekeeping operations and other programs;[51]
- foreign military financing for the procurement of defense articles and services, as well as design and construction services;[52] and
- issuance of licenses for direct commercial sales of military equipment to countries listed in the current TIP Report for child soldiers recruitment and use.

(For further discussion about the CSPA's relationship to security cooperation programs and activities, see text box "FAQs on Child Soldiers Prohibitions" below.)

Exceptions and Presidential Determinations, Certifications, and Waivers

CSPA security assistance restrictions may not apply if one of four circumstances is invoked. (See *Table 7* below.)

---

[48] §110 of the TVPA, as amended with technical edits by §1212 of the 2013 VAWRA; 22 U.S.C. 7107.

[49] As authorized by §516 of the FAA, as amended; 22 U.S.C. 2321j.

[50] As authorized by §541 of the FAA, as amended; 22 U.S.C. 2347.

[51] As authorized by §551 of the FAA, as amended; 22 U.S.C. 2348.

[52] As authorized by §23 of the Arms Export Control Act, as amended; 22 U.S.C. 2763.

Peacekeeping Exception

Assistance may continue to child soldier countries for peacekeeping operations that support military professionalization, security sector reform, heightened respect for human rights, peacekeeping preparation, or the demobilization and reintegration of child soldiers.

International Military Education and Training and Nonlethal Supplies Exception

Assistance for international military education, training, and nonlethal supplies to child solider countries may continue for up to five years, if the President certifies to appropriate congressional committees that such assistance will directly support professionalization of the military. The President must also certify that the country is taking "reasonable steps to implement effective measures to demobilize child soldiers ... and is taking reasonable steps in the context of its national resources to provide demobilization, rehabilitation, and reintegration assistance to those former child soldiers."

National Interest Waiver

The President may waive the CSPA security assistance restrictions if it is determined that such a waiver is in the national interest of the United States and the President submits a notification and justification to appropriate congressional committees within 45 days of granting a waiver. The presidential determination is also typically published in the *Federal Register*, though the President's memorandum of justification is not. (See *Table 7* below.)

Reinstatement Certification

Security assistance otherwise prohibited by the CSPA may be reinstated if the President certifies to appropriate congressional committees that the government of the listed country has (1) implemented measures, including an action plan and actual steps to stop recruiting and using child soldiers, and (2) implemented policies and mechanisms to prohibit and prevent future use of child soldiers.

Table 7. Aid Restrictions and Waivers to Child Soldier Countries, Pursuant to the CSPA, FY2011-FY2017

Fiscal Year	Aid Restricted	Full National Interest Waivers	Partial National Interest Waivers	Waivers Due to Subsequent Compliance
FY2011	Burma, Somalia	Chad, Democratic Republic of Congo, Sudan, Yemen	None	None
FY2012	Burma, Somalia, Sudan	Yemen	Democratic Republic of Congo	Chad
FY2013	Burma, Sudan	Libya, South Sudan, Yemen	Democratic Republic of Congo, Somalia[a]	None
FY2014	Burma, Central African Republic, Rwanda, Sudan, Syria	Chad, South Sudan, Yemen	Democratic Republic of Congo, Somalia	
FY2015	Burma, Sudan, Syria	Rwanda, Somalia, Yemen	Central African Republic, Democratic Republic of Congo, South Sudan	
FY2016	Burma, Sudan, Syria, Yemen	Democratic Republic of Congo, Nigeria, Somalia	South Sudan	
FY2017	Syria, Yemen, Sudan	Burma, Iraq, Nigeria	Democratic Republic of Congo, Rwanda, Somalia, South Sudan	

Sources: Determination of the President of the United States, Nos. 2011-4 (75 FR 75855), 2012-01 (76 FR 65927), 2012-18 (77 FR 61509), 2013-17 (78 FR 63367), 2014-18 (79 FR 69755), 2015-13 (80 FR 62431), 2016- 14 (81 FR 72683).

[a] Following the President's delegation of authority on August 2, 2013 (see 78 FR 72789), the Secretary of State revised Presidential Determination No. 2012-18 on August 14, 2013, to partially waive restrictions on Somalia to allow for assistance under the Peacekeeping Operations authority for logistical support and troop stipends in FY2013. This State Department decision was not published in the Federal Register. In at least two other years, the President also delegated authority to the Secretary of State to make additional CSPA determinations with respect to Yemen: on September 29, 2015 (80 FR 62429), and on September 28, 2016 (81 FR 72681).

Security Assistance Restrictions in FY2017 Appropriations

The Consolidated Appropriations Act, 2017 (P.L. 115-31), contains two provisions that additionally prohibit certain types of security assistance from being used to support military training or operations that involve child soldiers. Similar provisions have also been included in prior appropriations measures in recent years.

- Section 8088 of the Department of Defense Appropriations Act, 2017 (Division C of P.L. 115-31), states that CSPA-listed countries may not receive certain funds appropriated by this act "to support any military training or operation that includes child soldiers" unless the President issues a determination pursuant to the CPSA that permits such assistance.[53]
- Section 7034(b)(1) of the Department of State, Foreign Operations, and Related Programs Appropriations Act, 2017 (Division J of P.L. 115-31), states that funds appropriated by this act "should not be used to support any military training or operations that include child soldiers."[54]

---

[53] Specified funds, subject to restriction in Section 8088 of the FY2017 Defense Department Appropriations Act, include those made available for excess defense articles, assistance under Section 1206 of the National Defense Authorization Act for Fiscal Year 2006, and peacekeeping operations. Similar provisions have been included in recent past Defense Department Appropriations Acts. For FY2016, see Section 8088 of P.L. 114-113; for FY2015, see Section 8092 of P.L. 113-235; for FY2014, see Section 8116 of P.L. 113-76; for FY2013, see Section 8115 of P.L. 113- 6; and for FY2012, see Section 8128 of P.L. 112-74.

[54] Similar provisions have been included in recent past Department of State, Foreign Operations, and Related Programs Appropriations Acts. For FY2016, see Section 7034(b)(1) of P.L. 114-113; for FY2015 see "peacekeeping operations" heading under Title IV of P.L. 113-235; for FY2014, see "peacekeeping operations" heading under Title IV of P.L. 113-76; for FY2013, see Section 1101 (extending Department of State, Foreign Operations, and Related Programs Appropriations Act, 2012) of Title I, Division F of P.L. 113-6; for FY2012, see "peacekeeping operations" heading under Title IV of P.L. 112-74; and for FY2011, see Section 2111 (adding a child soldiers provision to the extension of FY2010 appropriations provisions for "peacekeeping operations") of Title XI of P.L. 112-10.

FAQs on Child Soldiers Prohibitions

Are countries that recruit and use child soldiers eligible to receive DOD security assistance?

Despite the CSPA and recent provisions in annual appropriations acts, it may be possible for CSPA-listed countries to receive U.S. security assistance. One category of such assistance may include security cooperation programs and activities authorized in Title 10 of the U.S. Code (Armed Forces), funded in annual Defense Appropriations, and executed by the U.S. Department of Defense (DOD). Although the FY2017 Defense Department Appropriations Act prohibits a few types of security assistance, most Title 10 security cooperation authorities are not addressed.

Has the President waived or partially waived DOD security assistance in annual CSPA determinations?

Presidential determinations to waive or partially waive CSPA security assistance restrictions have made reference in the past to some DOD security cooperation authorities that have been used to provide assistance to countries identified as recruiting and using child soldiers. In the most recent presidential determination with respect to the CSPA, issued by then-President Barack Obama on September 28, 2016, Somalia received a partial waiver to receive assistance in FY2017 authorized pursuant to 10 U.S.C. 2282.55 South Sudan received a partial waiver to receive assistance in FY2017 authorized pursuant to Section 1208 of the FY2014 NDAA.56

[55] See Determination of the President of the United States No. 2016-14 (81 FR 72683). 10 U.S.C. 2282, used by DOD to train, equip, and build the capacity of foreign security forces for counterterrorism and military or stability operations, may not be used to provide assistance "that is otherwise prohibited by any provision of law." Moreover, it may not be used to provide assistance "to any foreign country that is otherwise prohibited from receiving such type of assistance under any other provision of law."

[56] Section 1208 of the FY2014 NDAA, used by DOD to support operations to counter the Lord's Resistance Army, may not be used to provide assistance "that is otherwise prohibited by any provision of law.

Are security forces units that recruit and use children banned from assistance under the Leahy Laws?

The U.S. Leahy Laws—codified at 22 U.S.C. 2378d and 10 U.S.C. 362—prohibit U.S. security assistance otherwise provided by the U.S. Departments of State and Defense to foreign security forces when there is credible information that a recipient unit has committed a gross violation of human rights (GVHR). Although the recruitment and use of child soldiers is often described as a human rights concern, it is not specifically addressed by the Leahy Laws, which do not define GVHR. As a matter of policy, the U.S. government vets for credible information that indicates (1) torture, (2) extrajudicial killing, (3) enforced disappearance, or (4) rape under color of law.

Trade Restrictions in the TPA

Pursuant to the Bipartisan Congressional Trade Priorities and Accountability Act of 2015 (TPA), as amended, trade authorities procedures may not apply to any implementing bill submitted with respect to an international trade agreement involving the government of a country listed as Tier 3 in the most recent annual TIP Report.[57] The trade authorities procedures described in the TPA are critical for the fast-tracking of international trade agreements, such as a free trade agreement.

The Trade Facilitation and Trade Enforcement Act of 2015 created an exception to the TPA's initial prohibitions.[58] This exception authorizes trade agreement negotiations to proceed with Tier 3 countries, but only if the President specifies in a letter to appropriate congressional committees that the country in question has taken "concrete actions to implement the principal recommendations with respect to that country in the past recent

[57] §106 of the TPA added this statutory restriction; it was subsequently amended by §914 of the Trade Facilitation and Trade Enforcement Act of 2015; See 19 U.S.C. 4205.

[58] §914 of the Trade Facilitation and Trade Enforcement Act of 2015.

annual report on trafficking in persons."[59] The letter must include a description of the *concrete actions* and supporting documentation of *credible evidence* of each concrete action (e.g., copies of relevant laws, regulations, and enforcement actions take, as appropriate). Moreover, the letter must be made available to the public.

TIP REPORT METHODOLOGY

The TVPA created the Office to Monitor and Combat Trafficking in Persons (J/TIP) within the State Department, whose director holds the rank of Ambassador-at-Large.[60] The J/TIP director is charged with overseeing the annual publication of the TIP Report, among other responsibilities laid out in the TVPA. In parallel to the drafting of the introductory material and the country narratives, the department's Bureau of Democracy, Human Rights, and Labor (DRL) initiates the process for identifying countries to be included in the list of governments that recruit and use child soldiers. Although not specified in law, each TIP Report typically covers country developments beginning in April of each year and ending in March of the following year.

Information Sources

According to the State Department, information used to prepare the report is based on a variety of sources, including U.S. embassies, government officials, nongovernmental and international organizations, published reports, news articles, academic studies, and research trips. U.S. diplomatic posts and domestic agencies report on human trafficking issues throughout the year and the TIP Report incorporates information based on

---

[59] *Appropriate congressional committees* in §106 of the TPA, as amended, refer to the Senate Finance Committee, SFRC, House Ways and Means Committee, and HFAC (the TVPA, in contrast, uses the term to refer to the SFRC, SJUD, HFAC, and HJUD). The definition was added by §914 of the Trade Facilitation and Trade Enforcement Act of 2015; 19 U.S.C. 4205. The President delegated this authority to the Secretary of State. See 81 FR 35579.

[60] §105 of the TVPA; 22 U.S.C. 7103.

meetings with government officials, local and international nongovernmental representatives, officials of international organizations, journalists, academics, and survivors.

Global Law Enforcement Data

Pursuant to the TVPA reauthorization of 2003, Congress added a new criterion for governments to achieve full compliance with the minimum standards for the elimination of severe forms of trafficking in persons: providing the State Department with data on trafficking investigations, prosecutions, convictions, and sentences.[61] (See *Figure 4* below.) Beginning with the 2004 TIP Report, the State Department has included this information in its TIP Reports—on a country-by-country basis, as well as in aggregate on a global and regional basis.

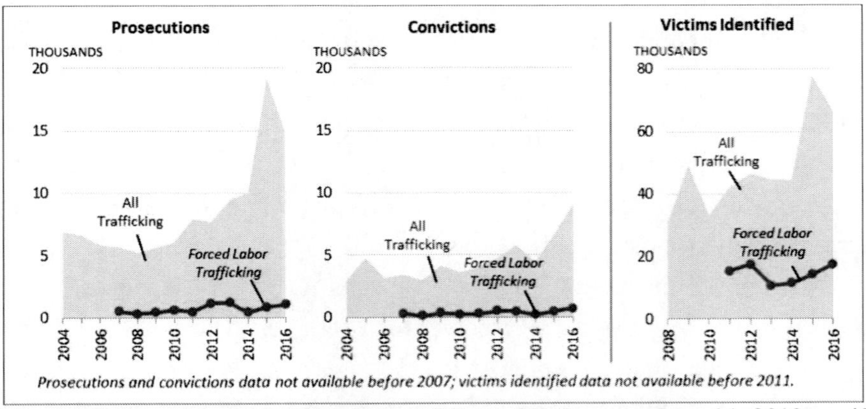

Source: CRS based on U.S. Department of State, TIP Reports, June 14, 2010, p. 45, and June 28, 2017, p. 34.

Notes: According to the most recent TIP Report (2017), with data covering the years 2009-2016:"The above statistics are estimates derived from data provided by foreign governments and other sources and reviewed by the Department of State. Aggregate data fluctuates from one year to the next due to the hidden nature of trafficking crimes, dynamic global events, shifts in government efforts, and a lack of uniformity in national reporting structures. The numbers in parentheses are those of labor trafficking prosecutions, convictions, and victims identified."

Figure 4. Global Law Enforcement Data from TIP Reports, 2004-2016.

---

[61] §108 of the TPVA, as amended by §6 of the 2003 TVPRA.

Information on Forced Labor

Pursuant to Title XII of the Violence Against Women Reauthorization Act of 2013, Congress requires the Departments of State and Labor to share information on forced labor, with the objective of informing both the State Department's TIP Report and the Labor Department's report on goods produced by forced or child labor in violation of international standards.[62]

Illustrative Draft Cycle

The annual process for drafting and releasing the TIP Report involves a period of worldwide information gathering, followed by an intense process of report drafting, led by J/TIP, but involving significant input from U.S. diplomatic missions and consular posts overseas as well as regional and functional bureaus. (See *Figure 5* below.) According to the State Department's Office of Inspector General (OIG), the annual rush to meet the report's statutory release deadline has often led to tensions and disagreements between bureaus and J/TIP regarding the draft country narratives and proposed tier rankings.[63]

Over time, the report draft cycle has evolved. Beginning with preparations for the 2010 TIP Report, for example, the State Department began to issue annual notices in the *Federal Register*, requesting information from nongovernmental groups on whether governments meet the TVPA's minimum standards for the elimination of trafficking.[64] A 2012 OIG inspection report of the J/TIP Office identified several other internal process changes that resulted in a significant reduction of tier ranking disputes.[65]

---

[62] §105 of the 2005 TVPRA, as amended by §1232 of the 2013 VAWRA; 22 U.S.C. 7112.

[63] U.S. Department of State and the Broadcasting Board of Governors, Office of Inspector General, *Inspection of the Office to Monitor and Combat Trafficking in Persons*, ISP-I-12-37, June 2012.

[64] For the 2017 TIP Report, see 81 FR 90039.

[65] Ibid, p. 8. Among the changes identified by the OIG report were the inclusion of footnotes in internal drafts and the use of SharePoint software to make country-specific information accessible across different parts of the State Department.

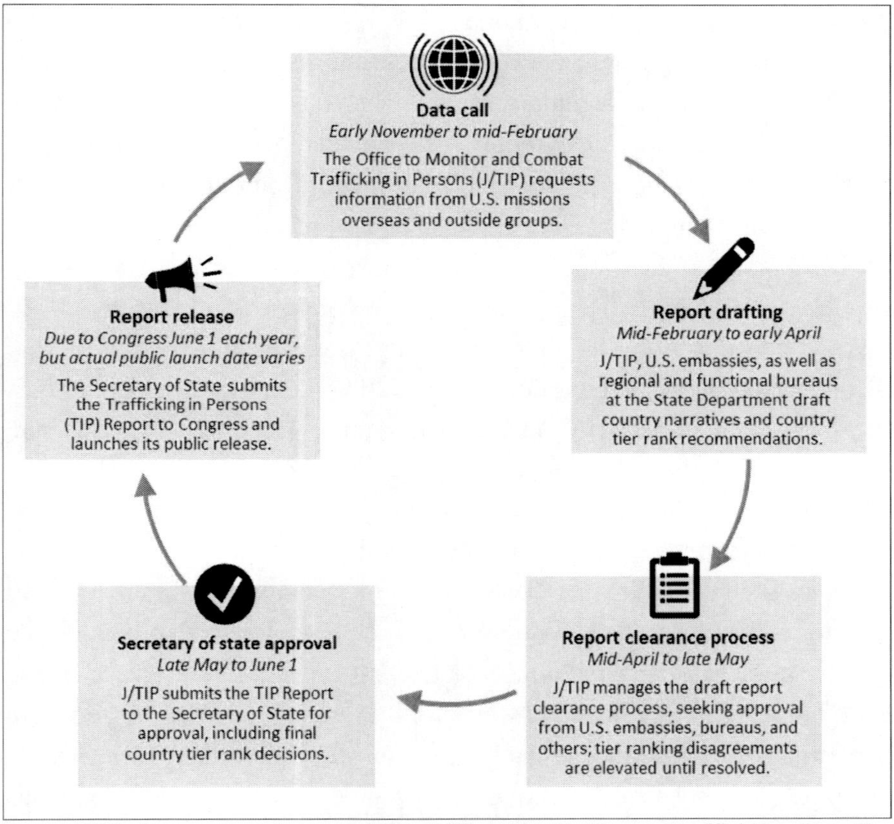

Source: U.S. Government Accountability Office (GAO), Human Trafficking: State Has Made Improvements in Its Annual Report but Does Not Explicitly Explain Certain Tier Rankings or Changes, GAO-17-56, December 2016 and U.S. Department of State and the Broadcasting Board of Governors, Office of Inspector General, Inspection of the Office to Monitor and Combat Trafficking in Persons, ISP-I-12-37, June 2012.

Figure 5. TIP Report: Typical Draft and Review Process.

Ranking Dispute Resolution

Although Congress has prescribed a range of expectations for the elimination of trafficking, ranking designations are not based on a concrete formula. Rather, country-specific considerations often leave State Department officials considerable discretion in categorizing countries.

Consequently, some country rankings, initially proposed by J/TIP in early drafts of the TIP Report, have reportedly been disputed by other parts of the State Department, including regional bureaus and senior leadership. According to the 2012 OIG report, "the number of tier-ranking disputes between regional bureaus and J/TIP declined from 46 percent of all countries ranked in 2006 to 22 percent of those ranked in 2011."[66]

On August 3, 2015, a *Reuters* news article reported that tier-ranking disputes for 2015 TIP Report involved 17 countries and that the J/TIP Office "won only three of those disputes, the worst ratio in the 15-year history of the unit."[67] The article indicated that countries whose rankings were disputed included China, Cuba, India, Malaysia, Mexico, and Uzbekistan—all of which reportedly received better rankings than the J/TIP Office had recommended. The article further reported that, typically, J/TIP "wins more than half" of the tier-ranking disputes.

In testimony before the Senate Foreign Relations Committee, J/TIP Director and Ambassador-atLarge Susan Coppedge declined to identify the specific number of tier-ranking disputes that preceded the release of the 2016 TIP Report. She noted, however, that the "vast majority" of the State Department's staff recommendations to the Secretary of State—encompassing those of J/TIP and the regional bureaus—were consensus recommendations.[68] In testimony before the Senate Foreign Relations Committee on the 2017 TIP Report, Coppedge noted that department staff could not agree on five countries' tier rankings.[69]

On June 24, 2017, a *Reuters* news article reported that Secretary of State Tillerson removed Burma and Iraq from the child soldiers list, overruling his own staff's assessments that children remain in the ranks of the Burmese Army and Iraqi government-affiliated militias.[70] Advocacy

---

[66] Ibid.

[67] Jason Szep and Matt Spetalnick, "Special Report: State Department Watered Down Human Trafficking Report," *Reuters*, August 3, 2015.

[68] CQ transcript of SFRC hearing on "Review of the 2016 Trafficking in Persons Report," July 12, 2016.

[69] CQ transcript of SFRC hearing on "Review of the 2017 Trafficking in Persons Report," July 13, 2017.

[70] Szep and Spetalnick, "Exclusive: Overruling Diplomats, U.S. to Drop Iraq, Myanmar from Child Soldiers' List," *Reuters*, June 24, 2017.

groups have also long suggested that Afghanistan be included on the child soldiers list—a proposal that was reportedly floated within the State Department this year as well.[71] According to the same *Reuters* article, an anonymous official stated that Tillerson's decision to leave Iraq and Afghanistan off the list was "made following pressure from the Pentagon to avoid complicating assistance to the Iraqi and Afghan militaries."

Allegations of Political Influence in Country Rankings

Although many observers view the TIP Report as a credible reflection of global efforts to address human trafficking, some have been critical of the methodology used to evaluate foreign country efforts and assign tier rankings. In a 2012 OIG report, the TIP Report was praised as having "gained wide credibility for its thoroughness" and "recognized as the definitive work by the anti-trafficking community on the status of anti-trafficking efforts."[72] The OIG report, however, also noted that some view the TIP Report as subjective and influenced by political pressures.

In December 2016, the U.S. Government Accountability Office (GAO) issued a report assessing the State Department's TIP Report and country ranking procedures.[73] In general, the State Department describes its tier ranking designations as not based on a concrete formula, but rather country-specific considerations that leave department officials considerable discretion. In analyzing its TIP Report methodology, the December 2016 GAO report assessed that the State Department lacked consistent and explicit explanations to justify upgrades and downgrades, which the report found problematic. It stated: "The lack of an explicit explanation for most of State's decisions to upgrade or downgrade countries to a different tier could limit the ability of internal and external stakeholders to understand the justification for tier changes and, in turn, use the report as a diplomatic tool to advance efforts to combat trafficking."[74]

---

[71] See for example "U.S.: Return Burma, Iraq to Child Soldier List," *Human Rights Watch*, June 26, 2017.

[72] ISP-I-12-37 (June 2012).

[73] GAO-17-56 (December 2016).

[74] Ibid.

FAQ: How has Congress reacted to Malaysia's ranking in recent TIP reports?

Many observers alleged that Malaysia's rankings in the 2015 and 2016 TIP Reports were influenced by factors unrelated to the Malaysian government's efforts to eradicate human trafficking. After four consecutive years on the Tier 2 Watch List from 2010 through 2013, Malaysia was downgraded in 2014, as required by law, to Tier 3 for lack of significant progress to combat human trafficking. In 2015 and 2016, however, the State Department ranked Malaysia as a Tier 2 Watch List country (see Figure 6 below).

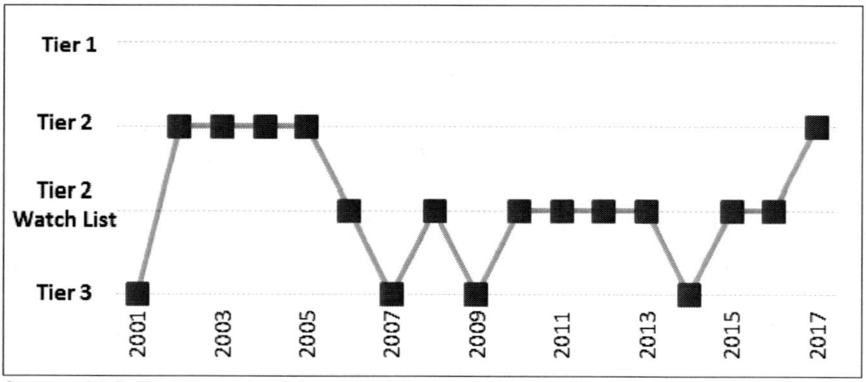

Source: U.S. Department of State, TIP Reports, 2001-2017.

Notes: Malaysia received full waivers from aid restrictions when it was rated Tier 3 in 2007, 2009, and 2014.

Figure 6. Malaysia: Historical TIP Rankings, 2001-2017.

Following the June 30, 2016, release of the 2016 TIP Report, in which Malaysia remained on the Tier 2 Watch List for a second consecutive year, several Members of Congress continued to express concerns over Malaysia's ranking. In the 2017 TIP Report, the department upgraded Malaysia to Tier 2. While Malaysian officials point to this year's TIP Report ranking as proof of the country's improved commitment to combating human trafficking, advocacy groups have expressed skepticism.

Report Release

Although not required by law, the State Department has always publicly released the report and the Secretary of State has personally presided over the launch of the annual TIP Report. The report, however, has never been published by its statutory June 1 deadline.[75] In addition to the statutory deadline for the annual release of the report, current law includes two other provisions related to the TIP Report's release, one that requires its translation and a second that connects the report's release with the presentation of the *Presidential Award for Extraordinary Efforts to Combat Trafficking in Persons*.

Translation Requirement

Pursuant to the Advance Democratic Values, Address Nondemocratic Countries, and Enhance Democracy Act of 2007, the Secretary of State is required to "expand the timely translation of applicable parts" of the TIP Report, among other reports prepared by the State Department.[76] Current law further specifies that the applicable parts of the TIP Report are to be translated "into the principal languages of as many countries as possible, with particular emphasis on nondemocratic countries, democratic transition countries, and countries in which extrajudicial killings, torture, or other serious violations of human rights have occurred."[77]

---

[75] Publications dates of the TIP Report were as follows: July 12, 2001; June 19, 2002; June 11, 2003; June 14, 2004; June 3, 2005; June 5, 2006; June 12, 2007; June 4, 2008; June 16, 2009; June 14, 2010; June 27, 2011; June 19, 2012; July 11, 2013; June 20, 2014; July 27, 2015; June 30, 2016; and June 28, 2017.

[76] See §2122 of Title XXI of the Advance Democratic Values, Address Nondemocratic Countries, and Enhance Democracy Act of 2007 (P.L. 110-53); 22 U.S.C. 8222. See also §107 of the 2008 TVPRA; 22 U.S.C. 7107 note.

[77] The provision, codified at 22 U.S.C. 8222, additionally required the Secretary of State to submit annual reports to appropriate congressional committees in 2008 through 2010 on the status of the law's implementation.

FAQ: What other required reports address international human trafficking matters?

Congress requires the executive branch to prepare and submit several other reports that address, at least in part, human trafficking matters. These include reports prepared by the Departments of State, Justice, and Labor.

- *State Department.* The TVPA and the CSPA require the State Department's annual Country Reports on Human Rights Practices to include information on human trafficking and child soldiers. In practice, the State Department satisfies this requirement by including a heading on Trafficking in Persons for each country in the report and a subheading on Child Soldiers for the CSPA-listed countries, referring and hyperlinking to the TIP Report. The most recent version of this report was released in 2017, covering human rights practices in 2016.
- *Justice Department.* The TVPA's reauthorization in 2003 added a provision to require the Attorney General to annually report, beginning in 2004, on U.S. government efforts to combat trafficking in persons.[78] The most recent publicly available edition of this report covers FY2015.
- *Labor Department.* The TVPA's reauthorization in 2005 added a provision to require the Bureau of International Labor Affairs to develop and make available a public list of goods from countries it has reason to believe are produced by forced labor or child labor in violation of international standards.[79] The list was most recently updated in September 2016. The Labor Department is also responsible for preparing an annual report on the Worst Forms of Child Labor.[80]

---

[78] §6 of the 2003 TVPRA amended §105 of the TPVA; it was also amended by §205 of the 2005 TVPRA, §§231 and 304 of the 2008 TVPRA, and §1231 of the 2013 VAWRA. See 22 U.S.C. 7103.

[79] §105 of the 2005 TVPRA, as amended by §§1232 and 1233 of the 2013 VAWRA; 22 U.S.C. 7112.

[80] §412 of the Trade and Development Act of 200 (P.L. 106-200) amended the Trade Act of 1974 (P.L. 93-618) to create this reporting requirement on the worst forms of child labor; 19 U.S.C. 2464.

Award Ceremony

Pursuant to the TVPA reauthorization of 2008, the timing of the TIP Report's release corresponds to a requirement for the Secretary of State to host an annual ceremony for recipients of the Presidential Award for Extraordinary Efforts to Combat Trafficking in Persons.[81]

Current law provides that the Secretary-hosted ceremony occur "as soon as practicable after the date on which the Secretary submits to Congress the TIP Report...."[82]

HUMAN TRAFFICKING TRENDS

An implicit objective of the TVPA was to leverage the country ranking process of the TIP Report as a foreign policy tool to motivate foreign governments to prioritize and address human trafficking. Some suggest the TIP Report can be used as a potent form of soft power as both a "name-and-shame" or "blacklist" process and a mechanism for country-by-country monitoring of antitrafficking progress. In theory, publications like the TIP Report can mobilize domestic and international pressure for policy change.[83] In practice, while some countries appear to be responsive to the TIP Report, others remain intractable.

Out of 187 countries ranked in the 2017 TIP Report, 36 countries were ranked Tier 1 and more than 80% of the ranked countries in this year's TIP Report remained noncompliant with the minimum standards laid out by the TVPA for eliminating trafficking in persons.

Pathways to the Top. Several countries' rankings have improved from noncompliant to Tier 1, including

---

[81] §112B of the TVPA, as added by §109 of the 2008 TVPRA; 22 U.S.C. 7109b.

[82] The provision, codified at 22 U.S.C. 7109b, additionally authorizes the Secretary of State to pay the travel costs for each award recipient and for a guest of each recipient who attends the ceremony. For the fiscal years 2008 through 2011, Congress had authorized to be appropriated such sums as may be necessary to carry out the provision. This authority has since lapsed.

[83] Judith G. Kelley and Beth A. Simmons, "Politics by Numbers: Indicators of Social Pressure in International Relations," *American Journal of Political Science*, Vol. 59, No. 1 (January 2015), pp. 55-70.

- *Armenia,* which was rated Tier 3 in 2002 and eventually improved to Tier 1 by 2013.
- *Guyana*, which was rated Tier 3 in the 2004 and experienced multiple years on the Tier 2 Watch List before attaining a Tier 1 rating for the first time in 2017.
- *Israel*, which was rated Tier 3 in 2001 and eventually improved to Tier 1 by 2012.
- *South Korea*, which was rated Tier 3 in 2001 and immediately improved to Tier 1 the following year.

Progress in Reverse

Other countries, which used to be fully compliant with the minimum standards to eliminate trafficking (Tier 1), have since become noncompliant, including

- *Benin,* which attained Tier 1 status in 2003, but after many years on Tier 2, further declined to the Tier 2 Watch List in 2016 and 2017.
- *Bosnia and Herzegovina,* which began as a Tier 3 country in 2001, attained Tier 1 status in 2010, but later declined to Tier 2 Watch List in 2014. It has been a Tier 2 country since 2015.
- *Cyprus*, which attained Tier 1 status in 2016 after many years vacillating between Tier 2 and Tier 2 Watch List, dropped back down to Tier 2 in 2017.
- *Hong Kong*, which began as a Tier 1 country in 2001 and remained so until 2008. In 2009, it dropped to Tier 2 and dropped again in 2016 to Tier 2 Watch List, where it remained in 2017.
- *Hungary*, which attained Tier 1 status in 2007, but dropped to Tier 2 Watch List in 2017.
- *Iceland*, which attained Tier 1 status in 2012, but dropped to Tier 2 in 2017.

- *Mauritius*, which began as a Tier 1 country in 2003 and has since vacillated between compliant and noncompliant. After dropping to Tier 2 Watch List in 2015, it rose to Tier 2 in 2016, where it remained in 2017.
- *Morocco*, which attained Tier 1 status in 2003, but has been rated Tier 2 since 2015.
- *Nepal*, which attained Tier 1 status in 2005, but has since been rated Tier 2.
- *Nigeria*, which attained Tier 1 status in 2009, but dropped to Tier 2 Watch List in 2017.

No Change

The rankings of several other countries have been unchanged.

- *Unchanged Tier 1:* Australia, Austria, Belgium, Denmark, Germany, Italy, the Netherlands, New Zealand, Norway, Spain, United Kingdom, and United States.[84]
- *Unchanged Tier 2:* Aruba, Bhutan, El Salvador, Kosovo, Mongolia, Palau, and Uganda.[85]
- *Unchanged Tier 3:* Eritrea and North Korea.[86]

Of the 45 countries on the Tier 2 Watch List in the 2017 TIP Report, 22 had been Tier 2 Watch List in 2016 and 9 required waivers to remain on the Tier 2 Watch List for their third or fourth consecutive year. (See *Table 4* above for the list of Tier 2 Watch List countries in the 2017 TIP Report and discussion in section on "Watch List Downgrades" above.)

---

[84] Denmark and Norway were first ranked in 2003, Australia and New Zealand were first ranked in 2005, and the United States was first ranked in 2010.

[85] Mongolia was first ranked in 2005, Kosovo and Palau were first ranked in 2009, Aruba was first ranked in 2011, and Bhutan was first ranked in 2013.

[86] North Korea was first ranked in 2003 and Eritrea was first ranked in 2009.

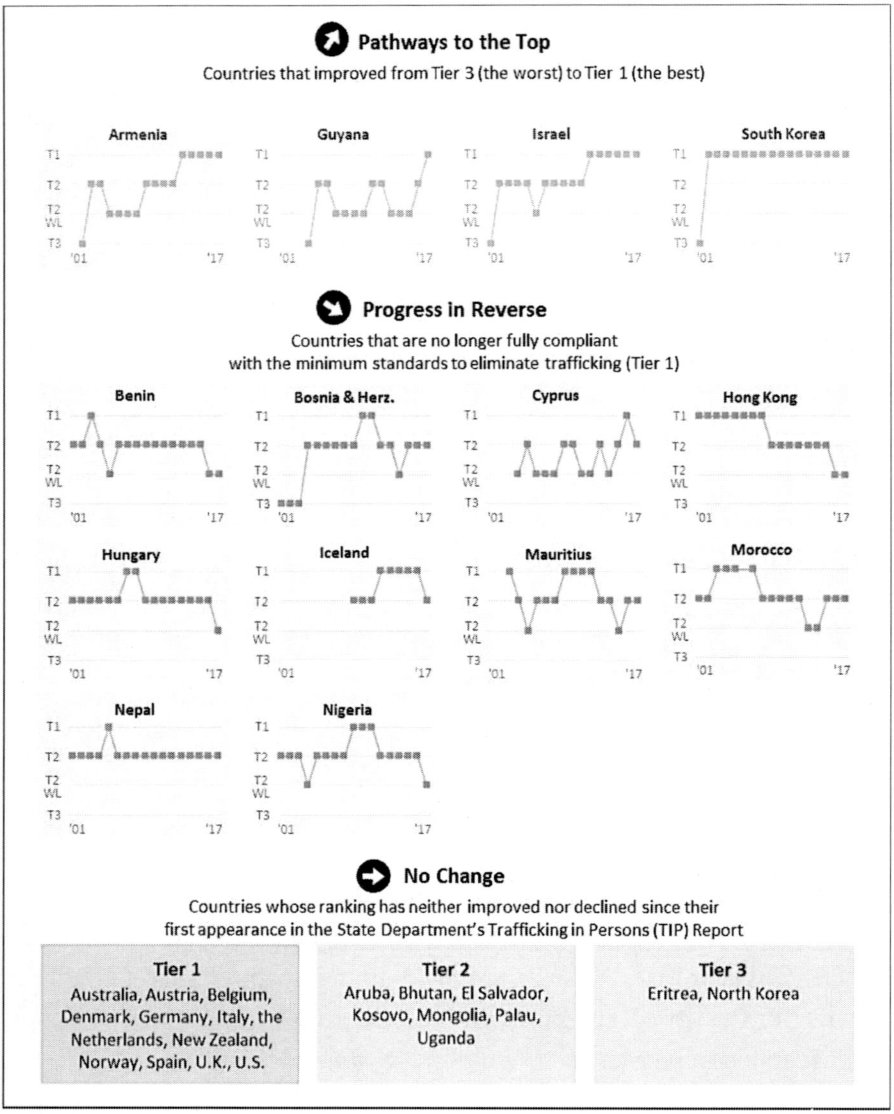

Source: U.S. Department of State, TIP Reports, 2001-2017.

Figure 7. Selected TIP Report Country Ranking Trends: Pathways, Progress, and Change, 2001-2017.

LEGISLATIVE OVERSIGHT AND OUTLOOK

The State Department's TIP Report is highly anticipated each year in Congress, with congressional oversight and evaluation taking the form of hearings, requests for GAO reports, and legislation.

Hearings

In recent years, the Senate Foreign Relations Committee has held closed briefings with State Department officials in anticipation of the TIP Report's release as well as public hearings after its publication.[87] The House Foreign Affairs Committee, particularly its Subcommittee on Africa, Global Health, Global Human Rights, and International Organizations, has also long held hearings on the TIP Report.[88]

Comptroller Reports

To date, GAO has prepared two reports that directly address the State Department's TIP Report, one in 2006 and a second in 2016.[89] Both contain GAO recommendations that remain pending or unimplemented.

---

[87] See SFRC hearings in the 115th and 114th Congresses: "Review of the 2017 Trafficking in Persons Report," July 13, 2017; "Closed: Preparing for the 2017 Trafficking in Persons Report," June 21, 2017; "Ending Modern Slavery: Building on Success," February 15, 2017; "Closed/Secret: Trafficking in Persons: Preparing the 2016 Annual Report," May 25, 2016; "Review of the 2016 Trafficking in Persons Report," July 12, 2016; "Closed Briefing: State Department Processes in Establishing Tier Rankings for the 2015 Trafficking in Persons Report," September 17, 2015; "Review of the 2015 Trafficking in Persons Report," August 6, 2015.

[88] See HFAC Subcommittee on Africa, Global Health, Global Human Rights, and International Organizations hearings in the 115th and 114th Congresses: "Winning the Fight Against Human Trafficking: The Frederick Douglass Reauthorization Act," May 2, 2017; "Accountability Over Politics: Scrutinizing the Trafficking in Persons Report," July 12, 2016; and "Demanding Accountability: Evaluating the 2015 Trafficking in Persons Report," November 4, 2015.

[89] GAO-17-56 (December 2016); GAO, *Human Trafficking: Better Data, Strategy, and Reporting Needed to Enhance U.S. Antitrafficking Efforts Abroad*, GAO-06-825, July 18, 2006.

Legislation in the 115th Congress

Several bills in the 115th Congress have been introduced to further modify requirements associated with the TIP Report, including H.R. 2200, the Frederick Douglass Trafficking Victims Prevention and Protection Reauthorization Act of 2017, which passed the House on July 12, 2017, and contains several changes to the TIP Report's country ranking process. Other bills introduced in the 115th Congress that, if passed, would modify requirements associated with the TIP Report include H.R. 436, the Human Trafficking Prioritization Act; S. 377, the Trafficking in Persons Report Integrity Act; H.R. 1191, the Child Soldier Prevention Act of 2017; and H.R. 2219 and S. 952, the End Banking for Human Traffickers Act of 2017.

Common themes in the legislative proposals to modify the TIP Report's methodology focus on reducing the prospects for political interference, while also increasing public transparency and congressional oversight into the State Department's country ranking process.

A key focus of the proposals involves changes to the special watch list or Tier 2 Watch List. Various bills seek to modify:

- the number of years a country may remain on the Tier 2 Watch List, from a maximum of four years (two consecutive years on Tier 2 Watch List, plus a maximum of two waivers to remain on the list for two more years) to three (two consecutive years on Tier 2 Watch List, plus one waiver);
- the conditions under which a country may remain on the Tier 2 Watch List (excluding those that have committed to take future antitrafficking steps, but have not already taken concrete steps to implement policies that would constitute significant efforts toward becoming compliant with the TVPA's minimum standards for eliminating trafficking);
- expectations for upgrading a Tier 2 Watch List country that exhausted its permitted time on that list and was subsequently downgraded to Tier 3 for lack of progress, including whether or

how long it would be permitted to return to the Tier 2 Watch List in the future;

- public documentation requirements to justify the continued listing of a country on the Tier 2 Watch List; and
- country narratives in the TIP Report to explicitly rationalize a country's upgrade or downgrade compared to its previous-year ranking.

Some bills also seek to further define key terms in the TVPA used by the State Department to determine country rankings, including proposed

- changes to the scope of foreign assistance subject to restriction;
- changes to the TVPA's four minimum standards for the elimination of trafficking;
- additions to the currently 12 criteria used to evaluate whether a country is making serious and sustained efforts to eliminate trafficking (the fourth minimum standard);
- revisions to what constitutes *significant efforts* to become compliant with the four minimum standards for the elimination of trafficking; and
- new definitions for the terms *concrete actions* and *credible evidence*.

If these proposals are enacted, they would constitute significant changes to the current TIP Report's methodology. A critical issue is whether changes to the TIP Report's methodology would motivate countries to do more to combat human trafficking or, in contrast, could undermine its value as a tool of soft power diplomacy. Some countries, which criticize the current ranking process as opaque, may prefer more detailed statutory instructions for how to assign tier rankings. Additional transparency in the TIP Report's rankings and country narratives could clarify expectations for future upgrades. Other countries, particularly those with limited resources and capabilities to address human trafficking, may have more difficulty proving progress in the report. If changes to the TIP

Report's ranking process result in more countries falling to Tier 3, additional policy question may arise, including whether the President would subject more Tier 3 countries to foreign aid restrictions or whether the Administration would use waivers to minimize the consequences of poor rankings in the TIP Report.

Chapter 4

STATUTE OF LIMITATION IN FEDERAL CRIMINAL CASES: AN OVERVIEW*

Charles Doyle
Senior Specialist in American Public Law

SUMMARY

A statute of limitations dictates the time period within which a legal proceeding must begin. The purpose of a statute of limitations in a criminal case is to ensure the prompt prosecution of criminal charges and thereby spare the accused of the burden of having to defend against stale charges after memories may have faded or evidence is lost.

There is no statute of limitations for federal crimes punishable by death, nor for certain federal crimes of terrorism, nor for certain federal sex offenses. Prosecution for most other federal crimes must begin within five years of the commitment of the offense. There are exceptions. Some types of crimes are subject to a longer period of limitation; some

---

* This is an edited, reformatted and augmented version of "Statute Limitation in Federal Criminal Cases: An Overview" by Charles Doyle that was originally published by the Congressional Research Service on November 14, 2017.

circumstances suspend or extend the otherwise applicable period of limitation.

Arson, art theft, certain crimes against financial institutions, and various immigration offenses all carry statutes of limitation longer than the five-year standard. Regardless of the applicable statute of limitations, the period may be extended or the running of the period suspended or tolled under a number of circumstances, such as when the accused is a fugitive or when the case involves charges of child abuse, bankruptcy, wartime fraud against the government, or DNA evidence.

Ordinarily, the statute of limitations begins to run as soon as the crime has been completed. Although the federal crime of conspiracy is complete when one of the plotters commits an affirmative act in its name, the period for conspiracies begins with the last affirmative act committed in furtherance of the scheme. Other so-called continuing offenses include various possession crimes and some that impose continuing obligations to register or report.

Limitation-related constitutional challenges arise most often under the Constitution's ex post facto and due process clauses. The federal courts have long held that a statute of limitations may be enlarged retroactively as long as the previously applicable period of limitation has not expired. The Supreme Court recently confirmed that view; the ex post facto proscription precludes legislative revival of an expired period of limitation. Due process condemns pre-indictment delays even when permitted by the statute of limitations if the prosecution wrongfully caused the delay and the accused's defense suffered actual, substantial harm as a consequence.

A list of federal statutes of limitation in criminal cases and a rough chart of comparable state provisions are attached. This report is available in an abbreviated form as CRS Report RS21121, *Statute of Limitation in Federal Criminal Cases: A Sketch*, without the attachments, footnotes, or attributions to authority found here.

INTRODUCTION

The Constitution's Speedy Trial Clause[1] protects the criminally accused against unreasonable delays between his indictment and trial. Before indictment, the statutes of limitation, and in extreme circumstances, the Due Process Clauses[2] protect the accused from unreasonable delays.

[1] U.S. CONST. amend. VI.
[2] *Id.* amends. V and XIV.

This is an overview of federal law relating to the statutes of limitation in criminal cases, including those changes produced by the act.

The phrase "statute of limitations" refers to the time period within which formal criminal charges must be brought after a crime has been committed.[3] "The purpose of a statute of limitations is to limit exposure to criminal prosecution to a certain fixed period of time following the occurrence of those acts the legislature has decided to punish by criminal sanctions. Such a limitation is designed to protect individuals from having to defend themselves against charges when the basic facts may have become obscured by the passage of time and to minimize the danger of official punishment because of acts in the far-distant past. Such a time limit may also have the salutary effect of encouraging law enforcement officials promptly to investigate suspected criminal activity."[4] Therefore, in most instances, prosecutions are barred if the defendant can show that there was no indictment or other formal charge filed within the time period dictated by the statute of limitations.[5]

Statutes of limitation are creatures of statute. The common law recognized no period of limitation.[6] An indictment could be brought at any time. Limitations are recognized today only to the extent that a statute or due process dictates their recognition.[7] Congress and most state legislatures

---

[3] *Statute of Limitations*, BLACK'S LAW DICTIONARY (10th ed. 2014).

[4] Toussie v. United States, 397 U.S. 112, 114-15 (1970).

[5] The statute of limitations is an affirmative defense that can be lost either explicitly, by pleading guilty, or by failure to raise it at or before trial. Musacchio v. United States, 136 S. Ct. 709, 717 (2016)("[T]he statutory text, context, and history establish that § 3282(a) imposes a nonjurisdictional defense that becomes part of a case only if a defendant raises it in the district court."); *see also* United States v. Fernandez, 722 F.3d 1, 27 (1st Cir. 2013) (signed waiver); United States v. Woodard, 675 F.3d 1147, 1150 (8th Cir. 2012) (waived by unconditional guilty plea); United States v. Wilbur, 674 F.3d 1160, 1177 (9th Cir. 2012) (waived if not raised at or before trial); United States v. Hsu, 669 F.3d 112, 117-18 (2d Cir. 2012) (waiver by guilty plea); United States v. Flood, 635 F.3d 1255, 1258 (10th Cir. 2011) (express waiver). *Musacchio* resolved a split in the circuits when it declared that "[a] defendant thus cannot successfully raise the statute-of-limitations defense in § 3282(a) for the first time on appeal." *Musacchio*, 136 S. Ct. at 718.

[6] *Doggett v. United States*, 505 U.S. 647, 667 (1992) (Thomas, J., dissenting) (citing *inter alia*, 2 JAMES FITZJAMES STEPHEN, A HISTORY OF THE CRIMINAL LAW OF ENGLAND 1, 2 (1883)).

[7] At some point events pass into history and due process restricts the extent to which they may be resurrected to build a criminal accusation, with or without an applicable statute of limitations, *United States v. Marion*, 404 U.S. 307, 324 (1971).

have enacted statutes of limitation, but declare that prosecution for some crimes may be brought at any time.[8]

Federal statutes of limitation are as old as federal crimes. When the Founders assembled in the First Congress, they passed not only the first federal criminal laws but made prosecution under those laws subject to specific statutes of limitation.[9] Similar provisions continue to this day.

Federal capital offenses may be prosecuted at any time,[10] but unless some more specific arrangement has been made a general five-year statute of limitations covers all other federal crimes.[11] Some of the exceptions to the general rule identify longer periods for particular crimes.[12] Others suspend or extend the applicable period under certain circumstances such as the flight of the accused,[13] or during time of war.[14]

Prosecution at Any Time

Aside from capital offenses,[15] crimes which Congress associated with terrorism may be prosecuted at any time if they result in a death or serious

[8] Capsulized descriptions of the various state criminal statutes of limitation governing felony prosecutions are appended.

[9] Except for murder and forgery, the statute of limitations for the prosecution of all federal capital offenses was three

[10] 18 U.S.C. § 3281.

[11] "Except as otherwise expressly provided by law, no person shall be prosecuted, tried, or punished for any offense, not capital, unless the indictment is found or information is instituted within five years next after such offense shall have been committed," 18 U.S.C. § 3282.

[12] 18 U.S.C. § 3286.

[13] 18 U.S.C. § 3290.

[14] 18 U.S.C. § 3287.

[15] "An indictment for any offense punishable by death may be found at any time without limitation." 18 U.S.C. § 3281. Between the Supreme Court's decision in *Furman v. Georgia*, 408 U.S. 238 (1972), and passage of the Violent Crime Control and Law Enforcement Act of 1994, 108 Stat. 1796, the death penalty authorized by federal capital offense statutes could not be constitutionally imposed. The question arose whether the term "offenses punishable by death" in the statute of limitations referred to offenses made capital by statute or only to offenses for which the death penalty might constitutionally be imposed. The courts concluded that Congress intended the term to refer to offenses which it made capital by statute. *United States v. Emery*, 186 F.3d 921, 924 (8th Cir. 1999); *United States v. Edwards*, 159 F.3d 1117, 1128 (8th Cir. 1998); *United States v. Manning*, 56 F.3d 1188, 1196 (9th Cir. 1995). A list of the federal capital offenses is appended. The list includes

injury or create a foreseeable risk of death or serious injury.[16] Although the crimes were selected because they are often implicated in acts of terrorism, a terrorist defendant is not a prerequisite to an unlimited period for prosecution.[17] A third category of crimes that may be prosecuted at any time consists of various designated federal child abduction and sex offenses.[18]

LIMITS BY CRIME

Although the majority of federal crimes are governed by the general five-year statute of limitations, Congress has chosen longer periods for specific types of crimes—20 years for the theft of art work;[19] 10 years for

---

those crimes made capital by operation of other provisions of law such as 18 U.S.C. § 3559(f) (murder of a child during the course a federal crime of violence) and 18 U.S.C. § 2245 (murder committed during the course of designated federal sex offenses).

[16] 18 U.S.C. § 3286(b) ("Notwithstanding any other law, an indictment may be found or an information instituted at any time without limitation for any offense listed in Section 2332b(g)(5)(B), if the commission of such offense resulted in, or created a foreseeable risk of, death or serious bodily injury to another person"). A list of crimes cross referenced in 18 U.S.C. § 2332b(g)(5)(B) is appended.

[17] 18 U.S.C. § 2332b(g)(5) defines a federal crime of terrorism as "an offense that – (A) is calculated to influence or affect the conduct of a government by intimidation or coercion, or to retaliate against government conduct; and (B) is a violation of" one of list of terrorism-associated offenses. The list of crimes which Section 3286(b) makes prosecutable at any time consists of those crimes listed in 18 U.S.C. § 2332b(g)(5)(*B*)(emphasis added). Had Congress wished the waiver of the statutes of limitation to apply only to terrorists accused of these offenses presumably it would have referred to 18 U.S.C. § 2332b(g)(5), *i.e.,* both § 2332b(g)(5)(A) and (B), rather than simply to 18 U.S.C. § 2332b(g)(5)(B) as it did.

[18] 18 U.S.C. § 3299. The felonies in Chapters 109A, 110 and 117 include violations of 18 U.S.C. 2241 (aggravated sexual abuse), 2242 (sexual abuse), 2243 (sexual abuse of a ward or child), 2244 (abusive sexual contact), 2245 (sexual abuse resulting in death), 2250 (failure to register as a sex offender), 2251 (sexual exploitation of children), 2251A (selling or buying children), 2252 (transporting, distributing or selling child sexually exploitive material), 2252A (transporting or distributing child pornography), 2252B (misleading names on the Internet), 2260 (making child sexually exploitative material overseas for export to the U.S.), 2421 (transportation for illicit sexual purposes), 2422 (coercing or enticing travel for illicit sexual purposes), 2423 (travel involving illicit sexual activity with a child), 2424 (filing false immigration statement), 2425 (interstate transmission of information about a child relating to illicit sexual activity).

[19] "No person shall be prosecuted, tried, or punished for a violation of or conspiracy to violate Section 668 unless the indictment is returned or the information is filed within 20 years after the commission of the offense," 18 U.S.C. § 3294.

arson,[20] for certain crimes against financial institutions,[21] and for immigration offenses;[22] and 8 years for the nonviolent terrorist offenses that may be prosecuted at any time if committed under violent circumstances.[23] Investigative difficulties[24] or the seriousness of the crime[25] seem to have provided the rationale for enlargement of the time limit for prosecuting these offenses beyond the five-year standard.[26]

SUSPENSION AND EXTENSION

The five-year rule may yield to circumstances other than the type of crime to be prosecuted. For example, an otherwise applicable limitation

---

[20] "No person shall be prosecuted, tried, or punished for any non-capital offense under Section 81 [arson in the special maritime or territorial jurisdiction of the United States] or subsection (f), (h), or (i) of Section 844 [use of fire or explosives to commit a federal offense, and burning or bombing of federal property or property used in or in activities affecting interstate or foreign commerce] unless the indictment is found or the information is instituted not later than 10 years after the date on which the offense was committed," 18 U.S.C. § 3295.

[21] "No person shall be prosecuted, tried, or punished for a violation of, or a conspiracy to violate – (1) Section 215, 656, 657, 1005, 1006, 1007, 1014, 1033, or 1344; (2) Section 1341 or 1343 [mail and wire fraud], if the offense affects a financial institution; or (3) Section 1963 [(RICO) racketeer influenced and corrupt organizations], to the extent that the racketeering activity involves a violation of Section 1344 [bank fraud] – unless the indictment is returned or the information is filed within 10 years after the commission of the offense," 18 U.S.C. § 3293.

[22] "No person shall be prosecuted, tried, or punished for violation of any provision of Sections 1423 to 1428, inclusive, of Chapter 69 [nationality and citizenship offenses] and Sections 1541 to 1544, inclusive, of Chapter 75 [passport and visa offenses] of Title 18 of the United States Code, or for conspiracy to violate any of such Sections, unless the indictment is found or the information is instituted within 10 years after the commission of the offense," 18 U.S.C. § 3291. *See also* 18 US.C. § 3298.

[23] "Notwithstanding Section 3282, no person shall be prosecuted, tried, or punished for any noncapital offense involving a violation of any provision listed in Section 2332b(g)(5)(B) [terrorist offenses], or a violation 112, 351(e), 1361, or 1751(e) of this title, or Section 46504, 46505, or 46506 of Title 49, unless the indictment is found or the information is instituted within eight years after the offense was committed.... " 18 U.S.C. § 3286(a).

[24] *See e.g.,* H.R. Rep. No. 82-167, at 2-3 (1951); H.R. Rep. No. 98-907, at 2 (1984).

[25] *Administration's Draft Anti-Terrorism Act of 2001: Hearings Before the House Comm. on the Judiciary*, 107th Cong., 1st Sess. at 60 (2001).

[26] *E.g.*, H.R. Rep. No. 101-54, at 472 (1989) ("The longer period of limitations [in 18 U.S.C. § 3293] is necessary because of the enormous backlog of thousands of pending investigations and prosecutions and the complexity of many of these cases.").

period may be suspended or extended in cases involving child abuse,[27] the concealment of the assets of an estate in bankruptcy,[28] wartime fraud against the government,[29] dismissal of original charges,[30] fugitives,[31] foreign evidence,[32] or DNA evidence.[33]

Child Protection

The child protection section, 18 U.S.C. § 3283, permits an indictment or information charging kidnaping, or sexual abuse, or physical abuse, of a child under the age of 18 to be filed within the longer of 10 years or the life of the victim.[34] Section 3283 extends the statute of limitations in sexual abuse cases generally and is not confined to the offenses found in sexual abuse chapter of the federal criminal code.[35] In contrast, 18 U.S.C. § 3299 eliminates the statute of limitations in child sexual abuse cases arising under the specific statutory provisions it cites.[36]

---

27 18 U.S.C. § 3283.
28 18 U.S.C. § 3284.
29 18 U.S.C. § 3287.
30 *Id.* §§ 3288, 3289.
31 *Id.* § 3290.
32 *Id.* § 3292.
33 *Id.* §§ 3282(b), 3297.
34 "No statute of limitations that would otherwise preclude prosecution for an offense involving the sexual or physical abuse, or kidnaping, of a child under the age of 18 years shall preclude such prosecution during the life of the child, or for 10 years after the offense, whichever is longer." *Id.* § 3283.
35 Weingarten v. United States, 865 F.3d 48, 58-60 (2d Cir. 2017) (applying the limitations period in 18 U.S.C. § 3283 to a conviction under 18 U.S.C. § 2343 (foreign travel for the purpose of unlawful sexual activity with a child)); United States v. Schneider, 801 F.3d 186, 196-97 (3d Cir. 2015) (same); United States v. Diehl, 775 F.3d 714, 720 (5th Cir. 2015) (applying the limitations period in 18 U.S.C. § 3283 to a conviction under 18 U.S.C. § 2251 (production of child pornography)) (citing United States v. Carpenter, 680 F.3d 1101, 1103-1104 (9th Cir. 2012) and United States v. Coutentos, 651 F.3d 809, 816-17 (8th Cir. 2011).
36 "Notwithstanding any other law, an indictment may be found or an information instituted at any time without limitation for any offense under Section 1201 [kidnaping] involving a minor victim, and for any felony under Chapter 109A [sexual abuse], 110 [child pornography] (except for Section 2257 and 2257A), or 117 [interstate or foreign travel for unlawful sexual purposes], or Section 1591 [sex trafficking of an adult by force or fraud or of a child]." 18 U.S.C.
§ 3299. *See e.g.*, United States v. Webster, 797 F.3d 531, 534 (8th Cir. 2015) (pointing out that there is no statute of limitations for a prosecution for sexual abuse under 18 U.S.C. §

DNA

There are two DNA provisions. One, 18 U.S.C. § 3297, suspends any applicable statute of limitations for the time required to identify an individual when DNA evidence implicates his involvement in a felony offense.[37] The other, 18 U.S.C. § 3282(b), suspends the statute of limitations for federal sexual abuse violations by means of an indictment using a DNA profile alone to identify the person charged.[38] Neither provision comes into play when the offense involves sexual abuse of a child or child abduction. As noted earlier, prosecution for such crimes may be brought at any time under 18 U.S.C. § 3299.

Section 3282(b) is the narrower of the two DNA provisions. It only applies to offenses proscribed in 18 U.S.C. ch. 109A. Chapter 109A outlaws abusive sexual contact, sexual abuse, and aggravated sexual abuse when any of these offenses is committed in a federal prison, or within the special maritime or territorial jurisdiction of the United States.[39] Section 3282(b) also suspends the provisions of the Speedy Trial Act that would otherwise come to life with the filing of an indictment in such cases.[40]

2241 found chapter 109A); United States v. Fritzsching, 245 F. Supp. 3d 1269, 1274 (D. Utah 2017) (making the same observation with respect to a prosecution for possession of child pornography under 18 U.S.C. § 2252 found in chapter 110); United States v. Reyna, 98 F. Supp. 3d 895, 899 (W.D. Tex. 2015) (same).

[37] 18 U.S.C. § 3297 ("In a case in which DNA testing implicates an identified person in the commission of a felony, no statute of limitations that would otherwise preclude prosecution of the offense shall preclude such prosecution until a period of time following the implication of the person by DNA testing has elapsed that is equal to the otherwise applicable limitation period.").

[38] *Id.* § 3282(b)("(1) In general. - In any indictment for an offense under chapter 109A for which the identity of the accused is unknown, it shall be sufficient to describe the accused as an individual whose name is unknown, but who has a particular DNA profile. (2) Exception. - Any indictment described under paragraph (1), which is found not later than 5 years after the offense under chapter 109A is committed, shall not be subject to - (A) the limitations period described under subsection (a); and (B) the provisions of chapter 208 until the individual is arrested or served with a summons in connection with the charges contained in the indictment. (3) Defined term. - For purposes of this subsection, the term 'DNA profile' means a set of DNA identification characteristics.").

[39] 18 U.S.C. §§ 2244, 2242, and 2241, respectively. Chapter 109A also criminalizes sexual abuse of a ward and aggravated sexual abuse of a child, but again those offenses may be prosecuted at any time by operation of 18 U.S.C. § 3299.

[40] *Id.* § 3282(b)(2)(B); *Id.* §§ 3161-3174 (Speedy Trial Act).

Section 3282(b), however, reaches only those cases in which the statute of limitations has not already expired.[41]

Section 3297 applies to any federal felony. Rather than suspend the statute of limitations, it marks the beginning of the period of limitation, not from the commission of the crime, but from the time when DNA testing implicates an individual.[42]

Concealing Bankruptcy Assets

The statute of limitations on offenses which involve concealing bankruptcy assets does not begin to run until a final decision discharging or refusing to discharge the debtor: "The concealment of assets of a debtor in a case under Title 11 shall be deemed to be a continuing offense until the debtor shall have been finally discharged or a discharge denied, and the period of limitations shall not begin to run until such final discharge or denial of discharge."[43] When a discharge determination is impossible, the statute of limitations runs from the date of the event when discharge becomes impossible for whatever reason.[44]

Wartime Statute of Limitations

Section 3287 establishes a suspension of the statute of limitations covering wartime frauds committed against the United States[45] that allows

---

[41] *Id.* § 3282(b)(2)(A). The Constitution prohibits revival of an expired statute of limitations, *Stogner v. California*, 539 U.S. 607 (2003).

[42] United States v. Lopez, 860 F.3d 201, 213 (4th Cir. 2017); United States v. Sylla, 790 F.3d 772, 774 (7th Cir. 2015).

[43] 18 U.S.C. § 3284.

[44] *United States v. Gilbert*, 136 F.3d 1451, 1454-455 (11th Cir. 1998); *United States v. Dolan*, 120 F.3d 856, 867-68 (8th Cir. 1997) (both citing United States v. Guglielmini, 425 F.2d 439 (2d Cir. 1970); and Rudin v. United States, 254 F.2d 45 (6th Cir. 1958)); *see also* United States v. Freeman, 864 F. Supp. 2d 1298, 1299 (M.D. Fla. 2012).

[45] "When the United States is at war or Congress has enacted a specific authorization for the use of the Armed Forces, as described in section 5(b) of the War Powers Resolution (50 U.S.C. 1544(b)), the running of any statute of limitations applicable to any offense (1) involving fraud or attempted fraud against the United States or any agency thereof in any manner, whether by conspiracy or not, or (2) committed in connection with the acquisition, care, handling, custody, control or disposition of any real or personal property of the United States, or (3) committed in connection with the negotiation, procurement, award,

for prosecution at any time up to five years after the end of the war.[46] At one time, it could be said with some conviction that Section 3287 "appears to have only been used in cases that involved conduct during or shortly after World War II" and none since.[47] That is no longer the case.[48]

In 2008, Congress amended the section to make it clear that the provision covers misconduct during both declared wars and periods of armed conflict for which Congress has explicitly authorized use of the Armed Forces.[49] The same amendment extended the period of suspension from three to five years.[50] The provision applies to crimes related to conduct of the conflict as well as those that are not.[51] The offense, however, must "involve the defrauding of the United States in [some] pecuniary manner or in a manner concerning property."[52] The provision's five-year clock begins to run with the end of the war or conflict, but there is some difference of opinion over whether a formal termination must come first.[53]

---

performance, payment for, interim financing, cancelation, or other termination or settlement, of any contract, subcontract, or purchase order which is connected with or related to the prosecution of the war or directly connected with or related to the authorized use of the Armed Forces, or with any disposition of termination inventory by any war contractor or Government agency, shall be suspended until 5 years after the termination of hostilities as proclaimed by a Presidential proclamation, with notice to Congress, or by a concurrent resolution of Congress. Definitions of terms in section 103 of title 41 shall apply to similar terms used in this section. For purposes of applying such definitions in this section, the term 'war' includes a specific authorization for the use of the Armed Forces, as described in section 5(b) of the War Powers Resolution (50 U.S.C. 1544(b))," 18 U.S.C. § 3287.

[46] "Although the language of [18 U.S.C. § 3287] would seem to allow the Government to indict any frauds against the United States that occurred up to the end of the suspension period plus the relevant statute of limitations, the Supreme Court in *United States v. Smith*, 342 U.S. 225 (1952), held that § 3287 only applied to crimes committed after the triggering of the suspension of limitation but before the termination of hostilities. *Id.* at 228." United States v. Pfluger, 685 F.3d 481, 484 (5th Cir. 2012) (parallel Supreme Court citations omitted).

[47] United States v. Shelton, 816 F.Supp. 1132, 1134-135 (W.D. Tex. 1993).

[48] *See e.g.*, United States v. Pfluger, 685 F.3d at 484 n.5, and the cases cited therein.

[49] P.L. 110-329, § 8117, 122 Stat. 3647 (2008), 18 U.S.C. § 3287.

[50] *Id*

[51] United States v. Prosperi, 573 F.Supp.2d 436, 441-42 (D. Mass. 2008) (citing United States v. Grainger, 346 U.S. 235 (1953)). Section 3287's limitation period does not, however, apply to civil cases such as qui tam actions under the False Claims Act. *See* Kellogg Brown & Root Services, Inc. v. United States *ex rel.* Carter, 135 S. Ct. 1970, 1978 (2015).

[52] Bridges v. United States, 346 U.S. 209, 220 (1953).

[53] *Pfluger*, 685 F.3d at 443-64 (holding that formal termination is required and noting a conflicting view in *Prosperi*, 573 F.Supp.2d at 454-55); *see also* United States v. Frediani,

Indictment or Information

The statute of limitations runs until an indictment or information is found and returned to the court.[54] There is, however, some question about the impact of sealing the indictment upon its return. The Federal Rules of Criminal Procedure allow the magistrate to whom the indictment is returned to seal it until the defendant is apprehended or released on bail.[55] Some courts seem troubled when they believe that the seal has been applied for purposes of tactical advantage rather than to prevent the escape of the accused.[56]

The statute of limitations remains tolled if the original indictment is replaced by a superseding indictment, as long as the superseding indictment does not substantially alter the original charge.[57]

---

790 F.3d 1196, 1201(11th Cir. 2015); United States ex rel. Carter v. Halliburton Co., 710 F.3d 171, 179 (4th Cir. 2013), *rev'd on other grounds sub nom., Kellogg, Brown & Root Services, Inc.*, 135 S. Ct. 1970. There has been at least one suggestion that the provisions should be construed narrowly in light of the possible duration of the conflicts. Paul D. Swanson, Note, *Limitless Limitations: How Wars Overwhelms Criminal Statutes of Limitations*, 97 CORNELL L. REV. 1575, 1584-85 (2012).

[54] *E.g.,* 18 U.S.C. § 3282(a) ("... [N]o person shall be prosecuted ... unless the indictment is found or the information is instituted within five years ..."); United States v. Liu, 731 F.3d 982, 996 (9th Cir. 2013); United States v. McMillian, 600 F.3d 434, 444 (5th Cir. 2010) ("Once an indictment is filed, the limitations period is tolled on the charges set forth in the indictment."); United States v. Milstein, 401 F.3d 53, 67 (2d Cir. 2005); United States v. Garcia, 268 F.3d 407, 411 (6th Cir. 2001).

[55] FED. R. CRIM. P. 6(e)(4).

[56] United States v. Ellis, 622 F.3d 784, 792 (7th Cir. 2010) ("The circuits are divided on whether the sealing of an indictment affects when the indictment is 'found' for purposes of the statute of limitations. The Tenth Circuit has held that an indictment is 'found' under §3284(a) whenever it is returned by the grand jury; sealing the indictment has no effect on this date. United States v. Thompson, 287 F.3d 1244, 1248-252 (10th Cir. 2002). But other circuits have held that sealing matters, at least in one sense; these circuits have held that an indictment is not 'found' for purposes of § 3284(a) if it was improperly sealed and the improper sealing prejudiced to the defendant. See, e.g. United States v. Bracy, 67 F.3d 1421, 1426 (9th Cir. 1995); United States v. Sharpe, 995 F.2d 49, 51-52 (5th Cir. 1993)(per curiam); United States v. Muse, 633 F.2d 1041, 1043-44 (2d Cir. 1980)(en banc)"); *see also* United States v. Richard, 943 F.2d 115, 118-19 (1st Cir. 1991); United States v. Larkin, 875 F.2d 168, 170-72 (8th Cir. 1989); United States v. Wright, 343 F.3d 849, 857 (6th Cir. 2003); John Stinson, *Secret Indictments: How to Discourage Them, How to Make Them Fair,* 2 DREXEL L. REV. 104, 145 (2009) (arguing that "[c]urrent sealing practice raises serious due process concerns").

[57] United States v. Yielding, 657 F.3d 688, 703-704 (8th Cir. 2011) ("For limitations purposes, a superseding indictment filed while the original indictment is validly pending relates back to the time of filing of the original indictment if it does not substantially broaden or amend

If the indictment or information is subsequently dismissed, federal law extends the statute of limitations an additional six months (30 days if the indictment or information is dismissed on appeal and there is a grand jury with jurisdiction in place).[58] Beyond the extension here, when a timely indictment is dismissed pursuant to a plea agreement under which the defendant pleads to other charges, the statute of limitations ordinarily

---

the original charges.... To determine whether a superseding indictment substantially broadens or amends a pending timely indictment, we agree with other courts that it is appropriate to consider whether the additional pleadings allege violations of a different statute, contain different elements, rely on different evidence, or expose the defendant to a potentially greater sentence. The touchstone of this analysis is whether the original indictment provided the defendant with fair notice of the subsequent charges against him."); *see also* United States v. Farias, 836 F.3d 1315, 1323 (11th Cir. 2016); United States v. Liu, 731 F.3d 982, 996- 97 (9th Cir. 2013); United States v. McMillan, 600 F.3d 434, 444 (5th Cir. 2010); *cf.* United States v. Edwards, 834 F.3d 180, 196 (2d Cir. 2016).

[58] "Whenever an indictment or information charging a felony is dismissed for any reason after the period prescribed by the applicable statute of limitations has expired, a new indictment may be returned in the appropriate jurisdiction within six calendar months of the date of the dismissal of the indictment or information, or, in the event of an appeal, within 60 days of the date the dismissal of the indictment or information becomes final, or, if no regular grand jury is in session in the appropriate jurisdiction when the indictment or information is dismissed, within six calendar months of the date when the next regular grand jury is convened, which new indictment shall not be barred by any statute of limitations. This section does not permit the filing of a new indictment or information where the reason for the dismissal was the failure to file the indictment or information within the period prescribed by the applicable statute of limitations, or some other reason that would bar a new prosecution." 18 U.S.C. § 3288. *E.g.,* United States v. Mathurin, 868 F.3d 921, 929 (11th Cir. 2017); United States v. Holden, 806 F.3d 1227, 1232-33; (9th Cir. 2015); *McMillan*, 600 F.3d at 444; *see also* United States v. Bert, 814 F.3d 70, 82 (2d Cir. 2016) (noting the options available to the government when an indictment is dismissed without prejudice) (citing Zedner v. United States, 547 U.S. 489, 499 (2006)). "Whenever an indictment or information charging a felony is dismissed for any reason before the period prescribed by the applicable statute of limitations has expired, and such period will expire within six calendar months of the date of the dismissal of the indictment or information, a new indictment may be returned in the appropriate jurisdiction within six calendar months of the expiration of the applicable statute of limitations, or, in the event of an appeal, within 60 days of the date the dismissal of the indictment or information becomes final or, if no regular grand jury is in session in the appropriate jurisdiction at the expiration of the applicable statute of limitations, within six calendar months of the date when the next regular grand jury is convened, which new indictment shall not be barred by any statute of limitations. This section does not permit the filing of a new indictment or information where the reason for the dismissal was the failure to file the indictment or information within the period prescribed by the applicable statute of limitations, or some other reason that would bar a new prosecution.," 18 U.S.C. § 3289.

begins again for the dismissed charges unless the defendant has waived as part of the plea agreement.[59]

Foreign Evidence

Section 3292 was enacted to compensate for the delays the Justice Department experienced when it sought to secure bank records and other evidence located overseas.[60] It provides the following:

(a) (1) Upon application of the United States, filed before return of an indictment, indicating that evidence of an offense is in a foreign country, the district court before which a grand jury is impaneled to investigate the offense shall suspend the running of the statute of limitations for the offense if the court finds by a preponderance of the evidence that an official request has been made for such evidence and that it reasonably appears, or reasonably appeared at the time the request was made, that such evidence is, or was, in such foreign country.
(2) The court shall rule upon such application not later than thirty days after the filing of the application.

(b) Except as provided in subsection (c) of this section, a period of suspension under this section shall begin on the date on which the official request is made and end on the date on which the foreign court or authority takes final action on the request.

---

[59] United States v. Gilchrist, 215 F.3d 333, 238-39 (3d Cir. 2000); United States v. Midgley, 142 F.3d 174, 177-79 (3d Cir. 1998); United States v. Podde, 105 F.3d 813, 818-20 (2d Cir. 1997). 18 U.S.C. § 3296(a) ("Notwithstanding any other provision of this chapter, any counts of an indictment or information that are dismissed pursuant to a plea agreement shall be reinstated by the District Court if - (1) the counts sought to be reinstated were originally filed within the applicable limitations period; (2) the counts were dismissed pursuant to a plea agreement approved by the District Court under which the defendant pled guilty to other charges; (3) the guilty plea was subsequently vacated on the motion of the defendant; and (4) the United States moves to reinstate the dismissed counts within 60 days of the date on which the order vacating the plea becomes final.").

[60] H.R. REP. NO. 98-907, at 2-3 (1984); *Foreign Evidence Rules Amendment: Hearing Before the Subcomm. on Criminal Justice of the House Comm. on the Judiciary*, 98th Cong., 2d Sess. 15 (1984) (testimony of Dep. Ass't Att'y Gen. Mark Richard).

(c) The total of all periods of suspension under this section with respect to an offense – (1) shall not exceed three years; and (2) shall not extend a period within which a criminal case must be initiated for more than six months if all foreign authorities take final action before such period would expire without regard to this section.

(d) As used in this section, the term "official request" means a letter rogatory, a request under a treaty or convention, or any other request for evidence made by a court of the United States or an authority of the United States having criminal law enforcement responsibility, to a court or other authority of a foreign country.

Construction of Section 3292 has been something less than uniform, thus far.[61] The courts are divided over whether the target of the grand jury or the subject of the foreign evidence sought may contest the government's application when it is filed or whether the application may be filed ex parte with an opportunity for the accused to contest suspension following indictment.[62] By the same token, it is less certain whether the phrase indicating that the application must be filed with "the district court before which a grand jury is impaneled to investigate the offense," means that the application must relate to a specific grand jury investigation or may be filed in anticipation of such an investigation.[63] On the related issue of when

---

[61] Abraham Abramovsky & Jonathan I. Edelstein, *Time for Final Action on 18 U.S.C. 3292*, 21 MICH. J. INT'L L. 941 (2000).

[62] *Compare In re* Grand Jury Investigation, 3 F. Supp. 2d 82, 83 (D. Mass. 1998) ("Nothing in section 3292, however, expressly contemplates secretly extending certain statutes of limitation as to certain individuals.... Moreover, this Court general eschews ex parte practice whenever possible, since action ex parte so fundamentally undercuts the values secured by the adversary process."), *with* United States v. Little, 667 F.3d 220, 225 (2d Cir. 2012) ("Nowhere in §3292 does it state that the party whose statute of limitation is being suspended is entitled to notice or a hearing"); United States v. Hoffecker, 530 F.3d 137, 168 (3d Cir. 2008); United States v. Torres, 318 F.3d 1058, 1061 (11th Cir. 2003) United States v. Wilson, 249 F.3d 366, 371 (5th Cir. 2001); DeGeorge v. U.S. District Court, 219 F.3d 930, 937 (9th Cir. 2000).

[63] *Compare* United States v. O'Neill, 952 F.Supp. 831, 833 (D.D.C. 1996)("The government can only request that statutes of limitation be tolled for offenses under investigation by the grand jury"), *with DeGeorge*, 219 F.3d at 939-40 (denial of mandamus) (characterizing the statement in *O'Neill* as dicta and declining to find clear error in a contrary lower court decision), *on appeal*, 380 F.3d 1203, 1214; *but see* United States v. Meador, 138 F.3d 986,

an application may be filed, one court has ruled that the government may seek the suspension either to allow it to obtain foreign evidence or to compensate it for time expended to acquire the evidence prior to the application.[64] Another has held that the extension cannot be had when the evidence sought by the government is in its possession at the time of the application.[65] Still others cannot agree on whether the request may revive an expired statute of limitations.[66]

The statute demands that the government bear the burden of establishing to the court its right to a suspension by a preponderance of the evidence.[67] The Second Circuit has pointed out, however, that the statute sets out two slightly different preponderance standards, a simple preponderance standard for the fact a request has been made, and slightly less demanding one (preponderance that it "reasonably appears") for the fact that the evidence sought exists overseas.[68] The government must do

---

994 (5th Cir. 1998) ("The purpose of §3292, apparent from its structure and legislative history, is to compensate for delays attendant in obtaining records from other countries. This provision should not be an affirmative benefit to prosecutors, suspending the limitations period, pending completion of an investigation, whenever evidence is located in a foreign land. It is not a statutory grant of authority to extend the limitations period by three years at the prosecutors' option.").

[64] United States v. Miller, 830 F.2d 1073, 1076 (9th Cir. 1987).

[65] United States v. Atiyeh, 402 F.3d 354, 362-67 (3d Cir. 2005).

[66] *Compare* United States v. Kozeny, 541 F.3d 166, (2d Cir. 2008) and United States v. Brody, 621 F.Supp.2d 1196, 1999-1201 (D. Utah 2009), *with* United States v. Bischel, 61 F.3d 1429 (9th Cir. 1995) and United States v. Hoffecker, 530 F.3d 137, 164 n.4 (3d Cir. 2008).

[67] 18 U.S.C. § 3292(a)(1); *Wilson*, 249 F.3d at 373; United States v. Trainor, 376 F.3d 1325, 1330 (11th Cir. 2004).

[68] United States v. Little, 667 F.3d 220, 225 (2d Cir. 2012) ("The statute therefore requires a district court to suspend the running of a statute of limitations upon an appropriate application showing: (1) that evidence of an offense being investigated by a grand jury is in a foreign country; and (2) that such evidence has been officially requested. According to the statute, the preponderance-of-the-evidence standard applies when determining whether the United States has made an official request. When deciding whether the evidence is in a foreign country, however, a lower standard applies: a court must 'find [] by a preponderance of the evidence ... that it reasonably appears, or reasonably appeared at the time the request was made, that such evidence is, or was, in a foreign country.' [§3292(a)(1)] (Emphasis added). In other words, this element is satisfied even if the court itself is not certain that a preponderance of the evidence shows that the evidence is in a foreign country, so long as a reasonable factfinder could have come to that conclusion.").

more than present unsworn, conclusory statements to meet its burden,[69] but "something of evidentiary value" on point will ordinarily do.[70]

As for the nature of the overseas evidence, it is no bar to suspension that the evidence might be obtained in this country or that without it the grand jury has enough evidence to indict.[71] On the other hand, the court may not suspend, if the government has already received the foreign evidence at the time when it submits its application for suspension.[72]

The suspension begins when the government submits its official request to a foreign source.[73] It ends when the foreign entity takes "final action" on the request.[74] When that occurs may be a matter of some dispute. Some courts suggest that final action occurs with a dispositive response, *i.e.*, when the United States is satisfied its request has been answered;[75] yet at least one believes that final action occurs when the foreign government believes it has provided a final response.[76]

Fugitives

A provision exempting fugitives accompanied passage of the first federal statute of limitations.[77] The language has changed little since,[78] but

---

[69] United States v. Trainor, 376 F.3d 1325, 1330-335 (11th Cir. 2004); United States v. Wilson, 322 F.3d 353,363 (5th Cir. 2003); DeGeorge v. U.S. District Court, 219 F.3d 930, 937 (9th Cir. 2000).

[70] United States v. Jenkins, 633 F.3d 788, 798 (9th Cir. 2011), quoting United States v. Trainor, 376 F.3d at 1332-33 ("[T]he government must meet a 'minimum evidentiary burden.' ... The government can satisfy its burden of proof under § 3289(a)(1) 'by including a sworn or verified application containing the necessary factual information, testimony by Government officials, affidavits, declarations, exhibits, or other materials of evidentiary value,' even including hearsay evidence."); see also *Little*, 667 F.3d at 224; United States v. Minter, 45 F. Supp. 3d 1390, 1398 (N.D. Ga. 2014).

[71] *Little*, 667 F.3d at 224-25.

[72] United States v. Atiyeh, 402 F.3d 354, 362-63 (3d Cir. 2005).

[73] 18 U.S.C. § 3292(b); *Jenkins*, 633 F.3d at 798-99.

[74] *Id.* § 3292(b).

[75] United States v. Bischel, 61 F.3d 1429, 1432-434 (9th Cir. 1995); United States v. Torres, 318 F.3d 1058, 1061-65 (11th Cir. 2003).

[76] United States v. Meador, 138 F.3d 986, 991-94 (5th Cir. 1998).

[77] 1 STAT. 119 (1790) ("[N]othing herein contained shall extend to any person or persons fleeing from justice.").

[78] 18 U.S.C. § 3290 ("No statute of limitations shall extend to any person fleeing from justice.").

its meaning remains a topic of debate.[79] Most circuits, taking their lead from *Streep v. United States*,[80] hold that the government must establish that the accused acted with an intent to avoid prosecution.[81] Yet two have held that mere absence from the jurisdiction is sufficient.[82] Even in the more demanding circuits, however, flight is thought to have occurred when the accused conceals himself within the jurisdiction;[83] remains outside the jurisdiction after becoming aware of the possibility of prosecution;[84] flees before an investigation begins;[85] departs after an investigation has begun but before charges are filed;[86] absconds to avoid prosecution on another matter;[87] or flees to avoid civil or administrative justice rather than criminal justice.[88]

---

[79] See generally, *What Constitutes "Fleeing From Justice" Within the Meaning of 18 U.S.C.A. §3290 Which Provides That No Statute of Limitations Shall Extend to Persons Fleeing From Justice*, 148 ALR FED 573.

[80] 60 U.S. 128 (1895).

[81] Choe v. Torres, 525 F.3d 733, 741 (9th Cir. 2008); United States v. Gibson, 490 F.3d 604, 608 (7th Cir. 2007); United States v. Florez, 447 F.3d 145, 150-51 (2d Cir. 2006); Ross v. U.S. Marshal, 168 F.3d 1190, 1193-194 (10th Cir. 1999); United States v. Greever, 134 F.3d 777, 780 (6th Cir. 1998); United States v. Foseca-Machado, 53 F.3d 1242, 1244 (11th Cir. 1995); Donnell v. United States, 229 F.2d 560, 565 (5th Cir. 1956); Brouse v. United States, 68 F.2d 294, 295 (1st Cir. 1933).

[82] *In re* Assarsson, 687 F.2d 1157, 1162 (8th Cir. 1982); McGowen v. United States, 105 F.2d 791, 792 (D.C. Cir. 1939). *Streep* declared that it "unnecessary, for the purposes of the present case, to undertake to give an exhaustive definition of these words [fleeing from justice]; for it is quite clear that any person who takes himself out of the jurisdiction, with the intention of avoiding being brought to justice for a particular offense, can have no benefit of the limitation, at least when prosecuted for that offense in a court of the United States," 160 U.S. at 133. In context, it might be thought unclear whether the Court meant flight with intent was required or merely sufficient.

[83] *Florez*, 447 F.3d at 152; *Greever*, 134 F.3d at 780.

[84] United States v. Fowlie, 24 F.3d 1070, 1072-73 (9th Cir. 1994); United States v. Rivera-Ventura, 72 F.3d 277, 283- 84 (2d Cir. 1995); United States v. Catino, 735 F.2d 718, 722-23 (2d Cir. 1984).

[85] *Ross*, 168 F.3d at 1194-195.

[86] *Choe*, 525 F.3d at 741 n.10.

[87] United States v. Morgan, 922 F.2d 1495, 1496-497 (10th Cir. 1991); United States v. Rivera-Ventura, 72 F.3d at 283; United States v. Gonzalez, 675 F.2d 1050, 1052-53 (9th Cir. 1982).

[88] *Rivera-Ventura*, 72 F.3d at 284.

CONSPIRACIES AND CONTINUING OFFENSES

Statutes of limitation "normally begin to run when the crime is complete,"[89] which occurs when the last element of the crime has been satisfied.[90] The rule for conspiracy is a bit different.[91] The general conspiracy statute consists of two elements: (1) an agreement to commit a federal crime or to defraud the United States and (2) an overt act committed in furtherance of the agreement.[92] Conspirators left uninterrupted will frequently continue on through several overt acts to the ultimate commission of the underlying substantive offenses which are the objectives of their plots. Thus, the statute of limitations for such conspiracies begins to run not with the first overt act committed in furtherance of the conspiracy but with the last.[93] The statute of limitations under conspiracy statutes that have no overt act requirement begins to run with the accomplishment of the conspiracy's objectives, with its

---

[89] Toussie v. United States, 397 U.S. 112, 115 (1970) (quoting Pendergast v. United States, 317 U.S. 412, 418 (1943)); *see also* United States v . Ongaga, 820 F.3d 152, 159-60 (5th Cir. 2016); United States v. Bennett, 765 F.3d 887, 893 (8th Cir. 2014); United States v. Perry, 757 F.3d 166, 173 (4th Cir. 2014); United States v. Venti, 687 F.3d 501, 503 (1st Cir. 2012); United States v. Eppolito, 543 F.3d 25, 46 (2d Cir. 2008); United States v. Reitmeyer, 356 F.3d 1313, 1317 (10th Cir. 2004); United States v. Najjor, 255 F.3d 979, 983 (9th Cir. 2001); United States v. Dees, 215 F.3d 378, 380 (3d Cir. 2000); United States v. Yashar, 166 F.3d 873, 875 (7th Cir. 1999); United States v. Lutz, 154 F.3d 581, 586 (6th Cir. 1998); United States v. Gilbert, 136 F.3d 1451, 1453 (11th Cir. 1998).

[90] *Ongaga*, 820 F.3d at 159-60; *Bennett*, 765 F.3d at 893; *Reitmeyer*, 356 F.3d at, 1317; United States v. Carlson, 235 F.3d 466, 470 (9th Cir. 2000); United States v. Crossley, 224 F.3d 847, 859 (6th Cir. 2000); *Yashar*, 166 F.3d at 875; United States v. Vebeliunas, 76 F.3d 1283, 1293 (2d Cir. 1996).

[91] *See generally, When Is Conspiracy Continuing Offense for Purposes of Statute of Limitations Under 18 USCS §3282*, 106 ALR FED. 616.

[92] "If two or more persons conspire either to commit any offense against the United States, or to defraud the United States, or any agency thereof in any manner or for any purpose, and one or more of such persons do any act to effect the object of the conspiracy, each shall be fined under this title or imprisoned not more than five years, or both.... " 18 U.S.C. § 371.

[93] Fiswick v. United States, 329 U.S. 211, 216 (1946); *see also* United States v. Martinez, 862 F.3d 223, 232-33 (2d Cir. 2017); United States v. Farias, 836 F.3d 1315, 1324 (11th Cir. 2016); United States v. Chhun, 744 F.3d 1110, 1122 (9th Cir. 2014); United States v. Stewart, 744 F.3d 17, 21 (1st Cir. 2014); United States v. Cunningham, 679 F.3d 355, 374 (6th Cir. 2012).

abandonment,[94] or with the defendant's effective withdrawal from the conspiracy.[95]

Concealment of the criminal plot after its completion is considered a natural component of all conspiracies. Consequently, overt acts of concealment after the objectives of the conspiracy have been accomplished may not be used to delay the running of the statute of limitations.[96] Overt acts of concealment which are among the original objectives of the conspiracy as charged in the indictment, however, may serve as the point at which the statute of limitations begins to run.[97] Distinguishing between the two is sometimes difficult.

There are other crimes, which, like conspiracy, continue on long after all the elements necessary for their prosecution fall into place. The applicable statute of limitations for these continuing crimes is delayed if either "the explicit language of the substantive criminal statute compels such a conclusion, or the nature of the crime involved is such that Congress must assuredly have intended that it be treated as a continuing one."[98] Continuing federal offenses for purposes of the statutes of limitation include the following:

---

[94] *Martinez*, 862 F.3d at 232 ("[T]he limitations period begins only when the purposes of the conspiracy have been accomplished or abandoned."); United States v. Wilbur, 674 F.3d 1160, 1176 (9th Cir. 2012); United States v. Nunez, 673 F.3d 661, 663 (7th Cir. 2012); United States v. Fishman, 645 F.3d 1175, 1191 (10th Cir. 2011); United States v. McNair, 605 F.3d 1152, 1213 (11th Cir. 2010).

[95] United States v. Smith, 568 U.S. 106, 107 (2013); Martinez, 862 F.3d at 232-33; United States v. Heard, 709 F.3d 413, 427 (5th Cir. 2013); United States v. Arias, 431 F.3d 1327, 1340 (11th Cir. 2005); United States v. Hitt, 349 F.3d 1010, 1015 (D.C. Cir. 2001); United States v. Monaco, 194 F.3d 381, 387 n.2 (2d Cir. 1999).

[96] Grunewald v. United States, 353 U.S. 391, 406 (1957); *see also* United States v. Qayyum, 451 F.3d 1214, 1219 (10th Cir. 2006); United States v. Grenoble, 413 F.3d 569, 575-76 (6th Cir. 2005); United States v. Arnold, 117 F.3d 1308, 1314 (11th Cir. 1997); United States v. Maloney, 71 F.3d 645, 659 (7th Cir. 1995); *cf.* United States v. Tanke, 743 F.3d 1296, 1304 (9th Cir. 2014).

[97] *Grunewald*, 353 U.S. at 406; *see also Qayyum*, 451 F.3d at 1219; United States v. Mann, 161 F.3d 840, 859 (5th Cir. 1998); United States v. Arnold, 117 F.3d at 1314; *Maloney*, 71 F.3d at 659-60; United States v. Rabinowitz, 56 F.3d 932, 934 (8th Cir. 1995).

[98] Toussie v. United States, 397 U.S. at 115; *see also* United States v. Ongaga, 820 F.3d 152, 160 (5th Cir. 2016); United States v. Holden, 806 F.3d 1227, 1231 (9th Cir. 2015); United States v. Smith, 373 F.3d 561, 563-64 (4th Cir. 2004); United States v. Reitmeyer, 356 F.3d 1313, 1322 (10th Cir. 2004). One commentator has characterized as "haphazard" the lower federal court's application of *Toussie*. *See* Jeffrey R. Boles, *Easing the Tension Between Statutes of Limitations and the Continuing Offense Doctrine*, 7 NW. J. L. & SOC. POL'Y 219, 256 (2012).

- escape from federal custody;[99]
- flight to avoid prosecution;[100]
- failure to report for sentencing;[101]
- possession of the skin and skull of an endangered species;[102]
- possession of counterfeit currency;[103]
- kidnaping;[104]

---

[99] "Whoever escapes or attempts to escape from the custody of the Attorney General or his authorized representative, or from any institution or facility in which he is confined by direction of the Attorney General, or from any custody under or by virtue of any process issued under the laws of the United States by any court, judge, or commissioner, or from the custody of an officer or employee of the United States pursuant to lawful arrest, shall, if the custody or confinement is by virtue of an arrest on a charge of felony, or conviction of any offense, be fined under this title or imprisoned not more than five years, or both; or if the custody or confinement is for extradition, or for exclusion or expulsion proceedings under the immigration laws, or by virtue of an arrest or charge of or for a misdemeanor, and prior to conviction, be fined under this title or imprisoned not more than one year, or both." 18 U.S.C. § 751(a); *United States v. Bailey*, 444 U.S. 394, 636 (1980).

[100] "Whoever moves or travels in interstate or foreign commerce with intent either (1) to avoid prosecution, or custody or confinement after conviction, under the laws of the place from which he flees, for a crime, or an attempt to commit a crime, punishable by death or which is a felony under the laws of the place from which the fugitive flees, or (2) to avoid giving testimony in any criminal proceedings in such place in which the commission of an offense punishable by death or which is a felony under the laws of such place, is charged, or (3) to avoid service of, or contempt proceedings for alleged disobedience of, lawful process requiring attendance and the giving of testimony or the production of documentary evidence before an agency of a State empowered by the law of such State to conduct investigations of alleged criminal activities, shall be fined under this title or imprisoned not more than five years, or both.... " 18 U.S.C. § 1073; United States v. Merino, 44 F.3d 749, 753-54 (9th Cir. 1994).

[101] "Whoever, having been released under this chapter knowingly – (1) fails to appear before a court as required by the conditions of release; or (2) fails to surrender for service of sentence pursuant to a court order; shall be punished as provided in subsection (b) of this section," 18 U.S.C. § 3146(a); United States v. Gray, 876 F.2d 1411, 1419 (9th Cir. 1989).

[102] "It is unlawful for any person subject to the jurisdiction of the United States to engage in any trade in any specimens contrary to the provisions of the Convention [on International Trade in Endangered Species], or to possess any specimens traded contrary to the provisions of the Convention, including the definitions of terms in article I thereof," 16 U.S.C. § 1538(c)(1); United States v. Winnie, 97 F.3d 975, 975-76 (7th Cir. 1996).

[103] "Whoever, with intent to defraud, passes, utters, publishes, or sells, or attempts to pass, utter, publish, or sell, or with like intent brings into the United States or keeps in possession or conceals any falsely made, forged, counterfeited, or altered obligation or other security of the United States, shall be fined under this title or imprisoned not more than 15 years, or both," 18 U.S.C. § 472; United States v. Kayfez, 957 F.2d 677, 678 (9th Cir. 1992).

[104] "(a) Whoever unlawfully seizes, confines, inveigles, decoys, kidnaps, abducts, or carries away and holds for ransom or reward or otherwise any person, except in the case of a minor by the parent thereof, when—(1) the person is willfully transported in interstate or foreign commerce, regardless of whether the person was alive when transported across a State boundary if the person was alive when the transportation began; (2) any such act against the

- failure to register under the Foreign Agents Registration Act;[105]
- failure to register under the Selective Service Act;[106]
- being found in the United States having reentered this country after deportation;[107]
- embezzlement under some circumstances;[108]

---

person is done within the special maritime and territorial jurisdiction of the United States; (3) any such act against the person is done within the special aircraft jurisdiction of the United States as defined in section 46501 of Title 49; (4) the person is a foreign official, an internationally protected person, or an official guest as those terms are defined in section 1116(b) of this title; or (5) the person is among those officers and employees described in section 1114 of this title and any such act against the person is done while the person is engaged in, or on account of, the performance of official duties; shall be punished by imprisonment for any term of years or for life and, if the death of any person results, shall be punished by death or life imprisonment." 18 U.S.C. § 1201(a); United States v. Denny-Shaffer, 2 F.3d 999, 1018-19 (10th Cir. 1993); United States v. Garcia, 854 F.2d 340, 343 (9th Cir. 1988) (the statute of limitations does not begin to run until the victim is released); if the victim is killed, the offense is a capital crime and the prosecution may be brought at any time.

[105] "Failure to file any such registration statement or supplements thereto as is required by either section 612(a) or section 612(b) of this title [relating to registration requirements] shall be considered a continuing offense for as long as such failure exists, notwithstanding any statute of limitation or other statute to the contrary," 22 U.S.C. § 618(e); United States v. McGoff, 831 F.2d 1071, 1071 (D.C. Cir. 1987).

[106] "No person shall be prosecuted, tried, or punished for evading, neglecting, or refusing to perform the duty of registering imposed by Section 3 of this title [50 U.S.C. § 3802] unless the indictment is found within five years next after the last day before such person attains the age of twenty-six, or within five years next after the last day before such person does perform his duty to register, whichever shall first occur." 50 U.S.C. § 3811(d); United States v. Kerley, 838 F.2d 932, 935 (7th Cir. 1988); United States v. Jacob, 781 F.2d 643, 648-49 (8th Cir. 1986).

[107] "Subject to subsection (b) of this section, any alien who – (1) has been denied admission, excluded, deported, or removed or has departed the United States while an order of exclusion, deportation, or removal is outstanding, and thereafter (2) enters, attempts to enter, or is at any time found in, the United States, unless (A) prior to his reembarkation at a place outside the United States or his application for admission from foreign contiguous territory, the Attorney General has expressly consented to such alien's reapplying for admission; or (B) with respect to an alien previously denied admission and removed, unless such alien shall establish that he was not required to obtain such advance consent under this chapter or any prior Act, shall be fined under Title 18, or imprisoned not more than two years, or both," 8 U.S.C. § 1326(a); United States v. Gomez, 38 F.3d 1031, 1035 (8th Cir. 1994);, United States v. Santana-Castellano, 74 F.3d 593, 597 (5th Cir. 1996) ("Likewise, the five year statute of limitations under Sec. 1326 begins to run at the time the alien is found barring circumstances that suggest that the INS should have known of his presence earlier, such as when he reentered the United States through an official border checkpoint in the good faith belief that his entry was legal."); United States v. DiSantillo, 615 F.2d 128, 132 (3d Cir. 1980).

[108] "We believe that the specific conduct at issue here is more properly characterized as a continuing offense rather than a series of separate acts. The facts found by the district court

- possession of unregistered pipe bombs;[109]
- failure to pay child support;[110]
- possession of an immigration document obtained fraudulently;[111]
- bank fraud;[112] and
- health care fraud.[113]

---

were sufficient to prove that he set into place and maintained an automatically recurring scheme whereby funds were electronically deposited in his account and retained for his own use without need for any specific action on his part." *Id. See also* United States v. Smith, 373 F.3d 561, 568 (4th Cir. 2004).

[109] "It shall be unlawful for any person ... (d) to receive or possess a firearm which is not registered to him in the National Firearms Registration and Transfer Record.... " 26 U.S.C. § 5861(d); "For the purpose of this chapter ... (a) ... The term 'firearm' means ... (8) a destructive device.... (f) ... The term 'destructive device' means (1) any explosive, incendiary, or poison gas (A) bomb,.... " 26 U.S.C. § 5845(d)(8), (f)(1); United States v. Berndt, 530 F.3d 553, 554-55 (7th Cir. 2008).

[110] "Any person who - (1) willfully fails to pay a support obligation with respect to a child who resides in another State, if such obligation has remained unpaid for a period longer than 1 year, or is greater than $5,000; (2) travels in interstate or foreign commerce with the intent to evade a support obligation, if such obligation has remained unpaid for a period longer than 1 year, or is greater than $5,000; or (3) willfully fails to pay a support obligation with respect to a child who resides in another State, if such obligation has remained unpaid for a period longer than 2 years, or is greater than $10,000; shall be punished as provided in subsection (c)." 18 U.S.C. § 228(a); United States v. Edelkind, 525 F.3d 388, 393-94 (5th Cir. 2008).

[111] "Whoever knowingly forges, counterfeits, alters, or falsely makes any immigrant or nonimmigrant visa, permit, border crossing card, alien registration receipt card, or other document prescribed by statute or regulation for entry into or as evidence of authorized stay or employment in the United States, or utters, uses, attempts to use, possesses, obtains, accepts, or receives any such visa, permit, border crossing card, alien registration receipt card, or other document prescribed by statute or regulation for entry into or as evidence of authorized stay or employment in the United States, knowing it to be forged, counterfeited, altered, or falsely made, or to have been procured by means of any false claim or statement, or to have been otherwise procured by fraud or unlawfully obtained.... Shall be fined under this title or imprisoned not more than.... " 18 U.S.C. § 1546(a); United States v. Krstic, 558 F.3d 1010, 1017-18 (9th Cir. 2009).

[112] Whoever knowingly executes, or attempts to execute, a scheme or artifice - (1) to defraud a financial institution; or (2) to obtain any of the moneys, funds, credits, assets, securities, or other property owned by, or under the custody or control of, a financial institution, by means of false or fraudulent pretenses, representations, or promises; shall be fined not more than $1,000,000 or imprisoned not more than 30 years, or both." 18 U.S.C. § 1344; United States v. Najjor, 255 F.3d 979, 983-84 (9th Cir. 2001).

[113] "Whoever knowingly and willfully executes, or attempts to execute, a scheme or artifice - (1) to defraud any health care benefit program; or (2) to obtain, by means of false or fraudulent pretenses, representations, or promises, any of the money or property owned by, or under the custody or control of, any health care benefit program, in connection with the delivery of or payment for health care benefits, items, or services, shall be fined under this title or imprisoned not more than 10 years, or both. If the violation results in serious bodily injury (as defined in section 1365 of this title), such person shall be fined under this title or imprisoned

CONSTITUTIONAL CONSIDERATIONS

Ex Post Facto

Historically, constitutional challenges to the application of various statutes of limitation have arisen most often under the ex post facto or due process clauses. The Constitution prohibits both Congress and the states from enacting ex post facto laws.[114] More precisely, the words of the Supreme Court in *Calder v. Bull*, it prohibits the following:

> 1st. Every law that makes an action done before the passing of the law, and which was innocent when done, criminal; and punishes such action. 2nd. Every law that aggravates a crime, or makes it greater than it was, when committed. 3rd. Every law that changes the punishment, and inflicts a greater punishment, than the law annexed to the crime, when committed. 4th. Every law that alters the legal rules of evidence, and receives less, or different, testimony, than the law required at the time of the commission of the offense, in order to convict the offender.[115]

The lower federal appellate courts had long felt that a statute that extended a period of limitation before its expiration did not offend the ex post facto clauses, but that the clauses do ban laws that attempt to revive and extend an expired statute of limitations.[116] Until the United States

---

not more than 20 years, or both; and if the violation results in death, such person shall be fined under this title, or imprisoned for any term of years or for life, or both." 18 U.S.C. § 1347(a); United States v. Holden, 806 F.3d 1227, 1231-32 (9th Cir. 2015) (citing United States v. Hickman, 331 F.3d 439, 445-46 (5th Cir. 2003)).

[114] "No Bill of Attainder or ex post facto Law shall be passed.... No State shall ... pass any Bill of Attainder, [or] ex post facto Law.... U.S. CONST. art. I, §§ 9, 10.

[115] *Stogner v. California*, 539 U.S. 607, 612 (2003), quoting *Calder v. Bull*, 3 Dall. (3 U.S.) 386, 390 (1798) (*seriatim* opinion of Chase, J.).

[116] *E.g.*, United States v. De La Mata, 266 F.3d 1275, 1286 (11th Cir. 2001); United States v. Morrow, 177 F.3d 272, 294 (5th Cir. 1999); United States v. Chandler, 66 F.3d 1460, 1467 (8th Cir. 1995); United States v. Taliaferro, 979 F.2d 1399, 1402-403 (10th Cir. 1992); United States v. Knipp, 963 F.2d 839, 844 (6th Cir. 1992); United States *ex rel.* Massarella v. Elrod, 682 F.2d 688, 689 (7th Cir. 1982); United States v. Richardson, 512 F.2d 105, 196 (3d Cir. 1975); United States v. Clemens, 266 F.2d 397, 399 (9th Cir. 1959); Falter v. United States, 23 F.2d 420, 425-26 (2d Cir. 1928).

Supreme Court confirmed that view in *Stogner v. California*,[117] however, there were well regarded contrary opinions. The California Supreme Court in *Frazer*, for example, at one point concluded that the ex post facto clauses in fact pose no impediment to the revival of an expired statute of limitations.[118] In so holding, the California court relied heavily on the United States Supreme Court's *Collins v. Youngblood* decision where the Court seemed to repudiate at least the evidentiary component of the traditional *Calder* understanding. As the California court read *Collins*, the Supreme Court had not only indicated that evidentiary changes were beyond the realm of ex post facto protection but that ex post facto protection reached no further than retroactive changes in a crime's elements or punishment.[119]

The Supreme Court subsequently warned that *Collins* should not be read as a repudiation of *Calder's* four prohibited classes, but instead that "*Collins* held that it was a mistake to stray *beyond Calder's* four categories."[120] In another case, the Court seemed to further signal its reluctance to reach beyond the limits of *Calder* when it declined to extend the ex post facto proscription to cover a retroactive application of a judicial (rather than a legislative) change in the law.[121] These developments did not necessarily undermine the California decision in *Frazer*, however, because its revival of a statute of limitations that had run did not appear to fit easily within any of the *Calder* categories. The *Frazer* analysis was in error nonetheless.

The United States Supreme Court in *Stogner* characterized the California legislative revival of an expired period of limitation as not only

---

[117] 539 U.S. 607 (2003).

[118] People v. Frazer, 982 P.2d 180, 194 (Cal. 1999).

[119] *Id.* at191-92 (citing Collins v. Youngblood, 497 U.S. 37, 43 n.3, 50 (1990)).

[120] Carmell v. Texas, 529 U.S. 513, 539 (2000) (emphasis in the original).

[121] *See* Rogers v. Tennessee, 532 U.S. 451, 462 (2001) ("Justice Scalia makes much of the fact that at the time of the framing of the Constitution, it was widely accepted ... that (according to Justice Scalia) there is no doubt that the ex post facto clause would have prohibited a legislative decision identical to the Tennessee court's decision here. This latter argument seeks at bottom merely to reopen what has long been settled by the constitutional text and our own decisions: that the ex post facto clause does not apply to judicial decisions.") *Rogers* arose when the Tennessee Supreme Court abrogated a previous common law rule that barred a murder prosecution unless the victim died within a year and a day of the defendant's assault upon the victim.

"manifestly unjust and oppressive," but among those laws that run afoul of *Calder's* second standard, i.e., "[e]very law that aggravates a crime, or makes it greater than it was, when committed."[122] As properly understood and alternatively characterized in *Calder*, this second category embraces statutes like the California statute that "inflicted punishments, where the party was not by law, liable to any punishment," at the time.[123]

Due Process

Retroactivity aside, the due process clauses may be implicated when a crime has no statute of limitations or when the period of limitation has not run. Although statutes of limitation alone generally govern the extent of permissible pre-indictment delay, extraordinary circumstances may trigger due process implications. The Supreme Court in *Marion* observed that even "the Government concedes that the Due Process Clause of the Fifth Amendment would require dismissal of [an] indictment if it were shown at trial that the pre-indictment delay ... caused substantial prejudice to [a defendant's] rights to a fair trial and that the delay was an intentional device to gain tactical advantage over the accused."[124] The Court declined to dismiss the indictment there, however, because the defendants failed to show they had suffered any actual prejudice from the delay or to show "that the Government intentionally delayed to gain some tactical advantage over [them] or to harass them."[125]

The Court later made clear that due process contemplates more than a claimant's showing of adverse impact caused by pre-indictment delay: "Thus *Marion* makes clear that proof of prejudice is generally a necessary

---

[122] *Stogner*, 539 U.S. at 611-12.

[123] *Id.* at 612 (quoting *Calder*, 3 Dall. (3 U.S.) at 389).

[124] United States v. Marion, 404 U.S. 307, 324 (1971); *see also* United States v. Gouveia, 467 U.S. 180, 192 (1984) ("But applicable statutes of limitations protect against the prosecution's bringing stale criminal charges against any defendant, and, beyond that protection, the Fifth Amendment requires the dismissal of an indictment, even if it is brought within the statute of limitations, if the defendant can prove that the Government's delay in bringing the indictment was a deliberate device to gain an advantage over him and that it caused him actual prejudice in presenting his defense.").

[125] *Marion*, 404 U.S. at 325.

but not sufficient element of a due process claim, and that the due process inquiry must consider the reasons for the delay as well as the prejudice to the accused."[126]

Perhaps because so few defendants have been able to show sufficient prejudice to necessitate further close inquiry,[127] the lower federal appellate courts seem at odds over exactly what else due process demands before it will require dismissal. Most have held that the defendant bears the burden of establishing both prejudice and government deficiency;[128] others, that once the defendant establishes prejudice the burden shifts to the government to negate the second prong;[129] and still others, that once the

---

[126] United States v. Lovasco, 431 U.S. 783, 790 (1977); *see also* Arizona v. Youngblood, 488 U.S. 51, 57 (1988) ("Our decisions in related areas have stressed the importance for constitutional purposes of good or bad faith on the part of the Government when the claim is based on the loss of evidence attributable to the Government.").

[127] United States v. Lively, 852 F.3d 549, 566 (6th Cir. 2017) ("The standard for pre-indictment delay is nearly insurmountable...") (quoting United States v. Rogers, 118 F.3d 466, 477 n.10); United States v. Gilbert, 266 F.3d 1180, 1187 (9th Cir. 2001) ("[T]he burden of showing actual prejudice is heavy and is rarely met.") (quoting United States v. Doe, 149 F.3d 945, 948 (9th Cir. 1998)); United States v. Cornielle, 171 F.3d 748, 752 (2d Cir. 1999). The defendant must show more than mere speculative harm; he "must specifically identify witnesses or documents lost during the delay properly attributable to the government, relate the substance of the testimony which would have been offered by the missing witnesses or the information contained in lost documents in sufficient detail to permit a court to assess accurately whether the information was material to his defense, and show that the missing testimony or other evidence is not available from alternative sources." United States v. Al-Muqsit, 191 F.3d 928, 938 (8th Cir. 1999); *see also* United States v. Irizarry-Colon, 848 F.3d 61, 70-1 (1st Cir. 2017); United States v. Beckman, 183 F.3d 891, 895 (8th Cir. 1999); United States v. Trammell, 133 F.3d 1343, 1351 (10th Cir. 1998); United States v. Crouch, 84 F.3d 1497, 1514-516 (5th Cir. 1996).

[128] *Irizarry-Colon*, 848 F.3d at 70 ("Even when an indictment is brought within the statute of limitations, 'excessive pre-indictment delay can sometimes , albeit rarely, violate the Fifth Amendment's Due Process Clause if the defendant shows *both* that the delay caused substantial prejudice to his right to a fair trial' *and* that 'the government intentionally delayed indictment ... to gain a tactical advantage'") (quoting United States v. Bater, 594 F.3d 51, 54 (1st Cir. 2010)) (emphasis in the original); *see also* United States v. Farias, 836 F.3d 1315, 1325 (11th Cir. 2016); United States v. Ross, 703 F.3d 856, 876 (6th Cir. 2012); United States v. Seale, 600 F.3d 473, 479 (5th Cir. 2010); United States v. Madden, 682 F.3d 920, 929 (10th Cir. 2012); United States v. Uribe-Rios, 558 F.3d 347, 358 (4th Cir. 2009); United States v. Corona-Verbera, 509 F.3d 1105, 1112 (9th Cir. 2007); United States v. Galdney, 474 F.3d 1027, 1030 (8th Cir. 2007); United States v. Beckett, 208 F.3d 140, 150 (3d Cir. 2000).

[129] United States v. Hagler, 700 F.3d 1091, 1099 (7th Cir. 2012); United States v. Benshop, 138 F.3d 1229, 1232 (8th Cir. 1998).

defendant shows prejudice the court must balance the harm against the justifications for delay.[130]

ATTACHMENT 1. PERIODS OF LIMITATION FOR SPECIFIC FEDERAL CRIMES (CITATIONS)

No Limitation

Death Penalty Offenses

- 8 U.S.C. § 1324(a)(1) (bringing in or harboring aliens where death results)[131]
- 15 U.S.C. § 1825(a)(2)(C) (killing those enforcing the Horse Protection Act)
- 18 U.S.C. §§ 32, 33, 34 (destruction of aircraft, commercial motor vehicles or their facilities where death results)
- 18 U.S.C. § 36 (drive-by shooting resulting in 1st degree murder)
- 18 U.S.C. § 37 (violence at international airports where death results)
- 18 U.S.C. §§ 43, 3559(f) (animal enterprise terrorism constituting murder of a child)

---

[130] United States v. Lopez, 860 F.3d 201, 213 (4th Cir. 2017) ("In order to prevail on a due process claim based on pretrial delay, a defendant first must show that he suffered actual prejudice. If that threshold requirement is met, then a court will consider the government's reasons for the delay, to evaluate whether there has been a violation of fundamental conceptions of justice or the community's sense of fair play and decency.") (internal citations omitted); *see also* United States v. Barken, 412 F.3d 1131, 1134 (9th Cir. 2005); United States v. DeGeorge, 380 F.3d 1203, 1210-211 (9th Cir. 2004)(internal quotation marks omitted) ("DeGeorge must satisfy a two-part test to establish that pre-indictment delay has violated his due process rights: 1) he must prove that he suffered actual, non-speculative prejudice from the delay; and 2) he must show that the delay when balanced against the government's reasons for it, offends those fundamental conceptions of justice which lie at the base of our civil and political institutions.").

[131] "An indictment for any offense punishable by death may be found at any time without limitation." 18 U.S.C. § 3281.

- 18 U.S.C. § 115 (kidnaping with death resulting of the member of the family of a federal official or employee to obstruct or retaliate)
- 18 U.S.C. § 115 (murder of the member of the family of a federal official or employee to obstruct or retaliate)
- 18 U.S.C. § 175 (development or possession of biological weapons)
- 18 U.S.C. §§ 175c, 3559(f) (variola virus offense constituting murder of a child)
- 18 U.S.C. §§ 229, 229A (use of chemical weapons where death results) 18 U.S.C. § 241 (conspiracy against civil rights where death results)
- 18 U.S.C. § 242 (deprivation civil rights under color of law where death results)
- 18 U.S.C. § 245 (discriminatory obstruction of enjoyment of federal protected activities where death results)
- 18 U.S.C. § 247 (obstruction of the exercise of religious beliefs where death results)
- 18 U.S.C. § 249 (hate crime resulting in death)[132]
- 18 U.S.C. § 351 (murder of a Member of Congress)
- 18 U.S.C. § 351 (conspiracy to kill or kidnap a Member of Congress if death results)
- 18 U.S.C. § 351 (kidnaping a Member of Congress if death results)
- 18 U.S.C. § 794 (espionage)
- 18 U.S.C. §§ 831, 3559(f) (nuclear material offense constituting murder of a child)
- 18 U.S.C. § 844(d) (use of fire or explosives unlawfully where death results)
- 18 U.S.C. § 844(f)(burning or bombing federal property where death results)
- 18 U.S.C. § 844(i)(burning or bombing property affecting interstate commerce where death results) 18 U.S.C. § 924(j)(1)

[132] There is no statute of limitations for a hate crime resulting in death notwithstanding the fact that the offense is not punishable by death. 18 U.S.C. § 249(d)(2).

(murder while in possession of a firearm during the commission of a crime of violence or drug trafficking)

- 18 U.S.C. § 930(c) (murder while in possession of a firearm in a federal building)
- 18 U.S.C. § 1091 (genocide)[133]
- 18 U.S.C. § 1111 (murder within the special maritime or territorial jurisdiction of the U.S.)
- 18 U.S.C. § 1121(b) (killing a state law enforcement officer by a federal prisoner or while transferring a prisoner interstate)
- 18 U.S.C. § 1114 (murder of a federal officer or employee)
- 18 U.S.C. § 1116 (murder of a foreign dignitary)
- 18 U.S.C. § 1118 (murder by a federal prisoner)
- 18 U.S.C. § 1119 (murder of an American by an American overseas)
- 18 U.S.C. § 1120 (murder by an escaped federal prisoner)
- 18 U.S.C. § 1121 (murder of one assisting in a federal criminal investigation)
- 18 U.S.C. § 1201 (kidnaping where death results)
- 18 U.S.C. § 1203 (hostage taking where death results)
- 18 U.S.C. §§ 1365, 3559(f) (tampering with consumer products constituting murder of a child)
- 18 U.S.C. § 1503 (murder committed to obstruction of federal judicial proceedings)
- 18 U.S.C. § 1512 (tampering with a federal witness or informant involving murder)
- 18 U.S.C. § 1513 (retaliating against a federal witness or informant involving murder)
- 18 U.S.C. §§ 1591, 2245 (murder committed during the course of sex trafficking by force, fraud or of a child)
- 18 U.S.C. §§ 1651, 1652, 3559(f) (piracy involving murder of a child)

---

[133] Genocide may be prosecuted at any time regardless of whether the offense results in a death. 18 U.S.C. § 1091(f).

- 18 U.S.C. § 1716 (mailing injurious articles with intent to injure or damage property where death results) 18 U.S.C. § 1751 (kidnaping the President where death results)
- 18 U.S.C. § 1751 (conspiracy to kill or kidnap the President where death results)
- 18 U.S.C. § 1751 (murder of the President)
- 18 U.S.C. §§ 1952, 3559(f) (travel in aid of racketeering involve the murder of child)
- 18 U.S.C. § 1958 (use of interstate facilities in furtherance of a murder-for-hire where death results)
- 18 U.S.C. § 1959 (murder in aid of racketeering activity)
- 18 U.S.C. § 1992 (terrorist attacks on trains and mass transit)
- 18 U.S.C. § 2113(e) (robbing a federally insured bank if death results)
- 18 U.S.C. §§ 2118, 3559(f) (robbery or burglary involving controlled substances constituting murder of a child)
- 18 U.S.C. § 2119 (carjacking where death results)
- 18 U.S.C. §§ 2199, 3559(f) (murder of a child by a stowaway)
- 18 U.S.C. §§ 2241, 2245 (aggravated sexual assault of a child under 12 years of age in the special maritime or territorial jurisdiction of the U.S. where death results)
- 18 U.S.C. §§ 2242, 2245 (coercing or enticing interstate travel for sexual purposes where death results)
- 18 U.S.C. §§ 2243, 2245 (transporting minors for sexual purposes resulting in the death of a child under 14 years of age)
- 18 U.S.C. §§ 2244, 2245 (abusive sexual contact where death results)
- 18 U.S.C. § 2251 (sexual exploitation of children where death results)
- 18 U.S.C. §§ 2251A, 2245 (selling or buying children where death results)
- 18 U.S.C. §§ 2260, 2245 (production of material depicting sexually explicit activities of a child where death results)

- 18 U.S.C. §§ 2261, 2261A, 2262, 3559(f) (murder of a child involved in interstate domestic violence, stalking, or interstate violation of a protective order)
- 18 U.S.C. § 2280 (violence against maritime navigation where death results)
- 18 U.S.C. § 2281 (violence against maritime fixed platform where death results)
- 18 U.S.C. § 2282A (interference with maritime commerce where death results)
- 18 U.S.C. § 2283 (transportation of explosive, nuclear, chemical, biological or radioactive material resulting in death)
- 18 U.S.C. § 2291 (destruction of a vessel or maritime facility)
- 18 U.S.C. § 2332 (terrorist murder of an American outside the U.S.)
- 18 U.S.C. § 2332a (use of weapons of mass destruction where death results)
- 18 U.S.C. § 2332b (acts of terrorism transcending national boundaries where death results)
- 18 U.S.C. § 2332f (bombing public places)
- 18 U.S.C. §§ 2332g, 3559(f) (anti-aircraft missile offense constituting murder of a child)
- 18 U.S.C. §§ 2332h, 3559(f) (radiological dispersal device offense constituting murder of a child)
- 18 U.S.C. § 2340A (torture where death results)
- 18 U.S.C. § 2381 (treason)
- 18 U.S.C. § 2441 (war crimes where death results)
- 18 U.S.C. §§ 2421, 2245 (transportation of illicit sexual purposes where death results)
- 18 U.S.C. §§ 2422, 2245 (coercion or inducement to travel for illicit sexual purposes where death results)
- 18 U.S.C. §§ 2423, 2245 (transportation of minors for illicit sexual purposes where death results)

- 18 U.S.C. §§ 2425, 2245 (interstate transportation of information concerning a minor where death results)
- 21 U.S.C. § 461 (killing a poultry inspector)
- 21 U.S.C. § 675 (killing a meat inspector)
- 21 U.S.C. §§ 848(c), 3591(b) (major drug kingpin violations)
- 21 U.S.C. § 848(e)(1) (killing in furtherance of a serious drug trafficking violation or killing a law enforcement official in furtherance of a controlled substance violation)
- 21 U.S.C. § 1041(c) (murder of an egg inspector)
- 42 U.S.C. § 2000e-13 (murder of EEOC personnel)
- 42 U.S.C. § 2283 (murder of federal nuclear inspectors)
- 49 U.S.C. § 46502 (air piracy where death results)
- 49 U.S.C. § 46506 (murder in the special aircraft jurisdiction of the United States)

Terrorism-Related Offenses Resulting in or Involving the Risk of Death or Serious Injury

- 18 U.S.C. § 32 (destruction of aircraft or aircraft facilities)[134]
- 18 U.S.C. § 37 (violence at international airports)
- 18 U.S.C. § 81 (arson within special maritime and territorial jurisdiction)
- 18 U.S.C. §§ 175, 175b (biological weapons offenses)
- 18 U.S.C. § 175c (variola virus)
- 18 U.S.C. § 229 (chemical weapons offenses)
- 18 U.S.C. § 351(a),(b),(c), or (d) (congressional, cabinet, and Supreme Court assassination and kidnaping)
- 18 U.S.C. § 831 (nuclear materials offenses)

---

134 "[A]n indictment may be found or an information instituted at any time without limitation for any offense listed in section 2332b(g)(5)(B), if the commission of such offense resulted in, or created a foreseeable risk of death or serious bodily injury to another person." 18 U.S.C. § 3286(b).

- 18 U.S.C. § 832 (participation in a foreign atomic weapons program)
- 18 U.S.C. § 842(m) or (n) (plastic explosives offenses)
- 18 U.S.C. § 844(f)(2) or (3)(arson and bombing of federal property risking or causing death)
- 18 U.S.C. § 844(i) (burning or bombing of property used in, or used in activities affecting, commerce) 18 U.S.C. § 930(c) (killing or attempted killing during an attack on a federal facility with a dangerous weapon)
- 18 U.S.C. § 956(a)(1) (conspiracy to murder, kidnap, or maim persons abroad)
- 18 U.S.C. § 1030(a)(1) (protection of computer systems containing classified information)
- 18 U.S.C. § 1030(a)(5)(A)(i) (resulting in damage defined in 1030(a)(5)(B)(ii) through (v) (protection of computers)
- 18 U.S.C. § 1114 (protection of officers and employees of the United States),
- 18 U.S.C. § 1116 (murder or manslaughter of foreign officials, official guests, or internationally protected persons)
- 18 U.S.C. § 1203 (hostage taking)
- 18 U.S.C. § 1361 (destruction of federal property)
- 18 U.S.C. § 1362 (destruction of communication lines, stations, or systems)
- 18 U.S.C. § 1363 (injury to buildings or property within special maritime and territorial jurisdiction of the United States)
- 18 U.S.C. § 1366(a) (destruction of energy facilities)
- 18 U.S.C. § 1751(a),(b),(c), or (d) (Presidential and Presidential staff assassination and kidnaping)
- 18 U.S.C. § 1992 (terrorist attacks on trains and mass transit)
- 18 U.S.C. § 2155 (destruction of national defense materials, premises, or utilities),
- 18 U.S.C. § 2156 (production of defective national defense material)

- 18 U.S.C. § 2280 (violence against maritime navigation)
- 18 U.S.C. § 2280a (violence against maritime navigation involving weapons of mass destruction)
- 18 U.S.C. § 2281 (violence against maritime fixed platforms)
- 18 U.S.C. § 2281a (addition offenses involving violence against maritime fixed platforms)
- 18 U.S.C. § 2332 (certain homicides and other violence against United States nationals occurring outside of the United States)
- 18 U.S.C. § 2332a (use of weapons of mass destruction)
- 18 U.S.C. § 2332b (acts of terrorism transcending national boundaries)
- 18 U.S.C. § 2332f (bombing public places)
- 18 U.S.C. § 2332g (anti-aircraft missiles)
- 18 U.S.C. § 2332h (radiological dispersal devices)
- 18 U.S.C. § 2332i (acts of nuclear terrorism)
- 18 U.S.C. § 2339 (harboring terrorists)
- 18 U.S.C. § 2339A (providing material support to terrorists)
- 18 U.S.C. § 2339B (providing material support to terrorist organizations)
- 18 U.S.C. § 2339C (financing terrorism)
- 18 U.S.C. § 2339D (receipt of military training from a foreign terrorist organization)
- 18 U.S.C. § 2340A (torture committed under color of law)
- 21 U.S.C. § 960A (narcoterrorism)
- 42 U.S.C. § 2122 (atomic weapons)
- 42 U.S.C. § 2284 (sabotage of nuclear facilities or fuel)
- 49 U.S.C. § 46502 (aircraft piracy)
- 49 U.S.C. § 46504 (second sentence)(assault on a flight crew with a dangerous weapon)
- 49 U.S.C. § 46505(b)(3) or (c) (explosive or incendiary devices, or endangerment of human life by means of weapons, or aircraft)
- 49 U.S.C. § 46506 (if homicide or attempted homicide involved, application of certain criminal laws to acts on aircraft)

- 49 U.S.C. § 60123(b) (destruction of interstate gas or hazardous liquid pipeline facility)

Child Abduction and Sex Offenses

- 18 U.S.C. § 1201 (kidnaping a child)[135]
- 18 U.S.C. § 1591 (sex trafficking by force, fraud or of a child)
- 18 U.S.C. ch.109A
- 18 U.S.C. § 2241 (aggravated sexual abuse)
- 18 U.S.C. § 2242 (sexual abuse)
- 18 U.S.C. § 2243 (sexual abuse of a ward or child)
- 18 U.S.C. § 2244 (abusive sexual contact)
- 18 U.S.C. § 2245 (sexual abuse resulting in death)
- 18 U.S.C. § 2250 (failure to register as a sex offender)
- 18 U.S.C. ch. 110
- 18 U.S.C. § 2251 (sexual exploitation of children)
- 18 U.S.C. § 2251A (selling or buying children)
- 18 U.S.C. § 2252 (transporting, distributing or selling child sexually exploitive material)
- 18 U.S.C. § 2252A (transporting or distributing child pornography)
- 18 U.S.C. § 2252B (misleading names on the Internet)
- 18 U.S.C. § 2260 (making child sexually exploitative material overseas for export to the U.S.)
- 18 U.S.C. ch. 117
- 18 U.S.C. § 2421 (transportation of illicit sexual purposes)
- 18 U.S.C. § 2422 (coercing or enticing travel for illicit sexual purposes)
- 18 U.S.C. § 2423 (travel involving illicit sexual activity with a child)

---

[135] "[A]n indictment may be found or an information instituted at any time without limitation for any offense under section 1201 involving a minor victim, for any felony under chapter 109A, 110 (except section 2257 and 2257A), or 117, or section 1591." 18 U.S.C. § 3299.

- 18 U.S.C. § 2424 (filing false immigration statement)
- 18 U.S.C. § 2425 (interstate transmission of information about a child relating to illicit sexual activity)

20 Years

- 18 U.S.C. 668 (major art theft)[136]

10 Years

- 18 U.S.C. § 81 (arson in the special maritime or territorial jurisdiction of the United States not involving a risk of death or serious injury)*[137]
- 18 U.S.C. § 215 (receipt by financial institution officials of commissions or gifts for procuring loans)**[138] 18 U.S.C. § 656 (theft, embezzlement, or misapplication by bank officer or employee)**
- 18 U.S.C. § 657 (embezzlement by lending, credit and insurance institution officers or employees)**
- 18 U.S.C. § 844(f) (burning or bombing federal property not involving a risk of death or serious injury)* 18 U.S.C. § 844(h) (carrying explosives during the commission of a federal offense or using fire or explosives to commit a federal offense)*
- 18 U.S.C. § 844 (i) (burning or bombing property used in or used in activities affecting commerce not involving a risk of death or serious injury)*
- 18 U.S.C. § 1005 (fraud concerning bank entries, reports and transactions)**
- 18 U.S.C. § 1006 (fraud concerning federal credit institution entries, reports and transactions)**

---

[136] 18 U.S.C. § 3294.
[137] * Pursuant to 18 U.S.C. §§ 3295, 3286(b).
[138] ** Pursuant to 18 U.S.C. § 3293.

- 18 U.S.C. § 1007 (fraud concerning Federal Deposit Insurance Corporation transactions)**
- 18 U.S.C. § 1014 (fraud concerning loan and credit applications generally; renewals and discounts; crop insurance)**
- 18 U.S.C. § 1033 (crimes by or affecting persons engaged in the business of insurance)**
- 18 U.S.C. § 1344 (bank fraud)**
- 18 U.S.C. § 1341 (mail fraud affecting a financial institution)**
- 18 U.S.C. § 1343 (wire fraud affecting a financial institution)**
- 18 U.S.C. § 1423 (misuse of evidence of citizenship or naturalization) (or conspiracy to commit)+[139] 18 U.S.C. § 1424 (personation or misuse of papers in naturalization proceedings) (or conspiracy to commit)+
- 18 U.S.C. § 1425 (procurement of citizenship or naturalization unlawfully) (or conspiracy to commit)+ 18 U.S.C. § 1426 (reproduction of naturalization or citizenship papers) (or conspiracy to commit)+
- 18 U.S.C. § 1427 (sale of naturalization or citizenship papers) (or conspiracy to commit)+ 18 U.S.C. § 1428 (surrender of canceled naturalization certificate) (or conspiracy to commit)+ 18 U.S.C. § 1541 (passport or visa issuance without authority) (or conspiracy to commit)+ 18 U.S.C. § 1542 (false statement in application and use of passport) (or conspiracy to commit)+ 18 U.S.C. § 1543 (forgery or false use of passport) (or conspiracy to commit)+
- 18 U.S.C. § 1544 (misuse of passport) (or conspiracy to commit)+
- 18 U.S.C. § 1581 (peonage; obstruction of justice)++[140]
- 18 U.S.C. § 1583 (enticement into slavery)++
- 18 U.S.C. § 1584 (sale into involuntary servitude)++
- 18 U.S.C. § 1589 (forced labor)++
- 18 U.S.C. § 1590 (slave trafficking)++

---

[139] + Pursuant to 18 U.S.C. § 3291.

[140] ++ Pursuant to 18 U.S.C. § 3298.

- 18 U.S.C. § 1592 (document offenses involving slave trafficking)++
- 18 U.S.C. § 1963 (RICO violation involving bank fraud)** 18 U.S.C. § 2442 (recruiting or using child soldiers)[141]
- 42 U.S.C. § 2274 (communication of restricted data)†[142]
- 42 U.S.C. § 2275 (receipt of restricted data)†
- 42 U.S.C. § 2276 (tampering with restricted data)†
- 50 U.S.C. § 783 (disclosure of classified information (with suspension until the end of any federal employment of the accused))[143]

8 Years Generally

- 18 U.S.C. § 112 (assaults upon diplomats)[144]
- 18 U.S.C. § 351(e) (assaulting a Member of Congress)
- 18 U.S.C. § 1751(e) (assaulting the President or presidential staff) 49 U.S.C. § 46506 (certain criminal laws to acts on aircraft)

Federal Crimes of Terrorism That Do Not Result in or Involve the Risk of Death or Serious Injury

- 18 U.S.C. § 32 (destruction of aircraft or aircraft facilities)[145]
- 18 U.S.C. § 37 (violence at international airports)

---

[141] 18 U.S.C. § 3300.

[142] † Pursuant to 42 U.S.C. § 2278.

[143] 50 U.S.C. § 783(d).

[144] "[N]o person shall be prosecuted, tried, or punished for any noncapital offense involving a violation of any provisions listed in section 2332b(g)(5)(b), or a violation of section 112, 351(e), 1361, or 1761(e) of this title, or section 46504, 46505, 46506 of title 49, unless the indictment is found or the information is instituted without 8 years after the offense was committed." 18 U.S.C. § 3286(a). Offenses listed in Section 2332b(g)(5)(B) that involve a risk of death or serious bodily injury may be prosecuted at any time. 18 U.S.C. § 3286(b).

[145] "[N]o person shall be prosecuted, tried, or punished for any noncapital offense involving a violation of any provisions listed in section 2332b(g)(5)(b), or a violation of section 112, 351(e), 1361, or 1761(e) of this title, or section 46504, 46505, 46506 of title 49, unless the indictment is found or the information is instituted without 8 years after the offense was committed."

- 18 U.S.C. § 81 (arson within special maritime and territorial jurisdiction)
- 18 U.S.C. § 175, 175b (biological weapons offenses)
- 18 U.S.C. § 175c (variola virus)
- 18 U.S.C. § 229 (chemical weapons offenses)
- 18 U.S.C. § 351(a),(b),(c), or (d) (congressional, cabinet, and Supreme Court assassination and kidnaping)
- 18 U.S.C. § 831 (nuclear materials offenses)
- 18 U.S.C. § 832 (participation in a foreign atomic weapons program)
- 18 U.S.C. § 842(m) or (n) (plastic explosives offenses)
- 18 U.S.C. § 844(f)(2) or (3) (arson and bombing of federal property)
- 18 U.S.C. § 844(i) (burning or bombing of property used in, or used in activities affecting, commerce)
- 18 U.S.C. § 956(a)(1) (conspiracy to murder, kidnap, or maim persons abroad)
- 18 U.S.C. § 1203 (hostage taking)
- 18 U.S.C. § 1361 (destruction of federal property)
- 18 U.S.C. § 1362 (destruction of communication lines, stations, or systems)
- 18 U.S.C. § 1363 (injury to buildings or property within special maritime and territorial jurisdiction of the United States)
- 18 U.S.C. § 1366(a) (destruction of energy facilities)
- 18 U.S.C. § 1751(a),(b),(c), or (d) (Presidential and Presidential staff assassination and kidnaping)
- 18 U.S.C. § 1992 (terrorist attacks on trains and mass transit)
- 18 U.S.C. § 2155 (destruction of national defense materials, premises, or utilities),
- 18 U.S.C. § 2156 (production of defective national defense material)
- 18 U.S.C. § 2280 (violence against maritime navigation)

- 18 U.S.C. § 2280a (violence against maritime navigation involving weapons of mass destruction)
- 18 U.S.C. § 2281 (violence against maritime fixed platforms)
- 18 U.S.C. § 2281a (addition offenses involving violence against maritime fixed platforms)
- 18 U.S.C. § 2332 (certain homicides and other violence against United States nationals occurring outside of the United States)
- 18 U.S.C. § 2332a (use of weapons of mass destruction)
- 18 U.S.C. § 2332b (acts of terrorism transcending national boundaries)
- 18 U.S.C. § 2332f (bombing public places)
- 18 U.S.C. § 2332g (anti-aircraft missiles)
- 18 U.S.C. § 2332h (radiological dispersal devices)
- 18 U.S.C. § 2232i (acts of nuclear terrorism)
- 18 U.S.C. § 2339 (harboring terrorists)
- 18 U.S.C. § 2339A (providing material support to terrorists)
- 18 U.S.C. § 2339B (providing material support to terrorist organizations)
- 18 U.S.C. § 2339C (financing terrorism)
- 18 U.S.C. § 2339D (receipt of military training from a foreign terrorist organization)
- 18 U.S.C. § 2340A (torture committed under color of law)
- 21 U.S.C. § 960A (narcoterrorism)
- 42 U.S.C. § 2122 (atomic weapons)
- 42 U.S.C. § 2284 (sabotage of nuclear facilities or fuel)
- 49 U.S.C. § 46502 (aircraft piracy)
- 49 U.S.C. § 46504 (second sentence) (assault on a flight crew with a dangerous weapon)
- 49 U.S.C. § 46505(b)(3) or (c) (explosive or incendiary devices, or endangerment of human life by means of weapons, or aircraft)
- 49 U.S.C. § 46506 (if homicide or attempted homicide involved, application of certain criminal laws to acts on aircraft)

- 49 U.S.C. § 60123(b) (destruction of interstate gas or hazardous liquid pipeline facility)

7 Years

- 18 U.S.C. § 247 (damage to religious property)[146]
- 18 U.S.C. § 249 (hate crime not resulting in death)[147]
- 18 U.S.C. § 1031 (major fraud against the United States)[148]

6 Years

- 15 U.S.C. § 77x (Securities Act violations)¤[149]
- 15 U.S.C. § 77yyy (Trust Indenture Act violations)¤
- 15 U.S.C. § 78ff(a) (Securities Exchange Act violations)¤
- 15 U.S.C. § 80a-48 (Investment Company Act violations¤
- 15 U.S.C. § 80b-17 (Investment Advisers Act violations)¤
- 18 U.S.C. § 1348 (securities and commodities fraud)¤
- 26 U.S.C. § 6531 (tax crimes)[150]

5 Years

- All crimes not otherwise provided for[151]

3 Years

- 31 U.S.C. § 333 (misuse of Treasury Department names, symbols, etc.)[152]

---

[146] 18 U.S.C. § 247(g).
[147] 18 U.S.C. § 249(d)(1).
[148] 18 U.S.C. §1031(f).
[149] 18 U.S.C. § 3301.
[150] 26 U.S.C. § 6531.
[151] 18 U.S.C. § 3282.

1 Year

- 18 U.S.C. § 402 (contempt of court)[153]

Attachment 2. Selected State Felony Statutes of Limitation

State	Felonies (Generally)	Various Exceptions (Not Exhaustive)
ALABAMA	3 years (Ala. Code § 15-3-1)	Any time: (a) capital offense; (b) felony involving: -arson; forgery; drug trafficking; death or serious injury; use, attempted use, or threat to use violence; or counterfeiting; or(c) sex offense w/ victim <16 (Ala. Code § 15-3-5)
ALASKA	5 years (Alaska Stat.§ 12.10.010)	(a) Any time: murder; kidnaping; class A, B, or unclassified felony sexual assault; felony sexual abuse of minor; various sexual offenses w/ a minor victim; (b) 10 years: 1stdegree indecent exposure; manslaughter (Alaska Stat.§ 12.10.010)
ARIZONA	7 years (Ariz. Rev. Stat. Ann. § 13-107)	Any time: attempted commission orcommission of -homicide; class 2 felony sex offense or sexual exploitation of children; violent sexual assault; misuse of public money; felony falsification of public records (Ariz. Rev. Stat. Ann. § 13-107)
ARKANSAS	(a) 6 years: Class Y or A crimes; (b) 3 years: Class B, C, D, or unclassified crimes (Ark. Code Ann. § 5-1-109)	Any time: murder and various sex offenses (Ark. Code Ann. § 5-1-109)

[152] 31 U.S.C. § 333 (d)(2).
[153] 18 U.S.C. § 3285.

State	Felonies (Generally)	Various Exceptions (Not Exhaustive)
CALIFORNIA	3 years (Cal. Penal Code § 801)	(a) Any time: crime punishable by death or life imprisonment; various sex offenses; or embezzlement of public money (b) 6 years: felony punishable by imprisonment for 8 years or more (Cal. Penal Code §§ 799, 800)
COLORADO	3 years (Colo. Rev. Stat. Ann. § 16-5-401)	Any time: committing, attempting, conspiring to commit, or soliciting commit -murder, treason, kidnaping, forgery, or sex offenses against a child (Colo. Rev. Stat. Ann. § 16-5-401)
CONNECTICUT	5 years (Conn. Gen. Stat. Ann. § 54-193)	Any time: capital or class A felony; arson-murder; or 1st degree escape (Conn. Gen. Stat. Ann. § 54-193)
DELAWARE	5 years (Del. Code Ann. tit. 11 § 205)	Any time: commit or attempt to commit murder, class A felony, or various sex offenses (Del. Code Ann.tit. 11 § 205)
FLORIDA	3 years (Fla. Stat. Ann. § 775.15)	(a) Any time: capital or life felony, felony resulting in death, or perjury in a capital case; (b) 10 years: felony from use of destructive device resulting in injury; (c) 4 years: 1st degree felony, (Fla. Stat. Ann. § 775.15)
GEORGIA	4 years (Ga. Code Ann. § 17-3-1)	(a)Any time: murder; (b) 15 years: rape; (c) 7 years: other crimes punishable by death or life imprisonment; or felonies w/ victims <14 (Ga. Code Ann. § 17-3-1)
HAWAII	3 years (Haw. Rev. Stat. § 701-108)	(a) Any time: commit, attempt, conspire to commit, or solicit murder; or sexual assault (b) 10 years: vehicular manslaughter; (c) 6 years: class A felony (Haw. Rev.Stat. § 701-108)

Attachment 2. (Continued)

State	Felonies (Generally)	Various Exceptions (Not Exhaustive)
IDAHO	5 years (Idaho Code § 19-402)	Any time: murder, voluntary manslaughter, rape, sexual abuse of a child, or terrorism (Idaho Code § 19-401)
ILLINOIS	3 years (720 Ill. Comp. Stat. Ann. § 5/3-5)	Any time: homicide, attempted murder, treason, arson, or forgery (720 Ill. Comp. Stat. Ann. § 5/3-5)
INDIANA	5 years (Ind. Code Ann. § 35-41-4-2)	Any time: murder or a 1st or 2nd level felony (Ind. Code Ann. § 35-41-4-2)
IOWA	3 years (Iowa Code Ann. § 802.3)	(a) Any time: murder; (b) 10 years: various sex offenses (Iowa Code Ann. §§ 802.1 to 802.3)
KANSAS	5 years (Kan. Stat. Ann. § 21-5107)	Any time: murder, terrorism, rape, or use of weapons of mass destruction (Kan. Stat. Ann. § 21-5107)
KENTUCKY	Any time (Ky. Rev. Stat. Ann. § 500.050)	
LOUISIANA	4 years (La. Code Crim. P. art. 572)	(a) Any time: crime punishable by death or life imprisonment; or 1stor 2d degree rape; (b) 30 years: various sex crimes against minors; (c) 6 years: felony punishable at hard labor) (La. Code Crim. P. arts. 571, 571.1. 572.)
MAINE	(a) 6 years: Class A, B, or C crime; (b) 3 years: Class C or D crime (Me. Rev. Stat. Ann. tit. 17-A § 8)	Any time: murder, 1stor 2d degree homicide, or various sexual offenses against a minor (Me. Rev. Stat. Ann. tit. 17-A § 8)
MARYLAND	Any time subject to occasional individual statutory exceptions, e.g., computer crimes (3 years) (Md. Cts. &Jud. Proc. § 5-601)	

State	Felonies (Generally)	Various Exceptions (Not Exhaustive)
MASSACHUSETTS	6 years (Mass. Gen. Laws Ann. ch. 277 § 63)	(a) Any time: murder (b) 15 years: commit or conspire to commit rape or assault w/ intent to rape or murder; (c) 10 years: commit or conspire to commit robbery or assault w/ intent to rob (Mass. Gen. Laws Ann. ch. 277 § 63)
MICHIGAN	6 years (Mich. Comp. Laws Ann. § 767.24)	(a) Any time: murder, terrorism, or 1stdegree sexual conduct; (b) 10 years: kidnaping, extortion, conspiracy or assault w/ intent to murder (Mich. Comp. Laws Ann. §767.24)
MINNESOTA	3 years (Minn. Stat. Ann. § 628.26)	Any time: crime resulting in death, kidnaping (Minn. Stat. Ann. § 628.26)
MISSISSIPPI	2 years (Miss. Code Ann. § 99-1-5)	Any time: murder, rape, kidnaping, arson, manslaughter, burglary, aggravated assault, forgery, counterfeiting, robbery, larceny, fraud, embezzlement, or various sexual offenses against minors (Miss. Code Ann. § 99-1-5)
MISSOURI	3 years (Mo. Ann. Stat. § 556.036)	Any time: murder, rape or a class A felony (Mo. Ann. Stat. § 556.036)
MONTANA	5 years (Mont. Code Ann. § 45-1-205)	(a) Any time: homicide (b) 10 years: sexual assault (Mont. Code Ann. § 45-1-205)
NEBRASKA	3 years (Neb. Rev. Stat. § 29-110)	Any time: treason, murder, arson, forgery or various sexual offenses (Neb. Rev. Stat. § 29-110)

Attachment 2. (Continued)

State	Felonies (Generally)	Various Exceptions (Not Exhaustive)
NEVADA	3 years (Nev. Rev. Stat. Ann. § 171.085)	(a) Any time: murder or terrorism; (b) 20 years: sexual assault; (c) 5 years: kidnaping, attempted murder; (d) 4 years: theft, arson, robbery, burglary, sexual assault, or forgery (Nev. Rev. Stat. Ann. §§ 171. 080, 171.083, 171.085)
NEW HAMPSHIRE	6 years (N.H. Rev. Stat. Ann. § 625:8)	Any time: murder (N.H. Rev. Stat. Ann. § 625:8)
NEW JERSEY	5 years (N.J. Stat. Ann. § 2C:1-6)	(a) Any time: murder, manslaughter, sexual assault (b) 10 years: environment offenses; (c) 7 years: bribery or certain other offenses involving misconduct in office (N.J. Stat. Ann. § 2C:1-6)
NEW MEXICO	(a) 6 years: 2d degree felony; (b) 5 years: 3d or 4thdegree felony (N.M. Stat. Ann. § 30-1-8)	Any time: capital or 1stdegree felony(N.M. Stat. Ann. § 30-1-8)
NEW YORK	5 years (N.Y. Crim. P. Law § 30.10)	Any time: class A felony or 1stdegree rape, sexual criminal act, or sexual conduct against a child (N.Y. Crim. P. Law § 30.10)
NORTH CAROLINA	Any time (no statute)	
NORTH DAKOTA	3 years (N.D. Cent. Code §29-04-02)	(a) Any time: murder (N.D. Cent. Code § 29-04-01) (b) 10 years: various sex offenses against a minor (N.D. Cent. Code § 29-04-03.1)
OHIO	6 years (Ohio Rev. Code Ann. § 2901.13)	(a) Any time: murder; (b) 20 years: commit, attempt, or aid and abet kidnaping, robbery, riot, manslaughter, sexual assault, burglary, or arson (Ohio Rev. Code Ann. § 2901.13)

State	Felonies (Generally)	Various Exceptions (Not Exhaustive)
OKLAHOMA	3 years (Okla. Stat. Ann. tit. 22 § 152)	(a) Any time: murder; (b) 12 years: rape, sodomy, or certain other sexual offenses (Okla. Stat. Ann. tit. 22 §§ 151, 152)
OREGON	3 years (Ore. Rev. Stat. § 131.125)	(a) Any time: commit, attempt, conspire to commit, or solicit murder; (b) variable: various sexual offenses against minors; (c) 6 years: arson (Ore. Rev. Stat. § 131.125)
PENNSYLVANIA	2 years (Pa. Stat. Ann. tit. 42 § 5552)	(a) Any time: commit, conspire to commit, or solicit murder; manslaughter; various sex offenses against a minor; or aggravate assault of a police officer; (b) 12years: major sex offenses; (c) 5 years: major offenses (Pa. Stat. Ann. tit. 42 §§ 5551, 5552)
RHODE ISLAND	3 years (R.I. Gen. Laws § 12-12-17)	(a) Any time: treason, homicide, arson, burglary, counterfeiting, forgery, robbery, rape, assault, drug trafficking, any other felony punishable by life imprisonment, or various sex offenses against a minor; (b) 10 years: larceny, bribery, racketeering, perjury, or extortion (R.I. Gen. Laws § 12-12-17)
SOUTH CAROLINA	Any time	
SOUTH DAKOTA	7 years (S.D. Cod. Laws § 23A-42-2)	Any time: Class A, B, or C felonies (S.D. Cod. Laws § 23A-42-1)

Attachment 2. (Continued)

State	Felonies (Generally)	Various Exceptions (Not Exhaustive)
TENNESSEE	(a) 15 years: Class A felony; (b) 8 years: Class B felony; (c) 4 years: Class C or D felony; (d) 2 years: Class E felony (Tenn. Code Ann. § 40-2-101)	Any time: crime punishable by death or life imprisonment (Tenn. Code Ann. § 40-2-101)
TEXAS	3 years (Tex. Code Crim. P. art. 12.01)	(a) Any time: murder, manslaughter, rape, certain human trafficking offenses, or various sexual offenses against minors; (b) 10 years: forgery, embezzlement, arson (Tex. Code Crim. P. art. 12.01)
UTAH	4 years (Utah Code Ann. § 76-1-302)	Any time: capital felony, murder, manslaughter, various sex offenses against a minor, or kidnaping (Utah Code Ann. § 76-1-301)
VERMONT	3 years (Vt. Stat. Ann. tit.13 § 4501)	(a) Any time: rape, murder, arson(causing death), or kidnaping; (b) 11 years: arson; (c) 6 years: certain sexual offenses, grand larceny, robbery, burglary, embezzlement, forgery, bribery, false claims, fraud, human trafficking, or felony tax offenses (Vt. Stat. Ann. tit.13 § 4501)
VIRGINIA	Any time	
WASHINGTON	3 years (Wash. Rev. Code Ann. § 9A.04.080)	(a) Any time: homicide; (b) 10 years: arson, rape, or certain offenses involving misconduct in office; (c) until the victim is 30 years of age: certain sexual offenses against minors (Wash. Rev. Code Ann. § 9A.04.080)
WEST VIRGINIA	Any time	

State	Felonies (Generally)	Various Exceptions (Not Exhaustive)
WISCONSIN	6 years (Wis. Stat. Ann. § 939.74)	(a) Any time: 1stdegree murder, felony murder (b) various times: certain sex offenses committed against a child (Wis. Stat. Ann. § 939.74)
WYOMING	Any time	

Source: CRS from the statutes cited above.

Note: Recently, state legislatures have regularly enlarged or eliminated the statute of limitations for a number of offenses.

Chapter 5

MISSING ADULTS: BACKGROUND, FEDERAL PROGRAMS, AND ISSUES FOR CONGRESS*

Adrienne L. Fernandes-Alcantara
Specialist in Social Policy

SUMMARY

Adults may go missing due to personal choice, an abduction, foul play, a mental or physical disability, or a natural catastrophe, among other reasons. Although no accurate estimates exist of the number of missing adults, the Federal Bureau of Investigation (FBI) reported that as of December 31, 2016, approximately 54,000 cases of missing adults (age 18 and older) were pending in the National Crime Information Center (NCIC) system, a federal computerized index with data on crimes and locator files for missing and unidentified persons. Certain adults are particularly vulnerable to missing episodes; for example, those with dementia are at risk for becoming disoriented while engaged in a routine activity and may not be able to determine where they are or get to where

* This is an edited, reformatted and augmented version of "Missing Adults: Background, Federal Programs, and Issues for Congress" by Adrienne L. Fernandes-Alcantara that was originally published by the Congressional Research Service on November 30, 2017.

they should be. Adults who engage in high-risk behaviors, including involvement in gang activity, may also be more prone to going missing.

Unlike children, adults have the legal right to go missing under most circumstances. As a result, families of missing adults may receive limited assistance from state and local law enforcement entities in recovering their loved ones. The federal government has not been involved in assisting law enforcement entities with missing adult cases in the same way it has with missing children cases. Further, cases of missing children and young adults under the age of 21 must be reported to the NCIC, while reporting missing adults to the database is voluntary. In recent years, however, the federal government has increasingly played a role in (1) preventing certain types of missing adult incidents; (2) working to recover adults who go missing, including those who are deceased and for whom only remains can be found; and (3) supporting databases, including NCIC, that maintain records of missing adults and unidentified remains.

Recognizing the needs of a growing aging population, Congress authorized funding for the Missing Alzheimer's Disease Patient Alert program under the Violent Crime Control and Law Enforcement Act of 1994 (P.L. 103-322). The purpose of the program is to locate and respond to those with Alzheimer's and dementia who go missing. Congress provided appropriations for the program of $750,000 to $2 million annually from FY1996 through FY2015. No funding was appropriated for FY2016 or FY2017. Grants had been awarded under the program to a variety of entities, including the International Association of Chiefs of Police (IACP), Alzheimer's Association, Project Lifesaver, and universities. In 2000, Congress passed Kristen's Act (P.L. 106-468) to authorize the Department of Justice (DOJ) to make grants to establish a national clearinghouse for missing adults and provide technical assistance to law enforcement agencies in locating these individuals. From FY2002 through FY2006, DOJ made grants for these purposes. In addition, the federal DNA Initiative has also supported efforts to recover missing persons and identify unidentified human remains by funding DNA analysis and related assistance.

In addition to the NCIC, the federal government maintains the National DNA Index System (NDIS), which stores criminal information as well as information on individuals believed to be missing, their relatives, and unidentified human remains; and the National Missing and Unidentified Persons System (NamUs), which includes databases for missing adults and unidentified remains. Records are submitted to most of the databases by law enforcement agencies, state missing persons clearinghouses, medical examiners and coroners, or DNA laboratories. The NDIS, NamUs, and NCIC databases can be accessed only by authorized law enforcement and other personnel; however, records in NamUs can also be reviewed by the public.

Policymakers and other stakeholders have increasingly focused on the coordination of the federal databases on missing persons, as well as the role of the federal government in providing assistance to states and localities to develop alert systems and technology to locate missing adults. Many states have developed alert systems to recover vulnerable adults who have gone missing.

INTRODUCTION

Adults may go missing due to personal choice; an abduction or foul play; a physical or developmental disability; natural catastrophes that displace individuals, such as a hurricane; or certain high-risk behaviors, including gang involvement or drug use, among other circumstances.

State and local laws govern how criminal justice entities respond to missing adult cases. This response is complicated by a number of factors. Unlike children, adults have the legal right to go missing in most cases and may do so to seek protection from a domestic abuser and other related reasons.[1] Further, law enforcement agencies may be hesitant to devote resources to missing adult cases, given competing priorities. Law enforcement agencies within and across states also respond differently to missing adult cases. Some states require at least a 24-hour waiting period after the person is believed to be missing before a police report may be filed, while others take reports without a waiting period.[2]

The federal government has played a role in both (1) seeking to prevent certain types of missing adult incidents and (2) recovering adults who go missing, including those who are deceased and for whom only remains provide clues to their identity and circumstances surrounding their disappearance. Congress authorized the Missing Alzheimer's Disease

---

[1] Guardians and the court system may limit the autonomy of some adults through conservatorship or guardianship arrangements.

[2] For information about state responses to missing adults, see U.S. Department of Justice, Office of Justice Programs, National Institute of Justice, National Missing and Unidentified Persons System (NamUs), Missing Person Database, "Resources," https://www.findthemissing.org/en/homes/resources; and International Association of Chiefs of Police, "IACP Alzheimer's Initiative: A State by State Guide to Missing Senior/Adult Public Alert Systems" http://www.theiacp.org/Missing-Alzheimers-Disease-Patient.

Patient Alert program under the Violent Crime Control and Law Enforcement Act of 1994 (P.L. 103-322) to assist in locating missing individuals with Alzheimer's disease and other forms of dementia through a patient identification program, as well as outreach and education efforts. This program was funded through FY2015. In 2000, Congress authorized the Department of Justice (DOJ), through Kristen's Act (P.L. 106-468), to make grants to establish a national clearinghouse for missing adults and provide technical assistance to law enforcement agencies in locating missing adults. This grant was funded from FY2002 through FY2006. The federal government has also supported efforts to establish databases to track and identify missing adults, their relatives, and unidentified human remains.

The first section of this report discusses demographics and record keeping of missing adults and unidentified remains, as well as some of the factors that may contribute to the disappearance of adults. This section also discusses federally funded databases that are used to track data on missing adults and unidentified individuals. The second section of the report describes the federal programs and initiatives to assist in locating missing adults, including funding data where applicable. Finally, the third section discusses issues about the federal role in missing adult cases.

WHY DO ADULTS GO MISSING?

Certain circumstances can make adults vulnerable to going missing. Adults may go missing because of an abduction or foul play. A physical or developmental disability or cognitive disorder, such as Alzheimer's disease and other forms of dementia, may also contribute to a missing episode. Adults with dementia have been identified as high-risk for going missing by advocates for older adults. According to the Alzheimer's Association, a nonprofit organization that provides research on Alzheimer's disease, 5.5 million people in the United States suffer from Alzheimer's disease and related dementia, and about 60% of those will wander away from their homes or health care facilities.[3] Further, a natural catastrophe can displace individuals and make their whereabouts unknown to others. Finally, other adults vulnerable to missing incidents may include those with high-risk lifestyles, such as individuals who abuse drugs or are gang involved, and those that have a history of victimization, including domestic violence.

DATA ON MISSING ADULTS AND UNIDENTIFIED REMAINS

There is no definitive estimate of the number of adults who go missing, because some adults are not known to be missing or are not reported to databases that compile data on missing persons. However, three federally supported data sources provide some insight into this number: the Missing Person File at the FBI's National Crime Information Center (NCIC); the FBI's National DNA Index System (NDIS), which stores information on offenders and arrestees, forensic evidence, as well as individuals believed to be missing, their relatives, and unidentified human remains; and the National Missing and Unidentified Persons System (NamUs), administered by DOJ's National Institute of Justice (NIJ).[4] Profiles of missing individuals entered into one database do not necessarily populate other databases, although some missing individuals may be reported to more than one of the databases. Therefore, numbers of missing persons should not be added across any of the databases.

The NCIC Unidentified Person File, NamUs, and NDIS contain information about unidentified decedents, or remains. However, the true number of unidentified missing adult cases is unknown because remains can go undiscovered, or if they are recovered, they may not be reported to the databases or retained. In a census conducted by DOJ in 2004, medical

[3] Alzheimer's Association, "2017 Alzheimer's Disease Facts and Figures," https://www.alz.org/documents_custom/ 2017-facts-and-figures.pdf/, and "Three out of Five People with Alzheimer's Disease Will Wander," https://www.alz.org/norcal/in_my_community_18411.asp.

[4] Some private organizations that advocate for missing adults and provide assistance to the families of missing adults maintain missing person records that can be accessed by the public. Such organizations include Let's Bring Them Home and the Doe Network.

examiners and coroners reported a total of 13,486 unidentified human remains on record, though about 51% of medical examiner and coroners' offices lacked policies for retaining records such as x-rays, DNA, or fingerprints that could identify missing individuals.[5] (The report also found that 90% of offices serving large jurisdictions did retain such records.) Further, medical examiners and coroners estimated that about 4,400 unidentified human decedents were reported in an average year, with approximately 1,000 (23.0%) remaining unidentified after one year. Another DOJ study estimated, using death records reported to the Centers for Disease Control and Prevention from 1980 through 2004, that as many as 10,300 of these records were for unidentified decedents. This number is an approximation, as states do not uniformly specify on the death certificate when a person's identity is not known.[6] In addition, the criteria used by DOJ to search the death records may have included individuals whose identities were known, as well as unidentified individuals who were later identified.

The discussion in the next section will show that the databases range in the number of profiles they contain, as well as the type of information they collect, such as basic demographic profiles, DNA profiles, etc. (*Note that only the data on missing persons and unidentified decedents, as reported in NCIC, are regularly updated in this report.*)

National Crime Information Center Missing Person and Unidentified Person Files

The NCIC within the FBI's Criminal Justice Information Services (CJIS) Division maintains statistics on missing adults and unidentified

---

[5] Matthew J. Hickman et al., *Medical Examiners and Coroners' Offices, 2004*, U.S. Department of Justice, Office of Justice Programs, Bureau of Justice Statistics, June 2007.

[6] Kristen Hughes, *Unidentified Human Remains in the United States, 1980-2004*, U.S. Department of Justice, Office of Justice Programs, Bureau of Justice Statistics, November 2007.

decedents.[7] The NCIC is a computerized index of documented information concerning crimes and criminals of nationwide interest and a locator file for missing and unidentified persons. Since October 1, 1975, the NCIC has maintained records of missing persons (known as the Missing Person File) who are reported to the FBI by federal, state, and local law enforcement agencies; foreign criminal justice agencies; and authorized courts. The Missing Person File was created in response to a request in 1974 from the NCIC Advisory Policy Board (APB).[8] The APB is composed of local, state, and federal criminal justice and national security agencies, and it advises the FBI on criminal justice information matters. The Missing Person File includes records for individuals who are missing because they

- have a proven physical or mental disability,
- are missing under circumstances indicating that they may be in physical danger,
- are missing under circumstances indicating their disappearance may not have been voluntary,
- are under the age of 21 and do not meet the above criteria,
- are missing after a catastrophe, or
- are 21 and older and do not meet any of the above criteria but for whom there is a reasonable concern for their safety.

These categories are presented in further detail in *Table A-1.* Pursuant to the National Child Search Assistance Act of 1990 (Title XXXVII of the Crime Control Act of 1990, P.L. 101-647), records of missing children under age 18 *must* be immediately entered into the Missing Person File.

---

[7] The FBI is authorized to maintain the NCIC under 28 U.S.C. 434. Unless otherwise noted, this information was provided to the Congressional Research Service by the U.S. Department of Justice, Federal Bureau of Investigation, Criminal Justice Information Services Division on January 25, 2008.

[8] The Missing Children Act of 1982 affirmed the need for the Missing Person File by requiring the FBI to "acquire, collect, classify, and preserve any information which would assist in the location of any missing person (including an unemancipated person as defined by the laws of the places of residence of such person) and provide confirmation as to any entry for such a person to the parent, legal guardian, or next of kin of that person." 28 U.S.C. 534(a). The FBI amended NCIC entry procedures in May 1999 to replace the phrase "unemancipated person" with "a person who is missing under the age of 18."

The act also requires the Attorney General to publish an annual statistical summary of the Missing Person File. Suzanne's Law, enacted by the Prosecutorial Remedies and Other Tools to End the Exploitation of Children Today Act of 2003 (PROTECT Act, P.L. 108-21), requires law enforcement to also immediately submit information about missing adults to the NCIC ages 18 through 20. Law enforcement agencies are not mandated under federal law to submit missing person records of adults over the age of 21 into the Missing Person File. Although records of missing adults are captured, the NCIC does not include the complete number of adults who go missing and are not reported to the database.

NCIC Missing Person Data[9]

As of December 31, 2016, there were 88,040 individual records (entered in 2016 and previous years) remaining in the Missing Person File. Of these, 54,334 (61.7%) were for missing adults ages 18 and older and 33,052 (38.3%) were for children ages 17 and younger.

In calendar year 2016, over 647,000 (647,435) individuals of all ages were reported missing to the NCIC. Of all individuals reported missing in 2016, a total of 181,759 (28.1%) were ages 18 and older. Also in 2016, nearly 585,000 missing person records were cleared or canceled; some of these records were entered prior to 2016. *Table A-1* summarizes the number of missing cases entered in 2012 through 2016 for individuals ages 18 and older under the six missing person categories listed previously. The highest number of missing adults went missing for an unspecified reason, but there was a reasonable concern for their safety.

Of all adults age 18 and older who were reported missing in 2016, most were male (59.1%). The majority of missing adults were white (66.0%), followed by individuals who were black (26.6%), of an unknown

[9] U.S. Department of Justice, Federal Bureau of Investigation, 2016 NIC Missing Person and Unidentified Person Statistics Pursuant to P.L. 101-647, 104 Statute 4967, Crime Control Act of 1990 Requirements. (Hereinafter, U.S. Department of Justice, Federal Bureau of Investigation, 2016 Missing Person and Unidentified Person Statistics.) Some numbers and percentages are based on calculations by CRS.

race (3.0%), Asian (3.1%),[10] and American Indian or Alaskan Native (1.3%). Relative to their share of the population generally, missing white and Asian adults appear to be underrepresented and missing African American adults appear to be overrepresented.[11] The NCIC does not report on the Hispanic origin of missing individuals, and NCIC users are instructed to enter records for Hispanic individuals using the race code (American Indian or Alaskan Native, Asian or Pacific Islander, black, or white) that most closely represents that individual as perceived by the law enforcement official.[12]

NCIC Unidentified Missing Persons Data[13]

Some individuals who go missing may be deceased, and their remains, intact or not, may be the only available clues concerning their identity and circumstances surrounding their disappearance. Since 1983, the NCIC has taken reports of unidentified missing persons, pursuant to the passage of the Missing Children Act of 1982 (P.L. 97-292). The act required the FBI to "acquire, collect, classify, and preserve any information which would assist in the identification of any deceased individual who has not been

[10] This includes individuals who identify as Native Hawaiian or Other Pacific Islander.

[11] For information about demographics of the general population, see Karen R. Humes, Nicholas A. Jones and Roberto R. Ramirez, Overview of Race and Hispanic Origin: 2010, U.S. Census Bureau, 2010 Census Briefs, March 2011.

[12] In October 1997, the Office of Management and Budget published revised standards for the reporting by federal agencies of statistics on race and ethnicity. The standards specify the racial categories of American Indian or Alaska Native, black or African American, Native Hawaiian or Other Pacific Islander, and white; and ethnic categories of Hispanic or Latino and Not Hispanic or Latino. However, the FBI received an exemption from this reporting requirement for the NCIC. According to the FBI, states are not required to comply with the racial and ethnic classifications, due to the uniqueness of crime data and the fact that the data are reported by state and local jurisdictions. This information was provided to the Congressional Research Service by the U.S. Department of Justice, Federal Bureau of Investigation, Criminal Justice Information Services Division on May 6, 2008.

[13] Unless otherwise noted, this information was provided to the Congressional Research Service by the U.S. Department of Justice, Federal Bureau of Investigation, Criminal Justice Information Services Division.

identified after the discovery of such deceased individual."[14] Pursuant to this requirement, the NCIC's Unidentified Remains File was established to take reports of unidentified deceased persons, persons of any age who are living and unable to determine their identity, and unidentified catastrophe victims. Reports may include information about bodies found shortly after death, when a person's remains may be fairly intact, as well as skeletal remains. For those individuals who are living and their identities are unknown, information entered about their appearances could help in reuniting them with relatives.

The total number of unidentified persons in the NCIC may represent just a fraction of the true number of missing remains. As of December 31, 2016, the Unidentified Remains File included 8,431 unidentified persons. During 2015, nearly 900 unidentified person records were entered into NCIC. Of those, about 80% were for deceased unidentified bodies; less than 1% was for unidentified victims of catastrophes; and approximately 19% were for living persons who could not be identified because they could not identify themselves (e.g., an individual with amnesia, infant).[15]

National DNA Index System[16]

Another database operated by the FBI stores DNA records, including for missing adults and unidentified remains, and was authorized under the DNA Identification Act of 1994 as part the Violent Crime Control and Law Enforcement Act of 1994 (P.L. 103-322). This database is known as NDIS. P.L. 103-322 specified that the FBI could establish an index of DNA identification records of persons convicted of crimes, analyses of DNA samples recovered from crime scenes, and analyses from unidentified

---

[14] 28 U.S.C. 534(a).

[15] U.S. Department of Justice, Federal Bureau of Investigation, *2016 Missing Person and Unidentified Person Statistics.*

[16] Unless otherwise noted, this information was provided to the Congressional Research Service by the U.S. Department of Justice, Federal Bureau of Investigation, Office of Congressional Affairs on June 18, 2008, and July 16, 2008.

human remains. A fourth category of records for relatives of missing persons was added in 1999 by the Consolidated Appropriations Act of 2000 (P.L. 106- 113). DNA laboratories may enter DNA information into NDIS that involves one of the four categories of records, as well as the records of missing adults.[17] The data are first entered by authorized users into the Local DNA Index System (LDIS), which can then populate the central laboratory for each state, known as a State DNA Index System (SDIS). Only SDIS laboratories may upload DNA profiles directly to the NDIS. LDIS or SDIS laboratories can conduct searches of their own databases prior to uploading the data to NDIS. Searches of data entered by other states into NDIS are conducted by the FBI Laboratory, which automatically searches new DNA data when profiles are submitted by the states.

NDIS contains approximately 15 million profiles in the five databases: offenders and arrestees database, forensic evidence database, missing unidentified human remains database, missing person database, and biological relatives of missing persons database.[18] Most of the DNA profiles are those stored in the criminal and forensic evidence databases. The three missing person databases are part of the FBI Laboratory's National Missing Person DNA Database (NMPDD) program, which works to identify missing and unidentified persons based on available DNA profiles and other clues.[19] The unidentified human remains database contains DNA profiles from the remains of individuals that cannot be identified by

---

[17] According to the FBI, the authority to include DNA from missing persons is derived from P.L. 103-322, because in order to identify unidentified remains, a search of missing person records must be conducted that compares those records to the records for unidentified remains. This information was provided to the Congressional Research Service by the Department of Justice, Federal Bureau of Investigation, Office of Congressional Affairs on August 8, 2008.

[18] This is as of September 2017. See, U.S. Department of Justice, Federal Bureau of Investigation, "CODIS-NDIS Statistics," http://www.fbi.gov/about-us/lab/codis/ndis-statistics. The convicted offender database and forensic database, can be searched against one another to assist law enforcement personnel in solving crimes.

[19] In addition to conducting DNA analysis, the FBI Laboratory also assists state and local law enforcement agencies with investigations of missing persons involving examinations of anthropology, trace evidence, facial reconstruction, and fingerprinting, among other types of assistance. These services are provided at no cost.

fingerprint; dental, medical, or anthropological examinations; and of individuals who are living, but are unidentifiable using typical investigative methods (e.g., children and others who cannot or refuse to identify themselves). The relatives of missing persons database contains DNA profiles that are voluntarily submitted by the relatives of known missing individuals. Finally, the missing person database contains DNA records of missing persons obtained from their belongings or derived from the profiles of their relatives.

The three missing person databases can be searched against one another. The Combined DNA Index System (CODIS) is the software in NDIS that compares various DNA profiles, and if a match is made between two sets of DNA profiles, the software sends an electronic message to the laboratories that contributed the samples. DNA analysts at the laboratories review the data to confirm the match. The laboratories are responsible for alerting the investigating law enforcement agency, medical examiner, coroner, or medical-legal authority of the results. The FBI is continuing to develop technology, including software to conduct kinship DNA analyses, and is using metadata (e.g., sex, date of last sighting, and age) that is intended to assist in locating missing persons.[20]

The National Missing and Unidentified Persons System (NamUs)[21]

The National Missing and Unidentified Persons System (NamUs) is an online repository for information about missing persons and unidentified remains that is overseen by DOJ's National Institute of Justice (NIJ). According to DOJ, NamUs was established in response to an overwhelming need for a central reporting system for unidentified human remains cases. In 2005, DOJ's National Institute of Justice convened stakeholders—medical examiners, coroners, law enforcement personnel, managers of state missing children clearinghouses, family members of

---

[20] U.S. Department of Justice, Federal Bureau of Investigation, "CODIS: Combined DNA Index System," http://www.fbi.gov/services/labratory/biometric-analysis/codis.

[21] Unless otherwise noted, this information is provided by U.S. Department of Justice, "About Missing Persons Database," NamUs, http://www.namus.gov/index.htm.

missing persons, forensic scientists, and policymakers—for a national strategy meeting called the "Identifying the Missing Summit." The summit focused on the challenges in investigating and solving missing person cases. After the summit, work began on the development of the online repository.[22] To further work on the feasibility of a database, DOJ appointed an expert panel of medical examiners and coroners, which ultimately confirmed the need for a central reporting system for unidentified human remains. These efforts also led DOJ to establish and fund NamUs. NamUs is composed of three databases: missing persons, unidentified remains, and unclaimed remains.[23] The system has been accessible via the web since 2009, and is operated through an NIJ grant to the University of North Texas (UNT) Health Center. NamUs users, including members of the public, can search across databases in an effort to identify unidentified human remains and solve missing person cases. Funding has been provided at $2.4 million in FY2016 (P.L. 114-113) and FY2017 (P.L. 115-31) for the "operationalization, maintenance, and expansion" of the system. NIJ has provided funding in previous years through appropriations for "DNA and other forensics."[24]

The missing person database serves as a repository for information on missing persons that can be entered by law enforcement agencies or members of the public. Profiles of missing individuals may include photographs and information about the circumstances around their

---

[22] According to the U.S. Department of Justice, there is no specific statutory authority for NamUs; however, the agency derives its authority to establish the database from statutes on the general authorities of the National Institute of Justice (NIJ, 42 U.S.C. 3721-3723), which manages the database, to support research and develop tools and technologies, as well as statutes concerning the general authorities of NIJ's Office of Science and Technology (6 U.S.C. 161-165). This information was provided to the Congressional Research Service by the U.S. Department of Justice, Office of Justice Programs on June 16, 2008.

[23] The database that became the Unidentified Remains database was initially developed in 2005 and 2006 as a public service project by the National Association of Medical Examiners (NAME). NIJ has since hosted NamUs focus group meetings to define additional requirements for the system. NIJ has partnerships with the National Center for Forensic Science and NAME for the unidentified remains database and with the National Forensic Science Technology Center for development of the missing persons database.

[24] Based on correspondence with U.S. Department of Justice, Office of Justice Programs, Office of Communications, May 2016.

disappearance, their dental records, DNA, physical appearance, and police contact information, among other items. Users of the website may search the database based on these attributes. The database also includes information about state statutes on recovering missing persons as well as links to state missing person clearinghouses, which are maintained by state law enforcement agencies or advocacy organizations and provide information about missing adults.

The unidentified remains database is available for medical examiners and coroners to upload their cases. Website users may view profiles of the unidentified remains; however, only law enforcement agencies and other authorized entities may enter information and review additional information and photographs that are not available to the public. Some of the profiles cover remains that are fully intact, whereas others include pieces of the missing person's body or information about the remains and where they were found. Website users can also search based on characteristics such as demographics, anthropologic analysis, the NCIC record number, dental information, and distinct body features.

The unclaimed remains database is available for medical examiners and coroners to upload profiles of deceased individuals who have been identified by name, but for whom no family members have been identified or located to claim the body. NamUs automatically performs comparisons of the various databases to determine matches or similarities between profiles of missing persons, unidentified persons, or unclaimed remains.

Comparison and Interaction of Databases

Records of missing persons or unidentified remains are submitted to most of the databases by authorized law enforcement agencies, state missing persons clearinghouses, medical examiners and coroners, or DNA laboratories. All of the databases can be accessed only by the federal government or authorized law enforcement and other personnel; however, records in NamUs and the NCMA database can also be reviewed by the public, though sometimes only on a limited basis for NamUs. *Table A-2* summarizes some of the features of the databases as well as others that store records of missing persons and unidentified remains.

FEDERAL ROLE IN RECOVERING MISSING ADULTS

In recent years, the federal government has played a role both in preventing certain types of missing adult incidents and in working to recover adults who go missing, including those who are deceased and for whom only remains provide clues to the circumstances surrounding their disappearance. In addition to funding or operating databases that track information about missing adults and unidentified remains, the federal government has undertaken other related efforts, including some that are no longer funded. These efforts are (1) the DNA Initiative, created under President George W. Bush, which focused on identifying the remains of unidentified deceased individuals; (2) National Missing Persons Task Force, with its emphasis on achieving greater cooperation among the various federal databases; (3) the Missing Alzheimer's Disease Patient Alert program to prevent missing episodes and locate missing individuals with Alzheimer's disease and related dementia; (4) activities funded under Kristen's Act to locate missing adults; and (5) the National Center for Missing and Exploited Children (NCMEC), which works to recover missing children and adults ages 18 to 21 who are reported to the agency as missing by law enforcement officials. The Missing Alzheimer's Disease Patient Alert program and activities funded under Kristen's Act have specifically received congressional appropriations for missing adult activities. The other activities have been funded under appropriations for initiatives or programs that encompass activities other than just those for missing adults.

DNA-Related Activities

In March 2003, President George W. Bush announced a new DNA Initiative to promote the use of forensic DNA technology to solve crimes, protect individuals from wrongful prosecution, and identify missing persons. Funding was provided under the initiative from FY2004 through FY2008.[25] Within the past several years, Congress has appropriated funding to DOJ to carry out the following activities to assist with locating missing adults and unidentified remains:[26]

- sample analysis of unidentified human remains and family reference samples;[27]
- standardized sample DNA collection kits for unidentified remains of missing persons;
- evaluation and implementation of advanced DNA technologies to facilitate the analysis of skeletal remains;
- focus group on using DNA technology to assist the identification of human remains;
- training and technical assistance on using DNA to identify missing persons and unidentified remains;

---

[25] For additional information about the DNA Initiative, see archived CRS Report RL33489, *An Overview and Funding History of Select Department of Justice (DOJ) Grant Programs*, by Nathan James (available upon request to CRS).

[26] The Justice for All Act of 2004 (P.L. 108-405) authorized funding for DNA technology to meet some of the activities set forth in the DNA Initiative. Sec. 308 of the act provides that the Attorney General may use DNA technology to identify missing persons and unidentified human remains. Sec. 308 further requires that each state or unit of local government that receives funding under the section is required to submit the DNA profiles of missing persons and unidentified human remains to the NDIS national missing persons database. According to the Department of Justice, no specific appropriation has been made pursuant to this section of the act. For further information about funding since FY2004, see U.S. Department of Justice, Office of Justice Programs, National Institute of Justice, "Funding to Identify Missing Persons," http://nij.gov/topics/forensics/investigations/missing-persons/Pages/funding-program.aspx.

[27] Laboratories that participate in NDIS conduct these sample analyses, and the DNA results are forwarded to the relevant missing person indexes in NDIS.

- census of medical examiners and coroners and inventory of unidentified remains; and
- NamUs databases.

National Missing Person's Taskforce[28]

As part of the DNA Initiative, in 2005, NIJ and FBI were directed by DOJ leadership to establish a national task force to assess how to better encourage, facilitate, and achieve greater use of federal missing person databases to solve missing persons cases and identify human remains. In response to this directive, NIJ and the FBI convened the National Missing Persons Taskforce, composed of a broad cross-section of criminal justice officials, forensic science experts, and victim advocates. The task force met July 2005 through January 2006 to address, among other issues, the federal databases that store information on missing persons and unidentified human remains. According to DOJ, members of the task force convened these meetings to better understand and improve the information sharing tools and DNA technologies available to solve cases involving missing persons and unidentified decedents. The task force also created model state legislation to encourage states to adopt laws that improve the ability of law enforcement to locate and return missing persons, identify human remains, and provide timely information to family members of missing persons.

Missing Alzheimer's Disease Patient Alert Program[29]

The Violent Crime Control and Law Enforcement Act of 1994 (P.L. 103-322) authorized the Missing Alzheimer's Disease Patient Alert

---

[28] This information was provided to the Congressional Research Service by the U.S. Department of Justice, Office of Justice Programs on June 16, 2008.

[29] This section was co-authored with Kirsten J. Colello, CRS Specialist in Gerontology.

program to provide grants to locally based organizations to protect and locate missing individuals with Alzheimer's disease and related dementia. Such individuals may be unable to think clearly; to recognize persons and landmarks; or to react rationally under normal circumstances. Those with Alzheimer's disease and dementia tend to hide or seclude themselves when they are in unfamiliar and disorienting situations. About 60% of missing persons with Alzheimer's disease and dementia who were found were located within the first 6 hours of going missing and about 30% within 6 to 12 hours.[30]

Funding was authorized for the program at $900,000 for each of FY1996, FY1997, and FY1998. Congress appropriated funding for the program from FY1996 through FY2015. Annual funding ranged from $750,000 to $2.0 million. Funding was not appropriated in FY2016 and FY2017.

The program is administered by DOJ's Bureau of Justice Assistance (BJA) within the Office of Justice Programs. Funding under the program has been awarded to a variety of entities, including the International Association of Chiefs of Police (IACP), Alzheimer's Association, MedicAlert Foundation Project Lifesaver, and universities. For example, IACP has used these funds to develop its Alzheimer's Initiative program. The program seeks to increase awareness among law enforcement agencies and the public in addressing the needs of missing persons with Alzheimer's disease. Their website provides a clearinghouse of information and resources for those who may come across missing persons, including a guide to state alert systems for missing seniors and adults. In addition, IACP provides training for public safety administrators, law enforcement officers, and others from the first responder community with training on Alzheimer's and dementia.[31]

BJA awarded funds through the Missing Alzheimer's Disease Patient Alert program to the Alzheimer's Association from FY1996 through 2015.

---

[30] International Association of Chiefs of Police, "Missing Persons with Alzheimer's Disease," Training Key #648, 2010.

[31] International Association of Chiefs of Police, "IACP Alzheimer's Initiative," http://www.theiacp.org/MissingAlzheimers-Disease-Patient.

These funds were used to establish and carry out the MedicAlert® + Alzheimer's Association Safe Return Program. The program is a nationwide emergency response service for individuals with Alzheimer's or a related dementia who wander or have a medical emergency. Enrollees receive a bracelet indicating that the individual is memory impaired and including a toll-free, 24-hour emergency response number to call if the person is found wandering or has a medical emergency.[32]

Kristen's Act

In 2000, Congress passed Kristen's Act (P.L. 106-468), named after Kristen Modafferi, who has been missing since 1997. Kristen was 18 when she disappeared and her family was unable to access services through the National Center for Missing and Exploited Children (NCMEC) because, at the time, the organization only provided assistance to missing incident cases for children under age 18. NCMEC now provides services for missing young adults ages 18 to 21, pursuant to Suzanne's Law, which requires law enforcement to also immediately submit information about missing adults ages 18 through 20 to the NCIC. Kristen's Act authorized $1 million in funding for each of FY2001 to FY2004 and permitted the Attorney General to make grants to assist law enforcement agencies in locating missing adults; maintain a database for tracking adults believed by law enforcement to be endangered due to age, diminished mental capacity, and possible foul play; maintain statistical information on missing adults; provide resources and referrals to the families of missing adults; and establish and maintain a national clearinghouse for missing adults.

---

[32] Wandering may pose a significant, if not life threatening, danger to the personal health, safety, and welfare of those with dementia. This may occur from exposure to the elements; lack of food; dehydration or lack of medication for extended periods of time; and general inability to think, act, or communicate in a way that could assist them. Nevertheless, it is not uncommon for persons with dementia to wander from their homes, sometimes repeatedly. The Alzheimer's Association reports that six out of 10 people with Alzheimer's disease will wander at least once during the course of the disease. Alzheimer's Association, "Wandering and Getting Lost," http://www.alz.org/care/alzheimersdementia-wandering.asp#who.

Kristen's Act grants were made from FY2002 through FY2006 through the Edward Byrne Discretionary Grant Program to the National Center for Missing Adults (NCMA), though funding authorization expired at the end of FY2004. Funding levels ranged from $150,000 to $1.7 million. NCMA began in 1995 as the missing adult division of the Nation's Missing Children Organization. NCMA received funding under Kristen's Act to expand its efforts to recover missing adults beginning in FY2002 and received this funding through FY2006. The organization merged with Let's Bring Them Home, a nonprofit organization that provides education and resources on missing persons.

National Center for Missing and Exploited Children

The National Center for Missing and Exploited Children is a primary component of the federally funded Missing and Exploited Children's Program.[33] Although NCMEC's mission is to recover missing children under age 18, it also provides services for missing young adults ages 18 through 20, pursuant to Suzanne's Law, which requires law enforcement to also immediately submit information about missing adults to the NCIC ages 18 through 20. This law changed the upper age limit of individuals who must be entered into the NCIC.

NCMEC processes young adult cases differently than cases for missing children.[34] NCMEC will accept a young adult case only if it is reported by a law enforcement entity—and not by parents, spouses, partners, or others—because the organization relies on law enforcement personnel to verify that the young adult is missing due to foul play or other reasons that would cause concern about the individual's whereabouts, such as diminished mental capacity. NCMEC then assists in recovery efforts for

---

[33] NCMEC receives federal funding through the Missing and Exploited Children's Program and other sources. For a full discussion of NCMEC activities, see CRS Report RL34050, *Missing and Exploited Children: Background and Policies*, by Adrienne L. Fernandes-Alcantara.

[34] This information was provided to the Congressional Research Service by the National Center for Missing and Exploited Children.

these adults as it would for children under age 18. A case manager in the Missing Children's Division is assigned to serve as the single point of contact for the searching family and to provide technical assistance to locate abductors and recover missing children and young adults.

ISSUES

Federal and state policymakers and other stakeholders have increasingly focused on three issues related to adults who go missing: (1) coordinating databases on missing persons; and (2) assisting states with building the capacity to develop both alert systems to inform the public about missing older adults and technology to recover these individuals.

Coordination of Federally Funded Databases on Missing Persons and Unidentified Decedents

The first section of this report discussed the various federally funded databases that store information on missing persons and unidentified decedents. These databases do not currently populate one another, although some of the databases indicate whether information about a particular individual is available in another database. This limitation raises the question about whether the federal government can and should develop technology to enable the databases to coordinate, although concerns about privacy and funding would likely need to be addressed.

Alert Systems

Silver or Senior Alerts[35]

Alert systems, known as Silver or Senior Alerts, have been established in multiple states.[36] These alert systems were created out of concern for the

[35] This section was co-authored with Kirsten J. Colello, Specialist in Gerontology.

safety of seniors and other at-risk adult populations who are prone to wandering due to a physical or cognitive disability or medical condition such as Alzheimer's or other forms of dementia. Some missing adult alert programs are modeled after the states' AMBER Alert system for abducted children.[37]

Issuing alerts to law enforcement agencies and the public for missing vulnerable adults in some the states appears to be at the discretion of the law enforcement agency—local or state or both— and is not required of the agency.[38] In addition, state alert systems vary in terms of the target population for issuing an alert (i.e., older adults with dementia versus any adult with a disability). Most law enforcement agencies have the ability to disseminate the alert to law enforcement agencies and media in the local area, region, statewide, and other states. For example, the Texas Division of Emergency Management disseminates information within the alert advisory area to local, state, and federal law enforcement agencies; primary media outlets; the Texas Department of Transportation; the Texas Lottery Commission; and the Independent Bankers Association of Texas.

Some stakeholders have raised concerns that alert systems may not be useful for some adults who go missing. For example, the media repeatedly

---

[36] For further information, see CRS Report R40552, *Alert Systems for Missing Adults in Eleven States: Background and Issues for Congress*, by Adrienne L. Fernandes-Alcantara and Kirsten J. Colello. The report was written in 2009, when 11 states were identified as having these systems. A journal article reported that 37 states had silver alert systems as of July 2012. See, Tobias D. Wasser and Patrick K. Fox, "For Whom the Bell Tolls: Silver Alerts Raise Concerns Regarding Individual Rights and Governmental Interests," The Journal of the American Academy of Psychiatry and the Law, vol. 41, no. 3 (September 2013) (Hereinafter, Wasser and Fox, "For Whom the Bell Tolls: Silver Alerts Raise Concerns Regarding Individual Rights and Governmental Interests".) The International Association of Chiefs of Police includes a map of states that denotes which states have silver alerts, alert programs for seniors, or other alert programs; or where an alert program is pending. The map notes that Idaho, Nebraska, North Dakota, and Vermont do not have any of these alert systems in place. See International Association of Chiefs of Police, "Alzheimer's Initiatives," http://www.theiacp.org/Missing-Alzheimers-Disease-Patient.

[37] AMBER Alert systems are voluntary partnerships among law enforcement agencies, broadcasters, and transportation agencies to activate messages in a targeted area when a child is abducted and believed to be in grave danger. For additional information, see CRS Report RL34050, *Missing and Exploited Children: Background and Policies*, by Adrienne L. Fernandes-Alcantara.

[38] This information is primarily based on the Congressional Research Service's review of authorizing legislation

reporting missing adult cases could desensitize the public to the issue of wandering. In addition, missing persons may not be found in a place that is well-trafficked. Among missing persons with Alzheimer's Disease, about three-quarters leave on foot; and of those found alive, about half are found 1 to 5 miles from where they originated.[39] For these reasons, policymakers may wish to consider Silver Alerts in combination with a combination of other policy approaches.[40]

Further, some stakeholders have raised concerns that broadcasting information about missing adults can infringe on their rights to privacy. Unlike incidents involving the AMBER Alert program, which was established to alert law enforcement and the public when a child is missing and criminal activity may be involved, it is not a crime for an adult to wander from home or purposely go missing. The stakeholders assert that states should have criteria for activating an alert that limits disclosure of information to the public only when it is absolutely necessary to preserve the missing person's life. They also assert that disclosure of this information should be reserved to the most limited geographic area possible. Further, concerns have been raised that having only selected criteria for the alert may be short-sighted. For example, some have argued that making age the primary factor for issuing an alert overlooks the possibility that age alone does not necessarily signal whether a person is endangered. Another consideration is the extent to which information about a missing person's health background can be broadcast to the public. The Health Insurance Portability and Accountability Act (HIPAA) Health Privacy Rule—the federal rule that regulates the use or disclosure of

---

[39] International Association of Chiefs of Police, "Missing Persons with Alzheimer's Disease," Training Key #648, 2010.

[40] For example, one such approach might be providing support to the caregivers of individuals with dementia, to better ensure that adults with the disease do not go missing. For information about current federal funding to assist caregivers, see CRS Report RL34123, *Family Caregiving to the Older Population: Background, Federal Programs, and Issues for Congress*, by Kirsten J. Colello.

protected health information—limits disclosure of health information by health care providers.[41]

In 2011, DOJ published a guide to assist states and communities in developing or enhancing what DOJ calls an Endangered Missing Advisory (EMA), or an advisory for individuals who do not meet the AMBER Alert criteria established by DOJ.[42] The guide suggests that EMAs can be issued for missing adults, or for children while law enforcement determines whether a case meets the AMBER Alert criteria. The guide outlines the steps states and communities can take in developing an EMA plan, including creating a task force—comprised of key AMBER Alert stakeholders, broadcasters and other representatives from the media, and law enforcement, among others—that can establish criteria and procedures for the EMA and oversee its operation and effectiveness. The guide suggests that adults may benefit from a different type of alert system than AMBER Alert, and that task forces should determine which elements of the AMBER Alert plan should be used to activate an EMA.[43]

Still, some states with alert systems could have difficulty coordinating with another state that lacks a similar system. States could also have challenges coordinating with states that have alert systems with different criteria for activating an alert. Although state and local governments have taken the lead in implementing alert systems, the federal government could play a role in coordinating efforts when a missing individual is believed to have crossed state lines as well as assist in the development of formal agreements or protocols for the use of interstate alerts. The federal government could model any policies to coordinate across state lines on the AMBER Alert program, which provides training and technical assistance to states on a number of issues related to abducted children. This

---

[41] Wasser and Fox, "For Whom the Bell Tolls: Silver Alerts Raise Concerns Regarding Individual Rights and Governmental Interests."

[42] For further information about the AMBER Alert program, see CRS Report RL34050, *Missing and Exploited Children: Background and Policies*, by Adrienne L. Fernandes-Alcantara.

[43] U.S. Department of Justice, Office of Justice Programs, Office of Juvenile Justice and Delinquency Prevention, *Guide for Implementing or Enhancing an Endangered Missing Advisory,* March 2011.

training addresses how jurisdictions, including those in different states, can work together to recover children who are abducted, among other topics. Through conference and training exercises, state AMBER Alert coordinators, state and local law enforcement agencies, and other stakeholders have opportunities to meet and exchange ideas, which may further facilitate coordination.

Tracking Technology

Electronic monitoring services for individuals who are susceptible to going missing are being implemented. One such electronic monitoring program is used by some state and local law enforcement agencies with technology developed by Project Lifesaver International, a nonprofit organization that administers the Project Lifesaver program and has received funding under the Missing Alzheimer's Disease Patient Alert program.[44] Project Lifesaver uses a personalized wristband that emits a signal to track individuals prone to going missing. The wristband is worn by the clients continuously, and each month, a law enforcement officer or trained volunteer visits with the clients to replace the wristband batteries and provide referrals to clients and their caregivers in need of social services. When family members or caregivers report to the designated Project Lifesaver agency—typically a local law enforcement or first responder agency—that the client is missing, a search and rescue team responds to the wanderer's area to search using a mobile locator tracking system.

Project Lifesaver grew out of local law enforcement experience with search and rescue efforts for missing persons with Alzheimer's and other forms of dementia. The target population of the program has expanded to include children with special needs such as autism and Down's syndrome and to anyone else that may be at risk of wandering for a medical reason.

---

[44] This information was provided to the Congressional Research Service by Project Lifesaver International. See also, "Project Lifesaver International," http://www.projectlifesaver.org/.

In addition to providing the technology, the program trains the designated agency to communicate with persons with Alzheimer's disease and other disorders. Project Lifesaver International reports that the tracking technology is used by hundreds of law enforcement agencies in nearly all states and the District of Columbia. According to Project Lifesaver International, the benefits from the program include saving law enforcement and search and rescue response time and resources in locating missing persons due to wandering.

The Alzheimer's Association also has a program, known as Comfort Zone that uses tracking technology. The program is a web application that includes a location-based mapping service. The enrolled individual carries a tracking device with global positioning system (GPS) technology. Caretakers can track the individual's whereabouts via a secure online website through the Alzheimer's Association. The website includes a map with addresses of the vicinity in which the person is located. Caretakers can also receive alerts and notifications of the individual's whereabouts, such as when the individual leaves a specified radius (e.g., beyond their house or some other location).[45]

Tracking technology raises questions about the rights to privacy and autonomy of individuals who are enrolled. These organizations appear to have taken steps to ensure that enrolled participants meet the eligibility criteria and to secure the consent of the enrolled individual, where possible. For individuals who participate in Project Lifesaver, consent usually comes from a caregiver having legal responsibility for the individual. In rare cases, the individual gives consent. Individuals enrolled in Comfort Zone give consent to be enrolled, and in some cases the caregiver with legal responsibility gives consent. According to the Alzheimer's Association, the program is ideally for individuals with early stages of dementia.

---

[45] Alzheimer's Association, Comfort Zone, "About Comfort Zone," http://www.alz.org/comfortzone/about_comfort_zone.asp.

APPENDIX.

Table A-1. National Crime Information Center (NCIC): Missing Entries of Adults Ages 18 and Older, 2012-2016

Category (as defined under the NCIC Operating Manual)	Number of Missing Adults and Share of Total Missing Adult Cases (2012)	Number of Missing Adults and Share of Total Missing Adult Cases (2013)	Number of Missing Adults and Share of Total Missing Adult Cases (2014)	Number of Missing Adults and Share of Total Missing Adult Cases (2015)	Number of Missing Adults and Share of Total Missing Adult Cases (2016)
Disability: a person of any age who is missing and under proven mental/physical disability or senile, thereby subjecting himself/herself or others to personal and immediate danger.a	26,699 (16.3%)	26,342 (15.9%)	27,243 (16.2%)	28,059 (16.1%)	28,342 (15.6%)
Endangered: a person of any age who is missing under circumstances indicating that his/her physical safety may be in danger.	37,745 (23.0%)	36,440 (22.0%)	34,259 (20.4%)	35,446 (20.3%)	36,608 (20.1%)

Table A-1. (Continued)

Category (as defined under the NCIC Operating Manual)	Number of Missing Adults and Share of Total Missing Adult Cases (2012)	Number of Missing Adults and Share of Total Missing Adult Cases (2013)	Number of Missing Adults and Share of Total Missing Adult Cases (2014)	Number of Missing Adults and Share of Total Missing Adult Cases (2015)	Number of Missing Adults and Share of Total Missing Adult Cases (2016)
Involuntary: a person of any age who is missing under circumstances indicating that the disappearance may not have been voluntary, i.e., abduction or kidnapping.	13,774 (8.4%)	13,958 (8.4%)	12,825 (7.6%)	13,550 (0.7%)	12,329 (6.8%)
Catastrophe: a person of any age who is missing after a catastrophe.[a]	215 (0.1%)	184 (0.1%)	178 (0.0%)	169 (0.0%)	188 (0.1%)
Juvenile: a person between ages 18 and 21 who is missing and does not meet any of the enter criteria set forth under the Disability, Endangered, Involuntary, or Catastrophe categories.	4,747 (2.9%)	4.589 (2.8%)	4,504 (2.7%)	4,213 (2.4%)	4,391 (2.4%)

Category (as defined under the NCIC Operating Manual)	Number of Missing Adults and Share of Total Missing Adult Cases (2012)	Number of Missing Adults and Share of Total Missing Adult Cases (2013)	Number of Missing Adults and Share of Total Missing Adult Cases (2014)	Number of Missing Adults and Share of Total Missing Adult Cases (2015)	Number of Missing Adults and Share of Total Missing Adult Cases (2016)
Other: a person age 21 and older who	81,086	83,831	89,197	92,772	99,901
does not meet any of the criteria in the other categories, but for whom there is a reasonable concern for his or her safety; or a person who is under age 21 who is declared emancipated by the laws of his or her state of residence.	(49.4%)	(50.7%)	(53.0%)	(53.3%)	(55.0%)
Total	164,266	165,344	168,206	174,209	181,759

Source: U.S. Department of Justice, Federal Bureau of Investigation, 2012, 2013, 2014, 2015, and 2016 Missing Person and Unidentified Person Statistics Pursuant to P.L. 101-647, 104 Statute 4967, Crime Control Act of 1990 Requirements.

Note: Percentages may not sum to 100 due to rounding.

[a] According to the FBI, "proven physical or mental disability" refers to an individual who could have suicidal tendencies or a drug addiction, is a hemophiliac or diabetic, or has previously escaped custody, among other possible characteristics. A "catastrophe" refers to a disaster, such as an airplane crash, terrorist attack, natural disaster, among other possible scenarios. This information was provided to the Congressional Research Service by the U.S. Department of Justice, Federal Bureau of Investigation, Criminal Justice Information Services Division on December 26, 2007.

Table A-2. Databases of Missing Adults and Unidentified Remains

Database—Administering Agency or Organization	Features	Access to Database
National Crime Information Center (NCIC) Missing Person File and Unidentified Persons File—Department of Justice (DOJ)/Federal Bureau of Investigation (FBI)	The database includes descriptive information about the missing individual or their remains. Individuals are classified under one of six missing person categories or one of three unidentified missing person categories. The databases indicate whether DNA and fingerprinting information are available.	Data are reported by, and available to, authorized federal, state, and local criminal justice and non-criminal justice agencies.
National DNA Index System (NDIS)—DOJ/FBI	The system includes three databases for the DNA of missing persons, unidentified remains, and relatives of missing persons.	Data are reported by state and local DNA laboratories, in cooperation with state and local law enforcement officials. All profiles can be accessed by the FBI; some profiles can be accessed by the state and local DNA laboratories.
National Missing and Unidentified Persons System (NamUs)—DOJ/National Institute of Justice (NIJ)	The system includes three databases—Missing Persons, Unidentified Persons, and Unclaimed Persons—for descriptive information, pictures, and dental records, DNA, and fingerprints where available.	Data are reported by, and available to, authorized federal, state, and local criminal justice and non-criminal justice agencies. Profiles can be accessed by these entities and the public, although the public may not have access to information and photographs for some profiles.

Database—Administering Agency or Organization	Features	Access to Database
Next Generation Identification (NGI), DOJ/FBI (replaced [as of 2014] the Integrated Automated Fingerprint Identification System [IAFIS])	The system includes fingerprints and corresponding criminal histories.	Data are reported by authorized international, federal, state, and local criminal justice and non-criminal justice agencies.
Violent Criminal Apprehension Program (ViCAP)—DOJ/FBI	The system includes information on crimes, including missing person cases where the circumstances indicate a strong possibility of foul play and the victim is still missing. The database entries are continuously compared on the basis of certain aspects of the crime.	Data are reported by authorized federal, state, and local criminal justice and non-criminal justice agencies.

Source: Congressional Research Service.

Chapter 6

MANDATORY MINIMUM SENTENCING OF FEDERAL DRUG OFFENSES*

Charles Doyle
Senior Specialist in American Public Law

SUMMARY

As a general rule, federal judges must impose a minimum term of imprisonment upon defendants convicted of various controlled substance (drug) offenses and drug-related offenses. The severity of those sentences depends primarily upon the nature and amount of the drugs involved, the defendant's prior criminal record, any resulting injuries or death, and in the case of the related firearms offenses, the manner in which the firearm was used.

The drug offenses reside principally in the Controlled Substances Act or the Controlled Substances Import and Export Act. The drug-related firearms offenses involve the possession and use of firearms in connection with serious drug offenses and instances in which prior drug

* This is an edited, reformatted and augmented version of "Mandatory Minimum Sentencing of Federal Drug Offenses" by Charles Doyle that was originally published by the Congressional Research Service on January 11, 2018.

convictions trigger mandatory sentences for unlawful firearms possession.

The minimum sentences range from imprisonment for a year to imprisonment for life. Although the sentences are usually referred to as mandatory minimum sentences, a defendant may avoid them under several circumstances. Prosecutors may elect not to prosecute. The President may choose to pardon the defendant or commute his sentence. The defendant may qualify for sentencing for providing authorities with substantial assistance or under the so-called "safety valve" provision available to low-level, nonviolent, first-time offenders.

Over time, defendants, sentenced to mandatory terms of imprisonment for drug-related offenses, have challenged Congress's legislative authority to authorize them and the government's constitutional authority to enforcement. The challenges have met with scant success. Generally, courts have concluded that the provisions fall within congressional authority under the Commerce, Necessary and Proper, Treaty, and Territorial Clauses of the Constitution. By and large, courts have also found no impediment to imposition of mandatory minimum sentences under the Due Process, Equal Protection, or Cruel and Unusual Punishment Clauses, or the separation-of-powers doctrine.

Proposals to amend drug-related mandatory minimum sentence provisions surfaced during the 114th Congress. In the 115th Congress, Senator Grassley introduced the successor to those proposals for himself and a bi-partisan list of co-sponsors as S. 1917, the Sentencing Reform and Corrections Act of 2017. Many of the same issues are addressed in H.R. 4261 introduced by Representative Scott of Virginia. This is an overview of the law from which those proposals spring.

This report is available in an abridged version, CRS Report R45075, *Mandatory Minimum Sentencing of Federal Drug Offenses in Short*, without the citations to authority and origin of quotations found here.

INTRODUCTION

This is a brief discussion of the law associated with the mandatory minimum sentencing provisions of federal controlled substance (drug) laws and drug-related federal firearms and recidivist statutes.[1] These mandatory

[1] The inventory includes: 21 U.S.C. §§ 841(a), 841(b) (manufacturing, distributing, dispensing, or possessing with the intent to do so various controlled substances); *id.* §§ 841(h), 841(b) (dispensing controlled substances by way of the Internet); *id.* §§ 844(a), 841(b) (simple possession of controlled substances by repeat offenders); *id.* §§ 846, 841(b) (attempt or conspiracy to commit an offense punishable by a mandatory minimum sentence); *id.* § 848

minimums, however, are not as mandatory as they might appear. The government may elect not to prosecute the underlying offenses. Federal courts may disregard otherwise applicable mandatory sentencing requirements at the behest of the government.[2] The federal courts may also bypass some of them for the benefit of certain low-level, nonviolent offenders with virtually spotless criminal records under the so-called "safety valve" provision.[3] Finally, in cases where the mandatory minimums would usually apply, the President may pardon offenders or commute their sentences before the minimum term of imprisonment has been served.[4] Be

(continuing criminal enterprise (drug kingpin)); *id.* §§ 849, 841(b) (distribution of controlled substances as truck stops); 21 U.S.C. §§ 859, 841(b) (distribution of controlled substances to an individual under 21 years of age); *id.* §§ 860, 841(b) (distribution of controlled substances at in or near schools, playgrounds, public housing projects, etc.); *id.* §§ 861, 841(b) (use of children in drug operations); 21 U.S.C. §§ 861(f), 841(b) (distribution of controlled substances to pregnant individuals); *id.* §§ 952, 960 (importing controlled substances into the U.S.); *id.* §§ 953, 960 (exporting controlled substances from the U.S.); *id.* §§ 955, 960 (possession of controlled substances aboard a ship arriving in or departing from the U.S.); *id.* §§ 959, 960 (possession abroad of controlled substances or listed substances for importation into the U.S. by vessel or plane); *id.* §§ 960a, 841(b) (narco-terrorism); *id.* §§ 963, 960 (attempt or conspiracy to commit an exporting or importing offense punishable by a mandatory minimum); 18 U.S.C. § 3261; 21 U.S.C. § 841(b) (military extraterritorial jurisdiction); 46 U.S.C. §§ 70503, 70506; 21 U.S.C. § 960 (maritime drug law enforcement act offenses). Here and throughout, the host of later amendments to the Controlled Substances Act and the Controlled Substances Import and Export Act counsel citation to the sections of those Acts as they appear in title 21 of the United States Code unless otherwise noted. 18 U.S.C. § 3559(c) (mandatory life imprisonment for defendants convicted of a serious violent felony who have a one or more prior serious drug convictions and one or more prior serious violent felony convictions); *id.* § 924(c) (mandatory minimum sentence for carrying a firearm in furtherance of a drug trafficking offense); *id.* § 924(e) (mandatory minimum sentence for conviction of unlawful possession of a firearm by a defendant with three or more prior violent felony or serious drug offense convictions). Here and throughout the terms "drug" and "controlled substance" are used interchangeably.

Various parts of the report are drawn from the author's earlier reports, principally CRS Report RL32040, *Federal Mandatory Minimum Sentencing Statutes*; CRS Report RL30281, *Federal Mandatory Minimum Sentencing Statutes: A List of Citations with Captions, Introductory Comments, and Bibliography*; CRS Report R42386, *Mandatory Minimum Sentencing for Federal Sex Offenses: An Overview*; CRS Report R41326, *Federal Mandatory Minimum Sentences: The Safety Valve and Substantial Assistance Exceptions*; CRS Report R41412, *Federal Mandatory Minimum Sentencing: The 18 U.S.C. 924(c) Tack-On in Cases Involving Drugs or Violence*; CRS Report R41461, *Three Strike Mandatory Sentencing (18 U.S.C. 3559(c)): An Overview.*

[2] 18 U.S.C. § 3553(e).

[3] *Id.* § 3553(f).

[4] U.S. CONST. art. II, § 2, cl. 1. E.g., President Obama Commutes Sentences of 95 Federal Drug Offenders, *The Washington Post*, Dec. 18, 2015, https://www.washingtonpost.com/

that as it may, sentencing in drug cases, particularly mandatory minimum drug sentencing, has contributed to an explosion in the federal prison population and attendant costs. This, the federal inmate population at the end of 1976 was 23,566, and at the end of 1986 it was 36,042.[5] On January 4, 2018, the federal inmate population was 183,493.[6] As of September 30, 2016, 49.1% of federal inmates were drug offenders and 72.3% of those were convicted of an offense carrying a mandatory minimum.[7] In 1976, federal prisons cost $183.914 million; in 1986, $550.014 million; and in 2016, $6.751 billion (est.).[8]

BACKGROUND

Federal mandatory minimum sentencing statutes have existed since the dawn of the Republic. When the first Congress assembled, it enacted several mandatory minimums, each of them a capital offense.[9] The drug mandatory minimums are of more recent origins. The first arrived in 1914, when Congress established a mandatory minimum of five years for the manufacture of opium for smoking purposes.[10] Shortly after mid-century, Congress began adding to the number of drug-related mandatory minimums. Prior to enactment of the Controlled Substances Act and the

---

world/national-security/president-obama-commutes-sentences-of-about-100-drug-offenders/2015/12/18/9b62c91c-a5a3-11e5-9c4e-be37f66848bb_story.html?utm_term =.19c2833a2a8c.

[5] U.S. Department of Justice, Bureau of Justice Statistics, *Sourcebook of Criminal Justice Statistics* – 1987, Table 6.52 (1987).

[6] Federal Bureau of Prisons, Statistics, https://www.bop.gov/about/statistics/population_ statistics.jsp.

[7] U.S. Sentencing Commission, Mandatory Minimum Penalties for Drug Offenses in the Federal Criminal Justice System, 4 (Oct. 2017), https://www.ussc.gov/sites/default/files/pdf/ research-and-publications/researchpublications/ 2017/20171025_Drug-Mand-Min.pdf.

[8] Budget Of The U.S. Government: Appendix for Fiscal Years 1978, 1988, and 2017, respectively.

[9] The Act of April 30, 1790 declared that "persons ... adjudged guilty of treason against the United States ... shall suffer death," 1 Stat. 112; the same sentence awaited those who committed murder within the exclusive jurisdiction of the United States, id. at 113, or engaged in piracy, id. at 113-14, or counterfeiting, id . at 115.

[10] Act of January 17, 1914, 38 Stat. 278 (1914).

Controlled Substances Import and Export Act in 1970,[11] federal law included mandatory minimums for violations of the narcotics or marijuana tax regimes;[12] smuggling narcotics or marijuana;[13] distributing heroin to a child;[14] possession of narcotics aboard a U.S. vessel;[15] and violations of federal drug laws using communications facilities.[16] The 1970s legislation eliminated them all.[17] Left in their place were only the mandatory minimums in the continuing criminal enterprise (drug kingpin) section.[18]

Then, in 1984, Congress enacted the Sentencing Reform Act that created the United States Sentencing Commission and authorized it to promulgate then binding sentencing guidelines.[19] In many instances, the resulting Guidelines operated essentially, but briefly, to establish a mandatory minimum term of imprisonment where none had existed before.[20] Soon thereafter, Congress began to repopulate federal drug laws

---

[11] The 1970 Comprehensive Drug Abuse Prevention and Control Act encompassed both the Controlled Substances Act and the Controlled Substances Import and Export Act, P.L. 91-513, 94 Stat. 1236 (1970).

[12] 26 U.S.C. § 7237 (1964 ed.) (imprisonment for not less than 2 years for the first offense, not less than 5 years for the second, and not less than 10 years for the third).

[13] 21 U.S.C. §§ 174, 176a (1964 ed.) (Imprisonment for not less than 5 years for the first offense and not less than 10 years for the second).

[14] *Id.* § 176b (1964 ed.) (Imprisonment for not less than 10 years for distributing heroin to a child).

[15] *Id.* § 184a (1964 ed.) (Imprisonment for not less than 5 years for the first offense and not less than 10 years for the second).

[16] 18 U.S.C. § 1403 (1964 ed.) (Imprisonment for not less than 2 years).

[17] Pub. L. No. 91-513, § 1101, 84 Stat. 1236, 1291-92 (1970).

[18] *Id.* § 408, 84 Stat. at 1265 (imprisonment for not less than 10 years for the first offense and not less than 20 years for the second).

[19] P.L. 98-473, title II, §§ 211, 217, 98 Stat. 1987, 2017 (1984). Although the Sentencing Guidelines still heavily influence the sentences imposed by federal courts, *see* Gall v. United States, 552 U.S. 38 (2007), the Guidelines are no longer binding, United States v. Booker, 543 U.S. 220 (2005).

[20] P.L. 98-473, title II, §§ 211, 217, 98 Stat. 1987, 2017 (1984). Although the Sentencing Guidelines still heavily influence the sentences imposed by federal courts, *see* Gall v. United States, 552 U.S. 38 (2007), the Guidelines are no longer binding, United States v. Booker, 543 U.S. 220 (2005). Aggravating or mitigating circumstance exists that was not adequately taken into consideration by the Sentencing Commission..."). *See, e.g.*, United States v. Johnson, 908 F.2d 396, 399 (8th Cir. 1990) (sentencing under 18 U.S.C. § 1014, false statements on a loan application, no statutory mandatory minimum) ("Limiting appellate review of a district court's refusal to depart from the guidelines, 18 U.S.C. 3742(e) (1988) provides that a reviewing court must uphold a sentence unless it was : (1) imposed in violation of the law; (2) imposed because the court incorrectly applied the guidelines; (3) outside the range of the applicable guideline and was unreasonable; or (4) imposed for an offense with no applicable guideline and is plainly unreasonable. This circuit has

with mandatory minimums, the bulk of which Congress inserted using the Anti-Drug Abuse Act of 1986.[21] The 1986 legislation, however, included substantial assistance provisions which allow the courts to disregard the mandatory minimums in the case of cooperative defendants.[22] In addition, shortly thereafter, Congress instructed the Sentencing Commission to provide it with a detailed report on federal mandatory minimum statutes.[23]

The Commission's 1991 report[24] observed that from 1984 to 1990 four drug-related statutes accounted for roughly 94 percent of the mandatory minimum offenses regularly prosecuted.[25] The Commission's initial report was quickly followed by a Department of Justice study that concluded that a substantial number of those sentenced under federal mandatory minimums were nonviolent, first-time, low-level drug offenders.[26] Congress responded with the safety valve provisions of 18 U.S.C. § 3553(f), under which the court may disregard various drug mandatory minimums and sentence an offender within the applicable sentencing guideline range as long as the offender was a low-level, nonviolent

---

determined that departures pursuant to section 3553(b) were intended by the Commission to be allowed only in rare cases."); United States v. Carey, 895 F.2d 318, 321, 326 (7th Cir. 1990) (sentencing under 18 U.S.C. § 1344, scheme to defraud a bank, no statutory mandatory minimum) ("At sentencing, the district court acknowledged that the pretrial service agency's calculation of the appropriate sentencing range at 12 to 18 months was accurate. The court, however, departed downward from the applicable range .... We share in the district court's apparent concern over any harshness the Guidelines create in the case at bar.... Nevertheless, the Guidelines seek to end the disparity in sentencing, *see* 28 U.S.C. § 991(b)(2)(B), and in doing so, mandate that departures be the exception and occur only when truly justified.").

[21] P.L. 99-570, 100 Stat. 3207 (1986). The Act established mandatory minimums in 21 U.S.C. §§ 841 (possession with intent to distribute controlled substances); 844 (simple possession); 845 (distribution of a person under 21 years of age); 845a (distribution near a school); 845b (use of child in a drug operation); 960 (controlled substance import or export offenses) (1988 ed.); and added drug offenses to the Armed Career Criminal Act (ACCA)'s predicate offense list, 18 U.S.C. § 924(e) (1988 ed.).

[22] P.L. 99-570, 100 Stat. 3207 (1986), 18 U.S.C. § 3553(e) (1988 ed.).

[23] P.L. 101-647, § 1703, 104 Stat. 4845 (1990).

[24] United States Sentencing Commission, *Mandatory Minimum Penalties in the Federal Criminal Justice System: Special Report to the Congress* (Aug. 1991) (*Commission Report I*).

[25] *Id.* at 10 ("[F]our statutes account for approximately 94 percent of the cases ... 21 U.S.C. § 841 (manufacture and distribution of controlled substances), 21 U.S.C. § 844 (possession of controlled substances), 21 U.S.C. § 960 (penalties for the importation/exportation of controlled substances), and 18 U.S.C. § 924(c) (minimum sentence enhancements for carrying a firearm during a drug or violent crime) ...").

[26] *United States Department of Justice: An Analysis of Non-Violent Drug Offenders with Minimal Criminal Histories*, *reprinted in*, 54 CRIM. L. REP. 2101 (1994).

participant with no prior criminal record who has cooperated fully with the government.[27]

The hate crime legislation enacted in 2009 directed the U.S. Sentencing Commission to submit a second report on federal mandatory minimums.[28] The Commission presented its second report in October 2011.[29] A number of things had changed between the first and second Commission reports. Sentencing under the Guidelines had been in place for only a relatively short period of time when the first report was written. By the time of the second report, the number of defendants sentenced by federal courts had grown to almost three times the number sentenced under the Guidelines when the Commission wrote its first report.[30] The judicial landscape has changed as well. When the Commission issued its first report, the Guidelines were considered binding upon sentencing judges.[31] After the Supreme Court's *Booker* decision and its progeny, the Guidelines became but the first step in the sentencing process.[32] In addition, the Fair

---

[27] P.L. 103-322, § 80001(a), 108 Stat. 1985 (1994).

[28] The Matthew Shepard and James Byrd, Jr. Hate Crime Prevention Act, P.L. 111-84, § 4713, 123 Stat. 2843 (2009).

[29] United States Sentencing Commission, *Mandatory Minimum Penalties in the Federal Criminal Justice System: Report to the Congress* (Oct. 2011) (*Commission Report II*).

[30] *Id.* at 66 ("The total number of federal cases has almost tripled from 29,011 in fiscal year 1990 to 83,947 in fiscal year 2010"); *see also Commission Report I, supra* note 20 at 51 (noting that 29,011 defendants were sentenced under the Guidelines in fiscal year 1990). Moreover, although the second report noted that many of the mandatory minimum offenses were rarely prosecuted, it identified 195 mandatory minimum statutes. *Commission Report II, supra* note 26 at 348. The first report had identified 60. *Commission Report I, supra* note 20 at 11.

[31] 18 U.S.C. § 3553(b)(1) (" ... [T]the court shall impose a sentence of the kind, and within the range, [dictated by the Sentencing Guidelines,] unless the court finds that there exists an aggravating or mitigating circumstance of a kind, or to a degree, not adequately taken into consideration by the Sentencing Commission in formulating the guidelines that should result in a sentence different from that described.").

[32] In United States v. Booker, 543 U.S. 220 (2005), the Court held that Sixth Amendment right to jury trial precluded mandatory application of the Guidelines, but permitted their discretionary application. Thereafter, it explained that "a district court should begin all sentencing proceedings by correctly calculating the applicable Guidelines range.... [T]he district judge should then consider all of the § 3553(a) factors to determine whether they support the sentence requested by a party." United States v. Gall, 552 U.S. 38, 49-50 (2007). Thereafter, "the appellate court must review the sentence under the abuse of discretion standard. It must first ensure that the district court committed no significant procedural error, such as failing to calculate (improperly calculating) the Guidelines range.... " *id.* at 51.

Sentencing Act, passed in 2010, reduced the powder cocaine-crack cocaine ratio from 100 to 10 to roughly 18 to 1.[33]

The second Commission report recommended that Congress consider expanding eligibility for the safety valve, and adjusting the scope, severity, and the prior offenses that trigger the recidivist provisions under firearm statute[34] and the two principal drug statutes, (21 U.S.C. § § 841 and 960).[35]

In October 2017, the Commission issued a third report devoted exclusively to mandatory minimum penalties for drug offenses, in which it made no recommendations.[36] Instead, the report provided an extensive statistical analysis, summarized in ten findings:

1. Drug mandatory minimum penalties continued to result in long sentences in the federal system.
2. Mandatory minimum penalties continued to have a significant impact on the size and composition of the federal prison population.
3. Offenses carrying a drug mandatory minimum penalty were used less often, as the number and percentages of offenders convicted of an offense carrying a mandatory minimum penalty has decreased since fiscal year 2010.
4. While fewer offenders were convicted of an offense carrying a mandatory minimum penalty in recent years, the offenses of those who were tended to be more serious.
5. Drug mandatory minimum penalties applied more broadly than Congress may have anticipated.

---

[33] P.L. 111-220, § 2(a), 124 Stat. 2372 (2010). Prior to enactment, 5000 grams of powder cocaine or 50 grams of crack cocaine triggered the Controlled Substances Act's 10-year mandatory minimum, 21 U.S.C. §§ 841(b)(1)(A)(ii) and (iii) (2006 ed.), and 500 grams of powder or 5 grams of crack triggered its 5-year mandatory minimum. *Id.* §§ 841(b)(1)(B)(ii) and (iii) (2006 ed.). The FSA established a 5000 grams to 280 gram ratio for the 10-year mandatory minimum, 21 U.S.C. §§ 841(b)(1)(A)(ii) and (iii), and a 500 grams to 28 gram ratio for the 5-year mandatory minimum. *Id.* §§ 841(b)(1)(B)(ii) and (iii).

[34] 18 U.S.C. § 924.

[35] *Commission Report II*, *supra* note 26 at 355, 356, 364.

[36] United States Sentencing Commission, *Mandatory Minimum Penalties for Drug offenses in the Federal Criminal Justice System* (Oct. 2017).

6. Statutory relief plays a significant role in the application and impact of drug mandatory minimum penalties, and results in significant reduced sentences when applied.
7. Additionally, drug mandatory minimum penalties appear to provide criminal defendants with a significant incentive to provide substantial assistance to the government pursuant to 18 U.S.C. § 3553(e) and the related guideline provisions of USSG §5K1.1.
8. However, neither the statutory safety valve provision at 18 U.S.C. § 3553(f), nor the substantial assistance provision of 18 U.S.C. § 3553(e) fully ameliorate the impact of drug mandatory minimum penalties on relatively low-level offenders.
9. There were significant demographic shifts in the data relating to mandatory minimum penalties.
10. Although likely due in part to an older age at release, drug trafficking offenders convicted of an offense carrying a drug mandatory minimum penalty had a lower recidivism rate than those drug trafficking offenders not convicted of such an offense.[37]

Although each house devoted considerable attention to mandatory minimum sentencing and associated issues, the 114th Congress ended without consensus.[38] Several proposals introduced in the 115th Congress address some of the same issues.[39]

MANDATORY MINIMUMS FOR DRUG CRIMES

Table 1 below describes the mandatory minimum sentencing provisions for various drug and drug-related offenses.[40]

---

[37] *Id.* at 4-8.

[38] *See generally* CRS Legal Sidebar, WSGL 1713, *Sentencing Reform at the End of the 114th Congress*, by Charles Doyle.

[39] *E.g.*, S. 1917 ("Sentencing Reform and Corrections Act of 2017"); S. 1933 ("Smart Sentencing Act of 2017"); H.R. 3800 ("Mandatory Minimum Reform Act of 2017"); H.R. 4261 ("Safe, Accountable, Fair, Effective Justice Act"").

[40] For a chart listing the penalties for all federal controlled substance offenses see, CRS Report RL30722, *Drug Offenses: Maximum Fines and Terms of Imprisonment for Violation of the Federal Controlled Substances Act and Related Laws*, by Brian T. Yeh.

Table 1. Federal Drug Offenses: Mandatory Minimum Terms of Imprisonment

Substance	Minimum	Maximum
Trafficking21 U.S.C. §841(b)(1)(A)/960(b)(1) substances(e.g.,1 kilo or more of heroin)	10 years	Life
If death or serious injury results	20 years	
With prior drug felony conviction	20 years	
With prior drug felony conviction if death or serious injury results, or with two or more drug felony convictions	Life	
Trafficking 841(b)(1)(B)/960(b)(2) substances(*e.g.*, 100 grams or more of heroin)	5 years	40 years
If death or serious injury results	20 years	Life
Repeat offender	10 years	
Repeat offender if death or serious injury results	Life	
Trafficking lesser amounts of 841(b)(1)/960(b) substances; other Schedule I or II substances; analogues; or date rape drugs: if death or serious injury results	20 years	
Repeat offender if death or serious injury results	Life	
Simple possession of a controlled substance with 1 prior conviction	15 days	2 years
Simple possession of a controlled substance with 2 or more priors	90 days	3 years
Drug kingpin	20 years	Life
Repeat offender	30 years	
Large operation (e.g., gross $10 million + per year)	Life	
Killing in furtherance	20 years	Life/death
Unless a higher minimum applies, distribution of a controlled substance to a pregnant woman, or using a child	1 year	2x usual penalty
Repeat offender	3 years	3x for repeat offenders
Unless a higher minimum applies, distribution of a controlled substance proximate to a school or other prohibited location	1 year	2x usual penalty
Repeat offender	3 years	3x usual penalty
Narco-terrorism involving 841(b)(1) substances	2x usual minimum	Life
Firearm possession in furtherance of drug trafficking(varying by use, firearm, recidivism)	7 years–life	
Unlawful firearm possession with 3 or more prior serious drug or violent felony convictions	15 years	
Serious violent felony with 2 or more prior serious drug and/or violent felony convictions	Life	

Source: CRS analysis of statutes cited below.

Note: The same minimum and maximum penalties generally apply to attempt, conspiracy, or aiding and abetting the offenses described above.

Features of Mandatory Minimum Drug Offenses

Domestic Manufacture or Distribution (21 U.S.C. § 841(a))

Section 841(a) outlaws knowingly or intentionally manufacturing, distributing, dispensing, or possessing with the intent to distribute or dispense controlled substances except as otherwise authorized by the Controlled Substances Act.

Knowingly or Intentionally

The government may establish the knowledge element of Section 841(a) in either of two ways. First, the "knowledge requirement may be met by showing that the defendant knew he possessed a substance listed on the [controlled substance] schedules."[41] Second, "[t]he knowledge requirement may also be met by showing that the defendant knew the identity of the substance he possessed. Take, for example, a defendant who knows that he is distributing heroin but does not know that heroin is listed on the schedules."[42] As long as the government proves the defendant knows he was dealing in heroin, it need not prove that the defendant knew the particular type or quantity of the controlled substance he intended to distribute.[43]

When a defendant claims no guilty knowledge, the circumstances may warrant a willful blindness instruction to the jury. The willful blindness instruction, sometimes called the deliberate ignorance or "ostrich head in the sand" instruction, is warranted if "(1) the defendant claims lack of knowledge; (2) the evidence would support an inference that the defendant

---

[41] McFadden v. United States, 135 S. Ct. 2298, 2304 (2015). *See also* United States v. Ways, 832 F.3d 887, 895 (8th Cir. 2016).

[42] *McFadden*, 135 S. Ct. at 2304; *Ways*, 832 F.3d at 895.

[43] United States v. Sanders, 668 F.3d 1298, 1310 (11th Cir. 2012) ("Although [for the mandatory minimums to apply] the jury must determine the quantity and type of drug involved, nothing in the statute, the Constitution, or *Apprendi* [*v. New Jersey*] requires the government to prove that the defendant had knowledge of the particular drug type or quantity for which a sentence is enhanced under § 841(b)"); *see also* United States v. Qattoum, 826 F.3d 1062, 1065 (8th Cir. 2016); United States v. Stanford, 823 F.3d 814, 834 (5th Cir. 2016); McPhearson v. United States, 675 F.3d 553, 561 (6th Cir. 2012); United States v. Branham , 515 F.3d 1268, 1275-76 (D.C. Cir. 2008); *cf.*, United States v. Gil-Cruz, 808 F.3d 274, 278-79 (5th Cir. 2015) (holding the same with respect to parallel provisions under the Controlled Substances Import and Export Act (21 U.S.C. § 960)).

consciously engaged in a course of deliberate ignorance; and (3) the proposed instruction, as a whole, could not lead the jury to conclude that an inference of knowledge is mandatory."[44]

Manufacture, Distribute, Dispense, or Possess

Manufacture

For purposes of Section 841(a), "'manufacture' means the production ... or processing of a drug, and the term 'production' includes the manufacture, planting, cultivation, growing, or harvesting of a controlled substance." [45]

Distribute or Dispense

The Controlled Substances Act defines the term "distribute" broadly. The term encompasses any transfer of a controlled substance other than dispensing it.[46] It reaches both sales and transfers without compensation.[47] To "dispense" is "to deliver a controlled substance to an ultimate user ...by,

---

[44] United States v. Ford, 821 F.3d 63, 74 (1st Cir. 2016). *See also* United States v. Trejo, 831 F.3d 1090, 1095 (8th Cir. 2016) ("A willful blindness or deliberate indifference instruction is appropriate when there is evidence to support the inference that the defendant was aware of a high probability of the existence of the fact in question and purposely contrived to avoid learning all of the facts."); United States v. Haire, 806 F.3d 991, 998 (8th Cir. 2015) ("We reject Haire's contention that the willful blindness instruction lowered the government's burden of proof, because the district court instructed the jury that it could not find he acted knowingly if he was merely negligent, careless, or mistaken as to the fact that his suitcase contained rug proceeds."); United States v. Salinas, 763 F.3d 869, 880 (7th Cir. 2014) ("Deliberate avoidance is more than mere negligence; the defendant must have deliberately avoided acquiring knowledge of the crime being committed by cutting off his curiosity through an effort of the will. Evidence merely supporting a finding of negligence – that a reasonable person would have been strongly suspicious, or that a defendant should have been aware of criminal knowledge – does not support an inference that a particular defendant was deliberately ignorant.").

[45] United States v. Reveles-Espinoza, 522 F.3d 1044, 1047 (9th Cir. 2008) (citing 21 U.S.C. § 802(15), (22)). *See also* United States v. Bernitt, 392 F.3d 873, 879 (7th Cir. 2004).

[46] United States v. Soto, 794 F.3d 635, 659 (6th Cir. 2015) ("Title 21 U.S.C. § 802(11) defines 'distribute' as 'to deliver (other than by administering or dispensing) a controlled substance.' Subsection eight defines 'deliver' as 'the actual, constructive, or attempted transfer of a controlled substance.'").

[47] United States v. Bobadilla-Pagan, 747 F.3d 26, 32 (1st Cir. 2014) ("Nothing in the statute limits distribution to sale; rather it is well accepted that drugs may be distributed by giving them away for free.").

or pursuant to the lawful order of, a practitioner..."[48] The Controlled Substances Act outlaws practitioner's proscribing controlled substances for other than legitimate medical purposes.[49]

Possession with Intent to Distribute or Dispense

The government may satisfy the possession element with evidence of either actual or constructive possession.[50] "Actual possession is the knowing, direct, and physical control over a thing."[51] "Constructive possession exists when a person knowingly has the power and intention at a given time to exercise dominion and control over an object either directly or through others."[52]

The escalating mandatory minimums that apply to offenders with "a prior conviction for a felony drug offense" extend to those offenses classified as misdemeanors under state law, but punishable by imprisonment for more than a year[53] They also apply even if the underlying state conviction has been expunged.[54] On the other hand, there is

---

[48] 21 U.S.C. § 802(10).

[49] United States v. Moore, 423 U.S. 122, 124 (1975) ("We ...hold that registered physicians can be prosecuted under § 841when their activities fall outside the usual course of professional practice."). *See also* United States v. Azmat, 805 F.3d 1018, 1034 (11th Cir. 2015).

[50] United States v. Ibarra-Diaz, 805 F.3d 908, 932 (10th Cir. 2015); United States v. Corrales-Portillo, 778 F.3d 823, 832 (8th Cir. 2015).

[51] *Id.*

[52] United States v. Apicelli, 839 F.3d 75, 79 (1st Cir. 2016). *See also* United States v. Simpson, 845 F.3d 1059-60 (10th Cir. 2017); United States v. Rebolledo-Delgadillo, 820 F.3d 870, 875 (7th Cir. 2016) ("Construction possession is a legal fiction hereby an individual is deemed to possess contraband items even when he does not actually have immediate, physical control of the objects...Constructive possession requires proof that the defendant had the power and intent to exercise ownership, dominion, authority, or control over the contraband."); United States v. Facen, 812 F.3d 280, 287 (2d Cir. 2016) (internal citations omitted) ("Mere presence at the location of contraband does not establish possession. However, presence under a particular set of circumstances whim from a reasonable jury could conclude that the defendant constructively possessed contraband located there can support a conviction. Courts have considered a number of actors in determining whether a person has the power and intention to exercise dominion and control over narcotics, including: the presence of documents pertaining to the defendant in the same location as the narcotics; the defendant's possession of a key to the location where the drugs are found; the defendant's reaction to the presence of police; whether the defendant has compete control over the narcotics; and whether the drugs are in plain view, suggesting that the defendant is a trusted member of the narcotics operation.").

[53] Burgess, v. United States, 553 U.S. 124, 126 (2008).

[54] United States v. Dyke, 718 F.3d 1282, 1292 (10th Cir. 2013).

apparently at least a division among the circuits over whether the government's failure to comply with the procedure for establishing a prior conviction,[55] and therefore to alert the defendant to the prospect of an enhanced mandatory minimum, precludes a sentencing court from taking prior conviction into account.[56]

Sentencing

Sentencing for violations of Section 841(a) is governed by the nature and volume of the substance involved, the defendant's criminal record, and injuries attributable to the offense.[57] The most severe penalties are reserved for high-volume trafficking of eight substances assigned to Controlled Substance Schedules I and II.[58]

The eight substances are heroin, powder cocaine, cocaine base (crack), PCP, LSD, fentanyl, methamphetamine, and marijuana. Criminal penalties related to each substance provide one set of mandatory minimums for trafficking in a very substantial amount listed in Section 841(b)(1)(A), and a second, lower set of mandatory minimums for trafficking in a lower but still substantial amount listed in Section 841(a)(1)(B). The first set (841(b)(1)(A) level) features the following thresholds:

- heroin - 1 kilogram;[59]
- powder cocaine - 5 kilograms;[60]

---

[55] 21 U.S.C. § 851.

[56] United States v, Isaac, 655 F.3d 148, 155-57 (3d Cir. 2011) (citing cases on either side of the divide).

[57] As noted later and in the chart above, the sentencing provisions for violations of the Controlled Substances Export and Import Act, 21 U.S.C. § 960(b), mirror those for violations of the Controlled Substances Act in Section 841(b).

[58] 21 U.S.C. § 812.

[59] *Id.* §§ 841(b)(1)(A)(i), 960(b)(1)(A) ("1 kilogram grams or more of a mixture or substance containing a detectable amount of heroin") (10 grams = .35 ounces; 1 kilogram (1,000 grams) = 2.2 lbs.).

[60] *Id.* §§ 841(b)(1)(A)(ii), 960(b)(1)(B) ("5 kilograms or more of a mixture or substance containing a detectable amount of- (I) coca leaves, except coca leaves and extracts of coca leaves from which cocaine, ecgonine, and derivatives of ecgonine or their salts have been removed; (II) cocaine, its salts, optical and geometric isomers, and salts of isomers; (III) ecgonine, its derivatives, their salts, isomers, and salts of isomers; or (IV) any compound, mixture, or preparation which contains any quantity of any of the substances referred to in subclauses (I) through (III)").

- crack - 280 grams;[61]
- PCP - 100 grams;[62]
- LSD - 10 grams;[63]
- fentanyl - 400 grams;[64]
- methamphetamine - 50 grams;[65]
- marijuana - 1,000 kilograms.[66]

The second set (841(b)(1)(B) level) has thresholds that are one-tenth of those of the higher set:

- heroin - 100 grams;[67]
- powder cocaine - 500 grams;[68]
- crack - 28 grams;[69]
- PCP - 100 grams;[70]

---

[61] *Id.* §§ 841(b)(1)(A)(iii), 960(b)(1)(C) ("280 grams or more of a mixture or substance described in clause (ii) which contains cocaine base").

[62] *Id.* §§ 841(b)(1)(A)(iv), 960(b)(1)(D) ("100 grams or more of phencyclidine (PCP) or 1 kilogram grams or more of a mixture or substance containing a detectable amount of phencyclidine (PCP)").

[63] *Id.* §§ 841(b)(1)(A)(v), 960(b)(1)(E) ("10 grams or more of a mixture or substance containing a detectable amount of lysergic acid diethylamide (LSD)").

[64] *Id.* §§ 841(b)(1)(A)(vi), 960(b)(1)(F) ("400 grams or more of a mixture or substance containing a detectable amount of N-phenyl-N- [1- (2-phenylethyl) -4-piperidinyl] propanamide or 10 grams or more of a mixture or substance containing a detectable amount of any analogue of N-phenyl-N-[1-(2-phenylethyl)-4-piperidinyl] propanamide").

[65] *Id.* §§ 841(b)(1)(A)(viii), 960(b)(1)(H) ("50 grams or more of methamphetamine, its salts, isomers, and salts of its isomers or 500 grams or more of a mixture or substance containing a detectable amount of methamphetamine, its salts, isomers, or salts of its isomers").

[66] *Id.* §§ 841(b)(1)(A)(vii), 960(b)(1)(G) ("1000 kilograms or more of a mixture or substance containing a detectable amount of marihuana, or 1000 or more marihuana plants regardless of weight").

[67] *Id.* §§ 841(b)(1)(B)(i), 960(b)(2)(A) ("100 grams or more of a mixture or substance containing a detectable amount of heroin") (10 grams = .35 ounces; 1 kilogram (1,000 grams) = 2.2 lbs.). *Id.* § § 841(b) and 960(b) use the same thresholds.

[68] *Id.* §§ 841(b)(1)(B)(ii), 960(b)(2)(B) ("500 grams or more of a mixture or substance containing a detectable amount of- (I) coca leaves, except coca leaves and extracts of coca leaves from which cocaine, ecgonine, and derivatives of ecgonine or their salts have been removed; (II) cocaine, its salts, optical and geometric isomers, and salts of isomers; (III) ecgonine, its derivatives, their salts, isomers, and salts of isomers; or (IV) any compound, mixture, or preparation which contains any quantity of any of the substances referred to in subclauses (I) through (III)").

[69] *Id.* §§ 841(b)(1)(B)(iii), 960(b)(2)(C) ("28 grams or more of a mixture or substance described in clause (ii) which contains cocaine base").

- LSD - 1 gram;[71]
- fentanyl - 40 grams;[72]
- methamphetamine - 5 grams;[73]
- marijuana - 100 kilograms.[74]

A Section 841(a) violation involving one of the eight drugs at the higher 841(b)(1)(A) level is punishable by imprisonment for:

- not less than 10 years;
- not less than 20 years if the offense results in death or serious bodily injury or if the offender has a prior felony drug conviction; and
- a mandatory term of life imprisonment if the offender has a prior felony drug conviction and the offense resulted in death or serious bodily injury or if the offender has two or more prior felony drug convictions.[75]

A Section 841(a) violation involving one of the eight drugs at the lower 841(b)(1)(B) level is punishable by imprisonment for:

- not less than 5 years;
- not less than 10 years, if the offender has a prior felony drug conviction;

---

[70] *Id.* §§ 841(b)(1)(B)(iv), 960(b)(2)(D) ("10 grams or more of phencyclidine (PCP) or 100 grams or more of a mixture or substance containing a detectable amount of phencyclidine (PCP)").

[71] *Id.* §§ 841(b)(1)(B)(v), 960(b)(2)(E) ("1 gram or more of a mixture or substance containing a detectable amount of lysergic acid diethylamide (LSD)").

[72] *Id.* §§ 841(b)(1)(B)(vi), 960(b)(2)(F) ("40 grams or more of a mixture or substance containing a detectable amount of N-phenyl-N- [1- (2-phenylethyl) -4-piperidinyl] propanamide or 10 grams or more of a mixture or substance containing a detectable amount of any analogue of N-phenyl-N-[1-(2-phenylethyl)-4-piperidinyl] propanamide").

[73] *Id.* §§ 841(b)(1)(B)(viii), 960(b)(2)(H) ("5 grams or more of methamphetamine, its salts, isomers, and salts of its isomers or 50 grams or more of a mixture or substance containing a detectable amount of methamphetamine, its salts, isomers, or salts of its isomers").

[74] *Id.* §§ 841(b)(1)(B)(vii), 960(b)(2)(G) ("100 kilograms or more of a mixture or substance containing a detectable amount of marihuana, or 100 or more marihuana plants regardless of weight.").

[75] *Id.* § 841(b)(1)(A).

- not less than 20 years if the offense results in death or serious bodily injury; and
- a mandatory term of life imprisonment if the offender has a prior felony drug conviction and the offense resulted in death or serious bodily injury.[76]

A Section 841(a) violation involving one of the eight drugs in lesser amounts, or some other Schedule I or II drug, or a date rape drug is punishable by imprisonment for:

- not less than 20 years if death or serious bodily injury results; and
- life if the offender has a prior felony drug conviction and death or serious bodily injury results.[77]

The felony drug convictions that trigger the sentencing enhancement include federal, state, and foreign convictions.[78] The "serious bodily injury" enhancement is confined to bodily injuries which involve "(A) a substantial risk of death; (B) protracted and obvious disfigurement; or (C) protracted loss or impairment of the function of a bodily member, organ, or mental faculty."[79] And, the "if death results" enhancement is available only if the drugs provided by the defendant were the "but-for" cause of death; it is not available if the drugs supplied were merely a contributing cause.[80] The same "but for" standard presumably applies with equal force to the "serious bodily injury" enhancement.

---

[76] *Id.* § 841(b)(1)(B).

[77] *Id.* § 841(b)(1)(C) ("In the case of a controlled substance in schedule I or II, gamma hydroxybutyric acid (including when scheduled as an approved drug product for purposes of section 3(a)(1)(B) of the Hillory J. Farias and Samantha Reid Date-Rape Drug Prohibition Act of 2000), or 1 gram of flunitrazepam, except as provided in subparagraphs (A), [or] (B) ...."). The penalty is imprisonment for not more 20 years and there is no mandatory minimum where neither death nor serious bodily injury result.

[78] *Id.*§ 802(44) ("The term 'felony drug offense' means an offense that is punishable by imprisonment for more than one year under any law of the United States or of a State or foreign country that prohibits or restricts conduct relating to narcotic drugs, marihuana, anabolic steroids, or depressant or stimulant substances.").

[79] *Id.* § 802(25).

[80] Burrage v. United States, 134 S. Ct. 881, 892 (2014); *see also* Santillana v. Upton, 846 F.3d 779, 781 (5th Cir. 2017); Krieger v. United States, 842 F.3d 490, 497 (7th Cir. 2016).

Attempt, Conspiracy, and Aiding and Abetting (21 U.S.C. § 846; 18 U.S.C. § 2)

The mandatory minimums of Section 841 apply with equal force to those who attempt to possess with intent to distribute;[81] who conspire to do so;[82] or who aid and abet a violation of Section 841 by others.[83]

Attempt

To prove an attempt to violate Section 841(a) "the government must establish beyond a reasonable doubt that the defendant (a) had the intent to commit the object crime and (b) engaged in conduct amounting to a substantial step towards its commission. For a defendant to have taken a substantial step, he must have engaged in more than mere preparation, but may have stopped short of the last act necessary for the actual commission of the substantive crime."[84]

Conspiracy

Conspiracy is an agreement to commit a crime.[85] "To establish that a defendant conspired to distribute drugs under 21 U.S.C. § 846, the government must prove: (1) that there was a conspiracy, *i.e.*, an agreement to distribute the drugs; (2) that the defendant knew of the conspiracy; and (3) that the defendant intentionally joined the conspiracy."[86] The existence of the conspiracy need not be shown by written agreement or any other form of direct evidence, but may be inferred from the circumstances.[87] Moreover, each of the conspirators need not be fully aware of the roles or

---

[81] 21 U.S.C. §§ 856, 963.

[82] *Id.*

[83] 18 U.S.C. § 2.

[84] United States v. Anderson, 747 F.3d 51, 73-4 (2d Cir. 2014) (internal citations omitted). *See also* United States v. Stallworth, 656 F.3d 721, 728 (7th Cir. 2011); United States v. Hunt, 656 F.3d 906, 912 (9th Cir. 2011).

[85] United States v. Lyle, 856 F.2d 191, 207 (2d Cir. 2017).

[86] United States v. Jackson, 856 F.3d 1187, 1192 (8th Cir. 2017); *see also* United States v. Chapman, 851 F.3d 363,375 (5th Cir. 2017); United States v. Cardena, 842 F.3d 959, 994-95 (7th Cir. 2016); United States v. Williams, 827 F.3d 1134, 1162 (D.C. Cir. 2016).

[87] United States v. Garcia-Lagunas, 835 F.3d 479, 490 (4th Cir. 2016) ("[G]iven the clandestine and covert nature of conspiracies, the government can prove the existence of a conspiracy by circumstantial evidence alone."); *Jackson*, 856 F.3d at 1192; *Chapman*, 851 F.3d at 375; United States v. Trotter, 837 F.3d 864, 867-68 (8th Cir. 2016); *Williams*, 827 F.3d at 1162.

activities of all of their cohorts.[88] Each conspirator, however, is punishable for the foreseeable offenses committed in furtherance of the common scheme.[89]

Although it technically demonstrates an agreement to distribute a controlled substance, proof of a small, one-time sale of a controlled substance is ordinarily not considered sufficient for a conspiracy conviction. "[T]he factors that demonstrate a defendant was part of a conspiracy rather than in a mere buyer/seller relationship with that conspiracy include: (1) the length of affiliation between the defendant and the conspiracy; (2) whether there is an established method of payment; (3) the extent to which transactions are standardized; (4) whether there is a demonstrated level of mutual trust; (5) whether the transactions involved large amounts of drugs; and (6) whether the defendant purchased his drugs on credit."[90]

Aiding and Abetting

Accomplices who aid and abet the crime of another receive the same punishment as the offender they assist.[91] To prove, aiding and abetting, the government must show that the defendant knowingly embraced and assisted in the commission of the crime.[92]

---

[88] United States v. Bailey, 840 F.3d 99, 108 (3d Cir. 2016); United States v. Morales, 813 F.3d 1058, 1065 (8th Cir. 2016); United States v. Santos-Soto, 799 F.3d 49, 58 (1st Cir. 2015).

[89] Pinkerton v. United States, 328 U.S. 640, 64748 (1946); United States v. Hare, 820 F.3d 93, 105 (4th Cir. 2016); United States v. Gadson, 763 F.3d 1189, 1214 (9th Cir. 2014).

[90] *Bailey*, 840 F.3d at108. *See also Trotter*, 837 F.3d at 867-68 ("While proof of a conspiracy requires evidence of more than simply a buyer-seller relationship, we have limited the buyer-seller relationship cases to those involving only evidence of a single transient sales agreement and small amounts of drugs consistent with personal use."); United States v. Lyle, 856 F.3d 191, 207-208 (2d Cir. 2017).

[91] 18 U.S.C. § 2.

[92] United States v. Negron-Sostre, 790 F.3d 295, 311 (1st Cir. 2015) (internal citations omitted) ("[A] defendant may be held indirectly responsible as an aider and abettor if he associated himself with the venture ... participated in it as something that he wished to bring about, and ... sought by his actions to make the venture succeed."); United States v. Sanchez, 789 F.3d 827, 838 (8th Cir. 2015); United States v. Boykin, 785 F.3d 1352, 1359 (9th Cir. 2015).

Special Circumstances

Trafficking offenses that ordinarily do not trigger mandatory minimum sentences may do so if they involve special circumstances. Thus, trafficking to pregnant women,[93] children,[94] or in proximity of a school, playground, or other prohibited location,[95] or using a child to manufacture or traffic, are punishable with a one-year mandatory minimum term of imprisonment and in most instances a three-year mandatory minimum for repeat offenders.[96]

Import/Export Offenses

Sections 960 and 963 of the Controlled Substances Import and Export Act,[97] and by cross- reference Section 70506 of the Maritime Drug Law Enforcement Act (MDLEA),[98] largely track the penalties found in Section 841(b) of the Controlled Substances Act, including the mandatory minimum sentences of imprisonment.

---

[93] 21 U.S.C. § 861(f), (b), (c).

[94] *Id.* § 859.

[95] *Id.* § 860 ("(a) Any person who violates section 841(a)(1) of this title ... by distributing, possessing with intent to distribute, or manufacturing a controlled substance in or on, or within one thousand feet of, the real property comprising a public or private elementary, vocational, or secondary school or a public or private college, junior college, or university, or a playground, or housing facility owned by a public housing authority, or within 100 feet of a public or private youth center, public swimming pool, or video arcade facility, is (except as provided in subsection (b) of this section) subject to.... Except to the extent a greater minimum sentence is otherwise provided by section 841(b) of this title, a person shall be sentenced under this subsection to a term of imprisonment of not less than one year. The mandatory minimum sentencing provisions of this paragraph shall not apply to offenses involving 5 grams or less of marihuana. (b) Any person who violates section 841(a)(1) of this title by distributing, possessing with intent to distribute, or manufacturing a controlled substance in or on, or within one thousand feet of, ... or within 100 feet of a public or private youth center, public swimming pool, or video arcade facility, after a prior conviction under subsection (a) of this section has become final is punishable.... Except to the extent a greater minimum sentence is otherwise provided by section 841(b) of this title, a person shall be sentenced under this subsection to a term of imprisonment of not less than three years.... ").

[96] *Id.* § 861(a), (b), (c).

[97] *Id.* §§ 960, 963.

[98] 46 U.S.C. § 70506.

Section 960

Section 960 sets the penalties for three categories of offenses: (1) importing or exporting a controlled substance in violation of 21 U.S.C. § 825 (labeling and packaging), § 952 (importing controlled substances), § 953 (exporting controlled substances), or § 967 (smuggling controlled substances); (2) possession of a controlled substance aboard a vessel or aircraft in violation of 21 U.S.C. § 955; and (3) possession with intent to distribute in violation of 21 U.S.C. § 959.

Of these, violations of Sections 952 and 959 appear to be the most commonly prosecuted. "To sustain a conviction for the importation of a controlled substance[under Section 952], the government must prove: (1) the defendant played a role in bringing a quantity of a controlled substance into the United States; (2) the defendant knew the substance was controlled; and (3) the defendant knew the substance would enter the United States."[99] The government, however, need not prove that the defendant knew which controlled substance was being imported or its quantity.[100]

Section 959 proscribes two offenses: manufacturing or distributing a controlled substance for import purposes[101] and possession aboard an aircraft by a U.S. citizen or aboard a U.S. aircraft.[102] The section specifically states that it governs offenses committed outside the territory of the United States.[103]

Attempt, Conspiracy, and Aiding and Abetting

Section 963 outlaws attempts and conspiracies to violate the prohibitions covered by Section 960, and calls for the same penalties, including mandatory minimums, as apply to the underlying substantive offenses.

---

[99] United States v. Lopez-Monzon, 850 F.3d 202, 206 (5th Cir. 2017).

[100] United States v. Gil-Cruz, 808 F.3d 274, 278-79 (5th Cir. 2015); United States v. Jefferson, 791 Fl.3d 1013, 1016- 18 (9th Cir. 2015).

[101] 21 U.S.C. § 959(a); *e.g.*, United States v. Rojas, 812 F.3d 382, 399-400 (5th Cir. 2016); United States v. Romero-Padilla, 583 F.3d 126, 129-30 (2d Cir. 2009).

[102] 21 U.S.C. § 959(b), *e.g.*, United States v. Lawrence, 727 F.3d 386, 390-95 (5th Cir. 2013).

[103] 21 U.S.C. § 959(c).

Maritime Drug Law Enforcement Act (MDLEA) (46 U.S.C. §§ 70503, 70506)

MDLEA outlaws possession of a controlled substance aboard a vessel subject to U.S. jurisdiction or attempting or conspiring to do so.[104] Here too, violations carry the same penalties, including mandatory minimums, as the underlying substantive offenses.[105]

The term "vessel subject to the jurisdiction of the United States" includes vessels within U.S. territorial or customs waters, and vessels of foreign registration or vessels located in foreign territorial waters when the foreign nation has consented to application of U.S. law, as well as vessels for which no claim of registration or false claim of registration is presented.[106] Most of the lower federal appellate courts to consider the issue have held that the government need not establish any other nexus to the United States.[107] The type and volume of controlled substances ordinarily involved in MDLEA cases usually trigger the more severe mandatory minimum sentences.[108]

Narco-Terrorism (21 U.S.C. § 960a)

Section 960a doubles the otherwise applicable mandatory minimum sentence for drug trafficking (including an attempt or conspiracy to traffic) when the offense is committed in order to fund a terrorist activity or terrorist organization.[109] The merge of drug trafficking and terrorism offenses in Section 960a does not preclude conviction of the defendant for

---

[104] 46 U.S.C. §§ 70503, 70506(b).

[105] *Id.* § 70506(a).

[106] *Id.* § 70502(c).

[107] United States v. Wilchcombe, 838 F.3d 1179, 1186 (11th Cir. 2016) (citing United States v. Suerte, 291 F.3d 366, 369-72 (5th Cir. 2002); United States v. Cardales, 168 F.3d 548, 553 (1st Cir. 1999); United States v. Martinez- Hidalgo, 993 F.2d 1052, 1056 (3d Cir. 1993); contra, United States v. Klimavicius-Viloria, 144 F.3d 1249, 1257 (9th Cir. 1998)).

[108] *E.g.*, United States v. Trinidad, 839 F.3d 112, 114 (1st Cir. 2016) (114 kilograms of cocaine); *Wilchcombe*, 838 F.3d at 1183 (more than five kilograms of cocaine and more than 100 kilograms of marijuana); United States v. Cruickshank, 837 F.3d 1182, 1187 (11th Cir. 2016) (more than five kilograms of cocaine); United States v. Cruz-Mendez, 811 F.3d 1172, 1173 (9th Cir. 2016) (568 kilograms of marijuana); United States v. Pena-Santo, 809 F.3d 686, 691-92 (1st Cir. 2015) (more than 150 kilograms of cocaine).

[109] 21 U.S.C. §§ 960a, 963.

drug trafficking and terrorism offenses as well.[110] Here, too, the controlled substances involved ordinarily carry their own mandatory minimum term of imprisonment.[111]

Drug Kingpin (21 U.S.C. § 848)

Conviction of a Continuing Criminal Enterprise (CCE or Drug Kingpin) offense results in imposition of a 20-year mandatory minimum; the mandatory minimum for repeat offenders is 30 years.[112] Drug kingpins of enormous enterprises, however, face a mandatory sentence of life imprisonment.[113]

To secure a conviction, the government must establish, "1) a felony violation of the federal narcotics laws; 2) as part of a continuing series of three or more related felony violations of federal narcotics laws; 3) in concert with five or more other persons; 4) for whom [the defendant] is an organizer, manager or supervisor; [and] 5) from which [the defendant] derives substantial income or resources."[114]

The homicide mandatory minimum found in the drug kingpin statute sets a 20-year minimum term of imprisonment for killings associated with a kingpin offense or for killings of law enforcement officers associated

---

[110] United States v. Garavito-Garcia, 827 F.3d 242, 244, 249-50 (2d Cir. 2016) (conviction under 21 U.S.C. § 960a, as well as, 21 U.S.C. § 963 (conspiracy to import cocaine), 18 U.S.C. § 2339B (conspiracy to provide material support to a terrorist organization), and 18 U.S.C. § 2332g (conspiracy to traffic in anti-aircraft missiles); *cf.* United States v. Mohammed, 693 F.3d 192, 197 (D.C. Cir. 2012) (conviction under 21 U.S.C. § 960a and 21 U.S.C. § 959 (distribution of controlled substances with the intent to import into the United States).

[111] *E.g., Garavito-Garcia*, 827 F.3d at 244 ("ton-quantities" of cocaine); *Mohammed*, 693 F.3d at 195 (two kilograms of heroin).

[112] 21 U.S.C. § 848(a).

[113] *Id.* § 848(b) ("Any person who engages in a continuing criminal enterprise shall be imprisoned for life and fined in accordance with subsection (a), if - (1) such person is the principal administrator, organizer, or leader of the enterprise or is one of several such principal administrators, organizers, or leaders; and (2)(A) the violation referred to in subsection (c)(1) involved at least 300 times the quantity of a substance described in subsection 841(b)(1)(B) of this title, or (B) the enterprise, or any other enterprise in which the defendant was the principal or one of several principal administrators, organizers, or leaders, received $10 million dollars in gross receipts during any twelve-month period of its existence for the manufacture, importation, or distribution of a substance described in section 841(b)(1)(B).").

[114] United States v. Lee, 687 F.3d 935, 940 (8th Cir. 2012); *see also*, United States v. Bostick, 791 F.3d 127, 1490 (D.C. Cir. 2015); United States v. Isaac, 655 F.3d 148, 154 (3d Cir. 2011).

with certain other controlled substance offenses.[115] Neither prohibition requires the defendant to have been manufacturing or distributing controlled substances at the time of the killing.[116]

Drug-Related Mandatory Minimums

Firearm Possession in Furtherance (18 U.S.C. § 924(c))

Mandatory minimums are found in two federal firearms statutes. One, the Armed Career Criminal Act, deals exclusively with recidivists.[117] The other, Section 924(c), attaches one of several mandatory minimum terms of imprisonment whenever a firearm is used or possessed during and in relation to a federal crime of violence or drug trafficking.[118]

---

[115] 21 U.S.C. § 848(e); United States v. Hager, 721 F.3d 167, 179-80 (4th Cir. 2013) (citing United States v. Aguilar, 585 F.3d 652, 657 (2d Cir. 2009) (internal citations and quotation marks omitted)("There are three prongs to this statue. The first prong covers those who intentionally kill someone while engaged in a CCE. The second prong concerns the one who intentionally kills another while working in furtherance of a CCE. And, the third prong envelops that person who intentionally kills another while engaged in an offense punishable under section 841(b)(1)(A) ... or section 960(b)(1)."). *Hager* and *Aguilar* describe 21 U.S.C. § 848(e)(1)(A). Section 848(e)(1)(B) establishes the same 20-year mandatory minimum for a killing of a police officer in the line of duty when committed in furtherance or to avoid punishment for any violation of the Controlled Substances or Controlled Substances Import and Export Acts.

[116] United States v. Barrett, 797 F.3d 1207, 1219 (10th Cir. 2015); United States v. Pierce, 785 F.3d 832, 839 (2d Cir. 2015) ("The government need only prove beyond a reasonable doubt that one motive for the killing ... was related to the drug conspiracy.").

[117] 18 U.S.C. § 924(e).

[118] *Id.* § 924(c). Section 924(c) has been the subject of repeated Supreme Court litigation and regular congressional amendment since its inception in 1968. However, the crime of violence prong of the section, rather than the drug trafficking prong, has been the scene of most of the activity. *See* United States v. O'Brien, 560 U.S. 218, 221 (2010) ("The Court must interpret, once again, §924(c) of Title 18 of the United States Code"); Dean v. United States, 137 S. Ct. 1170 (2017); Rosemond v. United States, 134 S. Ct. 1240 (2014); Alleyne v. United States, 133 S. Ct. 2151 (2013); United States v. Abbott, 562 U.S.18 (2010); Dean v. United States, 556 U.S. 568 (2009); Watson v. United States, 552 U.S. 74 (2007); Harris v. United States, 536 U.S. 545 (2002); Castillo v. United States, 530 U.S. 120 (2000); Mascarello v. United States, 524 U.S. 125 (1998); United States v. Gonzales, 520 U.S. 1 (1997); Bailey v. United States, 516 U.S. 137 (1995); Smith v. United States, 508 U.S. 223 (1993); Deal v. United States, 508 U.S. 129 (1993); P. L. 90-618, 82 Stat. 1223 (1968), 18 U.S.C. § 924(c)(1970 ed.); P. L. 91-644, §13, 84 Stat. 1889 (1971), 18

Section 924(c), in its current form, establishes one of several different minimum sentences when a firearm is used or possessed in furtherance of another federal crime of violence or drug trafficking. The mandatory minimums must be imposed in addition to any sentence imposed for the underlying crime of violence or drug trafficking and vary depending upon the circumstances:

- imprisonment for not less than five years, unless one of the higher mandatory minimums below applies;
- imprisonment for not less than seven years if a firearm is brandished;
- imprisonment for not less than 10 years if a firearm is discharged;
- imprisonment for not less than 10 years if a firearm is a short-barreled rifle or shotgun or is a semi-automatic weapon;
- imprisonment for not less than 15 years if the offense involves the armor piercing ammunition;
- imprisonment for not less than 25 years if the offender has a prior conviction for violation of Section 924(c);
- imprisonment for not less than 30 years if the firearm is a machine gun or destructive device or is equipped with a silencer; and
- imprisonment for life if the offender has a prior conviction for violation of Section 924(c) and if the firearm is a machine gun or destructive device or is equipped with a silencer.[119]

Features Firearm

Section 924(c) outlaws possession of a firearm in furtherance of, or use of a firearm during and in relation to, a predicate offense. A "firearm" for purposes of Section 924(c) includes not only guns ("weapons ... which will

---

U.S.C. § 924(c) (1976 ed.); P. L. §1005, 98 Stat. 2138 (1984), 18 U.S.C. § 924(c) (1982 ed.) (Supp. II); P.L. 99-308, 100 Stat. 457 (1986), 18 U.S.C. § 924(c) (1982 ed.) (Supp. IV); P.L. 100-690, §6460, 102 Stat. 4373 (1988), 18 U.S.C. § 924(c) (1988 ed.); P.L. 101-647, §1101,104 Stat. 4829 (1990), 18 U.S.C. § 924(c) (1988 ed.) (Supp. II); P.L. 105-386, §1, 112 Stat. 3469 (1998), 18 U.S.C. § 924(c) (2000 ed.); P.L. 109-92, §6(b), 119 Stat. 2102 (2005), 18 U.S.C. § 924(c)(2000 ed.) (Supp. V).

[119] 18 U.S.C. § 924(c)(1), (5).

or [are] designed to or may readily be converted to expel a projectile by the action of an explosive"), but silencers and explosives as well.[120] It includes firearms that are not loaded or that are broken.[121] It does not include toys or imitations.[122] Nevertheless, the government need not produce the gun itself at trial. It need do no more than "present sufficient testimony, including the testimony of lay witnesses, in order to prove beyond a reasonable doubt that a defendant used, possessed or carried a 'firearm' as that term is defined for purposes of §924(c)."[123] Yet conviction must rest on some evidence of the presence of a firearm.[124]

Predicate Offenses

Section 924(c) is triggered when a firearm is used or possessed in furtherance of a predicate offense. The predicate offenses are crimes of violence and certain drug trafficking crimes. The drug trafficking predicates include any felony violation of the Controlled Substances Act, the Controlled Substances Import and Export Act, or the Maritime Drug Law Enforcement Act.[125] A defendant may be convicted under Section

---

[120] *Id.* § 921(a)(3), (4) ("(3) The term 'firearm' means (A) any weapon (including a starter gun) which will or is designed to or may readily be converted to expel a projectile by the action of an explosive; ... (C) any firearm muffler or firearm silencer; or (D) any destructive device.... (4) The term 'destructive device' means - (A) any explosive, incendiary, or poison gas - (i) bomb, (ii) grenade, (iii) rocket having a propellant charge of more than four ounces, (iv) missile having an explosive or incendiary charge of more than one-quarter ounce, (v) mine, or (vi) device similar to any of the devices described in the preceding clauses ..."). *E.g.*, United States v. York, 600 F.3d 347, 354 (5th Cir. 2010) (Molotov cocktail constitutes a firearm for purposes of § 924(c)); United States v. Tomkins, 782 F.3d 338, 345 (7th Cir. 2015) (pipe bombs constitute firearms for purposes of § 924(c)).

[121] United States v. Cooper, 714 F.3d 873, 881 (5th Cir. 2013).

[122] United States v. Garrido, 596 F.3d 613, 617 (9th Cir. 2010) ("Possession of a toy or replica gun cannot sustain a conviction under § 924(c)"); *see also* United States v. Martinez-Armestica, 846 F.3d 436, 440 (1st Cir. 2017); United States v. Lawson, 810 F.3d 1032, 1039 (7th Cir. 2016).

[123] United States v. King, 751 F.3d 1268,1274 (11th Cir. 2014); *see also Lawson*, 810 F.3d at 1039-40; United States v. Sherer, 770 F.3d 407, 412 (6th Cir. 2014); United States v. Kamahele, 748 F.3d 984, 1010 (10th Cir. 2014).

[124] United States v. Feliciano, 761 F.3d 1202, 1212 (11th Cir. 2014).

[125] 18 U.S.C. § 924(c)(2), referring to 21 U.S.C. §§ 801-904, 21 U.S.C. §§ 951-971, and 46 U.S.C. §§ 70501-70507, respectively. *See, e.g.*, United States v. Chapman, 851 F.3d 363, 372-73 (5th Cir. 2017); United States v. RiveraRuperto, 846 F.3d 417, 423 (1st Cir. 2017).

924(c), however, even though not convicted or even prosecuted for the predicate offense.[126]

Possession in Furtherance

Section 924(c) has two alternative firearm-nexus elements: (a) possession in furtherance and (b) carrying or use.[127] The possession-in-furtherance version of the offense requires that the defendant "(1) committed a drug trafficking crime; (2) knowingly possessed a firearm; and (3) possessed the firearm in furtherance of the drug trafficking crime [or other predicate offense]."[128] The "possession" component may take the form of either actual or constructive possession. "Constructive possession exists when a person does not have possession but instead knowingly has the power and the intention at a given time to exercise dominion and control over an object, either directly or through others."[129]

The "in furtherance" component compels the government to show some nexus between possession of a firearm and a predicate offense – that is, to show that the firearm furthered, advanced, moved forward, promoted, or in some way facilitated the predicate offense.[130] This requires more than proof of the presence of a firearm in the same location as the predicate offense.[131]

---

[126] United States v. Galati, 844 F.3d 152, 155 (3d Cir. 2016); Davila v. United States, 843 F.3d 729, 730-31 (7th Cir. 2016).

[127] United States v. Burnett, 773 F.3d 122, 134 (3d Cir. 2014) ("Section 924(c) has two separate prongs, the violation of either standing alone is sufficient to support a conviction under the statute: (1) 'us[ing] or carry[ing]' a firearm 'during and in relation to' the underlying offense; or (2) 'possess[ing] a firearm 'in furtherance' of the underlying offense.... By making this distinction, Congress may well have intended 'in furtherance' to impose a more stringent standard than 'in relation to.'").

[128] United States v. Bobadilla-Pagan, 747 F.3d 26, 35 (1st Cir. 2014); *see also* United States v. Ramos, 852 F.3d 747, 753 (8th Cir. 2017); United States v. Bailey, 840 F.3d 99, 112 (3d Cir. 2016); United States v. Perez, 661 F.3d 568, 576 (11th Cir. 2011).

[129] United States v. Taylor, 800 F.3d 701, 709(6th Cir. 2015); *see also* United States v. Fernandez-Santos, 856 F.3d 10, 20 (1st Cir. 2017); United States v. Webster, 775 F.3d 897, 905-906 (7th Cir. 2015); United States v. Booker, 774 F.3d 928, 929-31 (8th Cir. 2014).

[130] United States v. Green, 835 F.3d 844, 854 (8th Cir. 2016); United States v. Ray, 803 F.3d 244, 263 (6th Cir. 20150; United States v. Pineda, 770 F.3d 313, 317 (4th Cir. 2014); United States v. Renteria, 720 F.3d 1245, 1255 (10th Cir. 2013); United States v. Eller, 670 F.3d 762, 765 (7th Cir. 2012); United States v. Pena, 586 F.3d 105, 113 (1st Cir. 2009); United States v. London, 568 F.3d 553, 559 (5th Cir. 2009); United States v. Lopez-Garcia, 565 F.3d 1306, 1322 (11th Cir. 2009).

[131] United States v. Russian, 848 F.3d 1239, 1250 (10th Cir. 2017); *Eller*, 670 F.3d at 765; United States v. Pena, 586 F.3d at 113; United States v. Penney, 576 F.3d 297, 315 (1st Cir. 2009).

Most circuits have identified specific factors that commonly allow a court to distinguish guilty possession from innocent "possession at the scene," particularly in a drug case, they include "(1) type of criminal activity that is being conducted; (2) accessibility of the firearm; (3) the type of firearm; (4) whether the firearm is stolen; (5) the status of the possession (legitimate or illegal); (6) whether the firearm is loaded; (7) the time and circumstances under which the firearm is found; and (8) the proximity to the drugs or drug profits."[132]

Although the Supreme Court has determined that acquiring a firearm in an illegal drug transaction does not constitute "use" in violation of Section 924(c),[133] several of the circuits have found that such acquisition may constitute "possession in furtherance."[134]

Use or Carry

The "use" outlawed in the use or carriage branch of Section 924(c) requires that a firearm be actively employed "during and in relation to" a predicate offense – that is, either a crime of violence or a drug trafficking

---

[132] *Russian*, 848 F.3d at 1250; *see also* United States v. Amaya, 828 F.3d 518 (7th Cir. 2016); United States v. Holley, 831 F.3d 322, 329 (5th Cir. 2016); *Renteria*, 720 F.3d at 1255; United States v. Brown, 715 F.3d 985, 993-94 (6th Cir. 2013); United States v. Johnson, 677 F.3d 138, 143 (3d Cir. 2012); *Lopez-Garcia*, 565 F.3d at 1322; United States v. Perry, 560 F.3d 246, 254 (4th Cir. 2009); *see also* United States v. Chavez, 549 F.3d 119, 130 (2d Cir. 2008) (noting after quoting the factors that, "while no conviction would lie for a drug dealer's innocent possession of a firearm, ... a drug dealer may be punished under § 924(c)(1)(A) where the charged weapon is readily accessible to protect drugs, drug proceeds, or the drug dealer himself"); *but see* United States v. Hector, 474 F.3d 1150, 1157 (9th Cir. 2007) (internal citations omitted) ("Although the Fifth Circuit has developed a non-exclusive list of factors ... we have concluded that this approach is not particularly helpful in close cases.... In our most recent case addressing the 'in furtherance question,' we reiterated the importance of the factual inquiry. We declined once again to adopt a checklist approach to deciding this issue and held that it is the totality of the circumstances, coupled with a healthy dose of a jury's common sense when evaluating the facts in evidence, which will determine whether the evidence suffices to support a conviction.").

[133] Watson v. United States, 552 U.S. 74 (2007).

[134] United States v. Gurka, 605 F.3d 40, 44 (1st Cir. 2010) ("We join the ... circuits holding that *Watson* does not affect the prong of 18 U.S.C. § 924(c)(1)(A) concerned with 'possession in furtherance.'") (citing United States v. Gardner, 602 F.3d 97, 103 (2d Cir. 2010) and United States v. Mahan, 586 F.3d 1185, 1189 (9th Cir. 2009)); *see also* United States v. Miranda, 666 F.3d 1280, 1282-284 (11th Cir. 2012); United States v. Dickerson, 705 F.3d 683, 688-90 (7th Cir. 2013).

offense.[135] A defendant "uses" a firearm during or in relation to a drug trafficking offense when he uses it to acquire drugs in a drug deal;[136] when he uses it as collateral in a drug deal;[137] or when he sells both drugs and firearms;[138] but not when he accepts a firearm in exchange for drugs in a drug deal.[139] The "carry[ing]" that the section outlaws encompasses instances when a firearm is carried on the defendant's person as well as when it is simply readily accessible in a vehicle during and in relation to a predicate offense.[140]

A firearm is used or carried "during and in relation" to a predicate offense when it has "some purpose or effect with respect" to the predicate offense; "its presence or involvement cannot be the result of accident or coincidence."[141] The government must show that the availability of the firearm played an integral role in the predicate offense.[142] It need not show that the firearm was used "in furtherance" of the predicate offense.[143]

---

[135] Bailey v. United States, 516 U.S. 137, 143 (1995); United States v. Isnadin, 742 F.3d 1278, 1307 (11th Cir. 2014); United States v. Haynes, 582 F.3d 686, 704 (7th Cir. 2009); United States v. Combs, 369 F.3d 925, 932 (6th Cir. 2004).

[136] Smith v. United States, 508 U.S. 223, 228 (1993); *Bailey*, 516 U.S. at 148.

[137] United States v. Cox, 324 F.3d 77, 82 (2d Cir. 2003).

[138] United States v. Benitiz, 809 F.3d 243, 248 (5th Cir. 2015).

[139] *Watson*, 552 U.S. at 78.

[140] Muscarello v. United States, 524 U.S. 125, 126 (1998) ("The question before us is whether the phrase 'carries a firearm' is limited to the carrying of firearms on the person. We hold that it is not so limited. Rather, it also applies to a person who knowingly possesses and carries a firearm in a vehicle, including locked in a glove compartment or trunk of a car, which the person accompanies"); United States v. Franklin, 561 F.3d 398, 403 (5th Cir. 2009); United States v. Winder, 557 F.3d 1129, 1138-139 (10th Cir. 2009); United States v. Robinson, 390 F.3d 853, 878 (6th Cir. 2005); United States v. Williams, 344 F.3d 365, 370 (3d Cir. 2003).

[141] United States v. Henry, 819 F.3d 856, 865 (6th Cir. 2016); United States v. Mashek, 606 F.3d 922, 930 (8th Cir. 2010) (quoting Smith v. United States, 508 U.S. 223, 238 (1993)); United States v. Roberson, 459 F.3d 39, 48 (1st Cir. 2006); *Williams*, 344 F.3d at 371.

[142] United States v. Burkley, 513 F.3d 1183, 1189-90 (10th Cir,. 2008) ("A firearm is carried during and in relation to the underlying crime when the defendant avails himself of the weapon and ... the weapon plays an integral role in the underlying offense.... Thus, the government must prove that the defendant intended the firearm to be available for use in the offense.").

[143] United States v. Burnett, 773 F.3d 122, 134 (3d Cir. 2014); *cf.* United States v. Barnes, 822 F.3d 914, 918 (6th Cir. 2016) (noting that "possession in furtherance" or "using or carrying during and in relation to" are two distinct crimes).

Discharge and Brandish

The basic five-year mandatory minimum penalty for using, carrying, or possessing a firearm in the course of a predicate offense becomes a seven-year mandatory minimum if a firearm was brandished during the course of the offense and becomes a 10-year mandatory minimum if a firearm was discharged during the course of the offense.[144] The discharge provision applies even if the firearm was discharged inadvertently.[145] Whether a firearm is discharged or brandished is a question that after *Alleyne v. United States* must be presented to the jury and proven beyond a reasonable doubt.[146] A firearm is brandished for these purposes when (1) it is displayed or its presence made known (2) in order to intimidate another.[147] Intimidation is a necessary feature of brandishing, but it is no less present when the fear is induced by using a gun as a club rather than merely displaying it.[148]

Short Barrels, Semiautomatics, Machine Guns, and Bombs

For some time, Section 924(c) consisted of a single long paragraph with brandishing, discharging, short barrels, semiautomatics, machine

---

[144] 18 U.S.C. § 924(c)(1)(A)(ii), (iii).

[145] Dean v. United States, 556 U.S. 568, 574 (2009); United States v. Mann, 786 F.3d 1244, 1251 (10th Cir. 2015).

[146] Alleyne v. United States, 133 S. Ct. 2151, 2163 (2013) ("Because the finding of brandishing increased the penalty to which the defendant was subjected, it was an element, which had to be found by the jury beyond a reasonable doubt"). *Alleyne* overruled *Harris*, which had held that brandishing was a sentencing factor that might be entrusted to the judge to find by a preponderance of the evidence (Harris v. United States, 535 U.S. 545, 556 (2002)); United States v. Cardena, 842 F.3d 959, 1000-1001 (7th Cir. 2016); United States v. Lewis, 802 F3.d 449, 454 (3d Cir. 2015); United States v. Hackett, 762 F.3d 493, 502 (6th Cir. 2014); United States v. King, 751 F.3d 1268, 1278-280 (11th Cir. 2014). The fact of a second or subsequent conviction, however, remains a sentencing factor, because the Supreme Court's holding in Almendarez-Torres v. United States, 523 U.S. 224 (1998), to that effect has not been withdrawn, *King*, 751 F.3d at 1280 (citing Alleyne v. United States, 133 S. Ct. at 2160 n.1); *Cardena*, 842 F.3d at 1000.

[147] 18 U.S.C. § 924(c)(4) ("For purposes of this subsection, the term 'brandish' means, with respect to a firearm, to display all or part of the firearm, or otherwise make the presence of the firearm known to another person, in order to intimidate that person, regardless of whether the firearm is directly visible to that person"); *Cardena*, 842 F.3d at 1001; United States v. Gonzales, 841 F.3d 339, 353 (5th Cir. 2016); United States v. Carter, 560 F.3d 1107, 1114 (9th Cir. 2009); United States v. Payne, 763 F.3d 1301, 1304-1305 (11th Cir. 2014).

[148] United States v. Bowen, 527 F.3d at 1075 (10th Cir. 2008).

guns, and bombs all in the same paragraph. When Congress added the "possession in furtherance" language, it parsed the section. Now, the general, brandish, and discharge mandatory penalties provisions appear in one part.[149] The provisions for offenses involving a short-barreled rifle or shotgun, a semiautomatic assault weapon, a silencer, a machine gun, or explosives appear in a second part.[150] The provisions for second and consequent convictions appear in a third part.[151]

The circuits are apparently divided over the question of whether the government must show that the defendant knew that the firearm at issue was of a particular type (*i.e.*, short-barreled rifle or shotgun, machine gun, or bomb).[152]

Prior to the division, the Supreme Court had identified as an element of a separate offense (rather than a sentencing factor) the question of whether a machine gun was the firearm used during and in relation to a predicate offense.[153] The use of a short-barreled rifle, semiautomatic assault weapon, silencer, machine gun, or bomb is not a sentencing factor, but an element of a separate offense to be charged and proved to the jury beyond a reasonable

---

[149] 18 U.S.C. § 924(c)(1) (emphasis added) ("(A) Except to the extent that a greater minimum sentence is otherwise provided by this subsection or by any other provision of law, any person who, during and in relation to any crime of violence or drug trafficking crime (including a crime of violence or drug trafficking crime that provides for an enhanced punishment if committed by the use of a deadly or dangerous weapon or device) for which the person may be prosecuted in a court of the United States, uses or carries a firearm, or who, in furtherance of any such crime, possesses a firearm, shall, in addition to the punishment provided for such crime of violence or drug trafficking crime - *(i) be sentenced to a term of imprisonment of not less than 5 years; (ii) if the firearm is brandished, be sentenced to a term of imprisonment of not less than 7 years; and (iii) if the firearm is discharged, be sentenced to a term of imprisonment of not less than 10 years ...*").

[150] 18 U.S.C. § 924(c)(1)(B) ("If the firearm possessed by a person convicted of a violation of this subsection - (i) is a short-barreled rifle, short-barreled shotgun, or semiautomatic assault weapon, the person shall be sentenced to a term of imprisonment of not less than 10 years; or (ii) is a machinegun or a destructive device, or is equipped with a firearm silencer or firearm muffler, the person shall be sentenced to a term of imprisonment of not less than 30 years.... ").

[151] *Id.* § 924(c)(1)(C) ("In the case of a second or subsequent conviction under this subsection, the person shall - (i) be sentenced to a term of imprisonment of not less than 25 years; and (ii) if the firearm involved is a machinegun or a destructive device, or is equipped with a firearm silencer or firearm muffler, be sentenced to imprisonment for life.").

[152] United States v. Burwell, 690 F.3d 500, 510-11 (D.C. Cir. 2012) (citing cases evidencing a split).

[153] Castillo v. United States, 530 U.S. 120, 121 (2000).

doubt.[154] The question of whether a second or subsequent conviction has occurred, however, remains a sentencing factor.[155]

Aiding, Abetting, and Conspiracy

As a general rule, anyone who commands, counsels, aids, or abets the commission of a federal crime by another is punishable as though he had committed the crime himself.[156] "In order to aid and abet another to commit a crime it is necessary that a defendant in some sort associate himself with the venture, that he participate in it as in something that he wishes to bring about, that he seek by his action to make it succeed." [157]

The Supreme Court has said in *Rosemond v. United States* that to aid or abet a violation of Section 924(c), the assistance may be shown to have advanced either the predicate offense or the firearm use.[158] However, the defendant must be shown to have intended his efforts contribute to the success of the Section 924(c) violation – that is, commission of a predicate offense while armed.[159] Thus, the defendant must be shown to have known before the commission of the predicate offense that his confederate was armed.[160]

---

[154] United States v. O'Brien, 560 U.S. 218, 235 (2010).

[155] United States v. Rivera-Rivera, 555 F.3d 277, 291 (1st Cir. 2009); United States v. Mejia, 545 F.3d 179, 207-208 (2d Cir. 2008). This is true even after *Alleyne*, because the Court continues to recognize a recidivist exception to the *Apprendi* rule, *see, e.g.*, Alleyne v. United States, 133 S. Ct. 2151, 2160 n.1 ("In *Almendarez-Torres v. United States*, 523 U.S. 224 (1998), we recognized a narrow exception to this general rule for the fact of a prior conviction. Because the parties do not contest that decision's vitality, we do not revisit it for purposes of our decision today.").

[156] 18 U.S.C. § 2.

[157] Nye & Nissen v. United States, 336 U.S. 613, 619 (1949); *see also* United States v. Centeno, 793 F.3d 378, 387 (3d Cir. 2015); United States v. Sosa, 777 F.3d 1279, 1292 (11th Cir. 2015) ("Thus, to convict under a theory of aiding and abetting, the government must prove that (1) someone committed the substantive offense; (2) the defendant contributed to and furthered the offense; and (3) the defendant intended to aid in its commission.").

[158] Rosemond v. United States, 134 S. Ct. 1240, 1247 (2014)("Rosemond therefore could assist in § 924(c)'s violation by facilitating either the drug transaction or the firearms use (or of course both.").

[159] *Id.* at 1248("[A] person aids and abets a crime when (in addition to taking the requisite act) he intends to facilitate that offense's commission.... [T]he intend must go to the specific and entire crime charged—so here, to the full scope (predicate crime plus gun use) of § 924(c).").

[160] *Id.* at 1249; United States v. Diaz-Rodriguez, 853 F.3d 540, 544-45 (1st Cir. 2017); United States v. Gooch, 850 F.3d 285, 287 (6th Cir. 2017).

In similar manner, conspirators are liable for any foreseeable crimes committed by any of their co-conspirators in furtherance of the conspiracy.[161] The rule applies when a defendant's coconspirator has committed a violation of Section 924(c).[162]

Sentencing Considerations

The penalties under Section 924(c) were once flat sentences. For example, the penalty for use of a firearm during the course of a predicate offense was a five-year term of imprisonment.[163] Now, they are simply mandatory minimums, each carrying an unspecified maximum term of life imprisonment.[164]

A court may not avoid the mandatory minimums called for in Section 924(c)(1) by imposing a probationary sentence,[165] or by ordering that a Section 924(c)(1) minimum mandatory sentence be served concurrently with some other sentence.[166] A court may, however, take Section 924(c)'s mandatory minimum into account when calculating the appropriate sentence for the underlying predicate offense.[167]

If a criminal episode involves more than one predicate offense, more than one violation of Section 924(c) may be punished.[168] Moreover, the

---

[161] Pinkerton v. United States, 328 U.S. 640, 646 (1946); Smith v. United States, 133 S. Ct. 718, 719 (2013).

[162] United States v. Bailey, 784 F.3d 99, 112 (3d Cir. 2016); United States v. Hare, 8120 F.3d 93, 105 (4th Cir. 2016); United States v. Soto, 794 F.3d 635, (6th Cir. 2015); United States v. Adams, 789 F.3d 713, 715 (7th Cir. 2015); United States v. Reed, 780 F.3d 272, 272 (4th Cir. 2015) ("A defendant may be convicted on a § 924(c) charge on the basis of a coconspirator's use of a gun if the use was in furtherance of the conspiracy and was reasonable foreseeable to the defendant.").

[163] 18 U.S.C. § 924(c) (1976 ed.).

[164] United States v. Lara-Ruiz, 781 F.3d 919, 924 (8th Cir. 2015); United States v. Diaz-Bermudez, 778 F.3d 309, 313- 14 (1st Cir. 2015); United States v. Shabazz, 564 F.3d 280, 289 (3d Cir. 2009) (citing United States v. Johnson, 507 F.3d 793, 798 (2d Cir. 2007); United States v. Dare, 425 F.3d 634, 642 (9th Cir. 2005); United States v. Avery, 295 F.3d 1158, 1170 (10th Cir. 2002); United States v. Cristobal, 293 F.3d 134, 147 (4th Cir. 2002); United States v. Sandoval, 241 F.3d 549, 551 (7th Cir. 2001); United States v. Pounds, 230 F.3d 1317, 1319 (11th Cir. 2000); United States v. Silas, 227 F.3d 244, 246 (5th Cir. 2000).

[165] 18 U.S.C. § 924(c)(1)(D)(i).

[166] *Id.* § 924(c)(1)(D)(ii). Dean v. United States, 137 S. Ct. 1170, 1174 (2017).

[167] *Id.* at 1178.

[168] United States v. Sandstrom, 594 F.3d 634, 658 (8th Cir. 2010) ("... [M]ultiple underlying offenses support multiple §924(c) convictions"); United States v. Catalan-Roman, 585 F.3d 453, 472 (1st Cir. 2009); United States v. Penny, 576 F.3d 297, 316 (6th Cir. 2009)

second or subsequent convictions which trigger enhanced mandatory minimum penalties need not be the product of separate trials, but may be part of the same verdict. Thus, a defendant charged and convicted in a single trial on several counts may be subject to multiple, consecutive, mandatory minimum terms of imprisonment.[169]

A number of defendants have sought refuge in the clause of Section 924(c), which introduces the section's mandatory minimum penalties with an exception: "[e]xcept to the extent that a greater minimum sentence is otherwise provided by this subsection or by any other provision of law." Defendants at one time argued that the mandatory minimums of Section 924(c) become inapplicable when the defendant was subject to a higher mandatory minimum under the predicate drug trafficking offense under the Armed Career Criminal Act (18 U.S.C. § 924(e)), or some other provision of law.[170] The Supreme Court rejected the argument in *Abbott v. United States*.[171] Thus, the clause means that the standard five-year minimum applies except in cases where the facts trigger one of Section 924(c)'s higher minimums.[172]

Armed Career Criminal Act (18 U.S.C. § 924(e))

> In the case of a person who violates section 922(g) of this title and has three previous convictions by any court referred to in section

("[W]hen two separate predicate offenses for triggering §924(c)(1) are charged and proved, a defendant may be convicted and sentenced for two separate crimes, even if both offenses were committed in the course of the same event"); United States v. Looney, 532 F.3d 392, 396 (5th Cir. 2008).

[169] Deal v. United States, 508 U.S. 129, 132 (1993); United States v. Gooch, 850 F.3d 285, 290 (6th Cir. 2017); United States v. Buck, 847 F.3d 267, 278 (5th Cir. 2017); United States v. Davis, 841 F.3d 1253, 1260 n. 9 (11th Cir. 2016); United States v. Cardena, 842 F.3d 959, 999 (7th Cir. 2016); United States v. Arline, 835 F.3d 277, 281-82 (2d Cir. 2016); United States v. Washington, 714 F.3d 962, 969-70 (6th Cir. 2013) (noting, however, that the stacking should be governed by the rule of lenity, so that, for example, the 25-year mandatory minimums for second offenses should be stacked starting with a seven-year brandishing sentence rather than a 10-year discharge sentence).

[170] United States v. Almany, 598 F.3d 238, 241-42 (6th Cir. 2010); United States v. Whitley, 529 F.3d 150, 153-56 (2d Cir. 2008).

[171] 562 U.S. 8, 13 (2010).

[172] *Id.*; United States v. Robles, 709 F.3d 98, 100-101 (2d Cir. 2013).

> 922(g)(1) of this title for a violent felony or a serious drug offense, or both, committed on occasions different from one another, such person shall be fined under this title and imprisoned not less than fifteen years....
> 18 U.S.C. § 924(e)(1).

Section 922(g) outlaws the possession of firearms by felons, fugitives, and various other categories of individuals.[173] The Armed Career Criminal Act (ACCA), quoted above, visits a 15- year mandatory minimum term of imprisonment upon anyone who violates Section 922(g), having been convicted three times previously of a violent felony or serious drug offense.[174] As the cases below suggest, the section most often ensnarls felons found in possession of a firearm who have three qualifying prior convictions. More often than not, the prior convictions are for violations of state law.[175]

Features

Section 924(e) begins with unlawful possession of a firearm ("a person who violates section 922(g)"). The threshold possession offense need not itself involve a drug or violent crime.[176] Section 924(e)'s 15-year mandatory minimum term of imprisonment instead flows as a consequence

---

[173] The disqualified categories cover felons, fugitives, drug addicts, mental defectives, unlawful aliens, dishonorably discharged members of the Armed Forces, individuals who have renounced their U.S. citizenship, those under a domestic violence restraining order, and those convicted of misdemeanor domestic violence, 18 U.S.C. § 922(g)(1)-(9).

[174] The ACCA is not to be confused with the federal three-strikes statute, 18 U.S.C. § 3559(c), which establishes a mandatory term of life imprisonment upon a third serious violent felony conviction, or with its two-strike counterpart in 18 U.S.C. § 3559(e), relating to mandatory life imprisonment for repeated child sex offenders.

[175] The vast majority of the Supreme Court's Section 924(e) cases involved at last one prior state conviction, *see, e.g.,* Mathis v. United States, 136 S. Ct. 2243 (2016); Welch v. United States, 136 S. Ct. 1257 (2016); Johnson v. United States, 135 S. Ct. 2551 (2015); Descamps v. United States, 570 U.S. 254 (2013); Sykes v. United States, 564 U.S. 1 (2011), overruled by *Johnson*, 135 S. Ct. 2551 (2015); McNeill v. United States v. 563 U.S. 816 (2011); Johnson v. United States, 559 U.S. 133 (2010); Chambers v. United States, 555 U.S. 122 (2009), overruled by *Johnson*, 135 S. Ct. 2551 (2015); United States v. Rodriquez, 553 U.S. 377 (2008); Begay v. United States, 553 U.S. 137 (2008), overruled by *Johnson*, 135 S. Ct. 2551 (2015); Logan v. United States, 552 U.S. 23 (2007); James v. United States, 550 U.S. 192 (2007), overruled by *Johnson*, 135 S. Ct. 2551 (2015); Shepard v. United States, 544 U.S. 13 (2005); Custis v. United States, 511 U.S. 485 (1994); Taylor v. United States, 495 U.S. 575 (1990).

[176] United States v. Raymond, 778 F.3d 716, 717 (8th Cir. 2015).

of the offender's prior criminal record ("three prior convictions ... referred to in section 922(g)(1) ... for a violent felony or a serious drug offense").[177] Not all violent felonies or serious drug offenses count. Certain convictions, principally those which have been overturned, pardoned, or otherwise set aside as a matter of state law, are exempt by definition.[178]

Moreover, qualifying violent felonies or serious drug offenses must have been committed on different occasions.[179] "[T]o trigger a sentence enhancement under the ACCA, a defendant's prior felony convictions must involve separate criminal episodes. However, offenses are considered distinct criminal episodes if they occurred on occasions different from one another," one court has observed.[180] And "two offenses are committed on occasions different from one another if it is possible to discern the point at which the first offense is completed and the second offense begins." [181] Thus, separate

---

[177] The statutory mandatory minimum takes precedence over a plea agreement calling for a sentence beneath the mandatory minimum. United States v. Symington, 781 F.3d 1308, 1313 (11th Cir. 2015) (citing United States v. Davis, 689 F.3d 349, 354 (4th Cir. 2012), and United States v. Moyer, 282 F.3d 1311, 1314 (10h Cir. 2002)).

[178] 18 U.S.C. § 921(20) ("The term 'crime punishable by imprisonment for a term exceeding one year' does not include- (A) any Federal or State offenses pertaining to antitrust violations, unfair trade practices, restraints of trade, or other similar offenses relating to the regulation of business practices, or (B) any State offense classified by the laws of the State as a misdemeanor and punishable by a term of imprisonment of two years or less. What constitutes a conviction of such a crime shall be determined in accordance with the law of the jurisdiction in which the proceedings were held. Any conviction which has been expunged, or set aside or for which a person has been pardoned or has had civil rights restored shall not be considered a conviction for purposes of this chapter, unless such pardon, expungement, or restoration of civil rights expressly provides that the person may not ship, transport, possess, or receive firearms."). *See* United States v. Sellers, 784 F.3d 876, 881-87 (2d Cir. 2015) (A New York youthful offender conviction set aside as a matter of New York law does not qualify as a predicate offense) (citing United States v. Collins, 61 F.3d 1379, 1382 (9th Cir. 1995), and United States v. Clark, 993 F.2d 402, 403 (4th Cir. 1993); and distinguishing, United States v. Ellis, 619 F.3d 72,75 (1st Cir. 2010) ("'It was not blatant error for the sentencing court to take [a defendant's] juvenile adjudication into consideration for the purpose of applying the ACCA' because 'juvenile adjudications [under Massachusetts law] are not "set aside" for the purpose of imposing sentence in later criminal proceedings.'")).

[179] 18 U.S.C. § 924(e)(1).

[180] United States v. Martin, 526 F.3d 926, 938-39 (6th Cir. 2008) (internal citations omitted).

[181] *Id. See also* United States v. Morris, 821 F.3d 877, 880 (7th Cir. 2016); United States v. Limney, 819 F.3d 747, 751 (4th Cir. 2016) (internal citations omitted) ("We have come to rely on five factors to determine whether predicate ACCA offenses were committed on different occasions: (1) whether the offenses arose in different geographic locations; (2) whether the nature of each offense was substantively different; (3) whether each offense involved different victims; (4) whether such offense involved different criminal objectives;

drug deals on separate days will constitute offenses committed on different occasions though they involve the same parties and location.[182] The fact that two crimes occurred on different occasions, however, must be clear on the judicial record; recourse to police records will not do.[183]

There is "no authority to ignore [an otherwise qualified] conviction because of its age or its underlying circumstances. Such considerations are irrelevant ... under the Act."[184] Moreover, application of Section 924(e) provides no opportunity to challenge the validity of the underlying predicate offenses.[185]

The section defines serious drug offenses as those violations of state or federal drug law punishable by imprisonment for 10 years or more.[186] Conviction under a statute which carries a 10-year maximum for repeat

---

and (5) whether the defendant had the opportunity after committing the first-in-time offense to make a conscious and knowing decision to engage in the next-in-time offense. Importantly, these five factors may be considered together or independently and the strong presence of any one factor can dispositively segregate an extended criminal episode into a serious of separate and distinct episodes."); United States v. Weeks, 711 F.3d 1255, 1261 (11th Cir. 2013) (internal citations omitted) ("To satisfy the ACCA's different-occasions requirement, a defendant must have at least three prior convictions for crimes that are temporally distinct. So long as the predicate crimes are successive rather than simultaneous, they constitute separate criminal episodes for purposes of the ACCA.").

[182] United States v. Abbott, 794 F.3d 896, 898 (8th Cir. 2015) ("We have repeatedly held that convictions for separate drug transactions on separate days are multiple AWCCA predicate offenses, even if the transactions were sales to the same victim or informant.").

[183] United States v. King, 853 F.3d 267, 279 (6th Cir. 2017); *Limney*, 819 F.3d at 751-52 (4th Cir. 2016); United States v. McCloud, 818 F.3d 591, 595-96 (11th Cir. 2016) (each citing Shepard v. United States, 544 U.S. 13 (2005)).

[184] United States v. Moody, 770 F.3d 577, 580 (7th Cir. 2014).

[185] Custis v. United States, 511 U.S. 485, 487 (1994) ("[A] defendant has no such right (with the sole exception of convictions obtained in violation of the right to counsel) to collaterally attack prior convictions."); Daniels v. United States, 532 U.S. 374, 378-82 (2001); United States v. Coleman, 655 F.3d 480, 485 (6th Cir. 2011); United States v. Greer, 607 F.3d 559, 565 (8th Cir. 2010); United States v. Dean, 604 F.3d 169, 174-75 (4th Cir. 2010); United States v. Covington, 565 F.3d 1336, 1345 (11th Cir. 2009); United States v. Buie, 547 F.3d 401, 403-404 (2d Cir. 2008); United States v. Krejcarek, 453 F.3d 1290, 1297 (10th Cir. 2006).

[186] 18 U.S.C. § 924(e)(2)(A) ("[T]he term 'serious drug offense' means - (i) an offense under the Controlled Substances Act (21 U.S.C. 801 et seq.), the Controlled Substances Import and Export Act (21 U.S.C. 951 et seq.), or chapter 705 of title 46, for which a maximum term of imprisonment of ten years or more is prescribed by law; or (ii) an offense under State law, involving manufacturing, distributing, or possessing with intent to manufacture or distribute, a controlled substance (as defined in section 102 of the Controlled Substances Act (21 U.S.C. 802)), for which a maximum term of imprisonment of ten years or more is prescribed by law.").

offenders qualifies, even though the maximum term for first-time offenders is five years.[187] It is the maximum permissible term which determines qualification, even when discretionary sentencing guidelines call for a term of less than 10 years,[188] or when the defendant was in fact sentenced to a lesser term of imprisonment.[189] To qualify as a predicate drug offense, the crime must have been at least a 10-year felony at the time of conviction for the predicate offense.[190]

The term "serious drug offense" includes attempts or conspiracies to commit a serious drug offense, as long as the attempt or conspiracy is punishable by imprisonment for 10 years or more.[191] By the same token, there is no need to prove that the defendant knew of the illicit nature of the controlled substance involved in his predicate serious drug offense if the serious drug offense satisfied the 10-year requirement and, in the case of state law predicate, involved the manufacture, distribution, or possession with intent to distribute a controlled substance.[192]

The Supreme Court in *Johnson v. United States* found unconstitutionally vague Section 924(e)'s violent felony residual clause ("the term 'violent felony' means any crime punishable by imprisonment for a term exceeding one year ... that ... involves conduct that presents a

---

[187] United States v. Rodriquez, 533 U.S. 377, 380 (2008). The record must make it clear, however, that the defendant was subject to any recidivist provision needed to reach the 10-year threshold, United States v. Lockett, 782 F.3d 349, 352-53 (7th Cir. 2015) ("Rodriquez requires the government to provide evidence from the record that the defendant was in fact subject to the enhanced recidivist penalties that could elevate his sentence past the ten-year mark.").

[188] United States v. Rodriquez, 533 U.S. at 390; United States v. Mayer, 560 F.3d 948, 963(9th Cir. 2009).

[189] United States v. Buie, 547 F.3d 401, 404 (2d Cir. 2008); United States v. Williams, 508 F.3d 724, 728 (4th Cir. 2007); United States v. Henton, 473 F.3d 467, 470 (7th Cir. 2004).

[190] McNeill v. United States, 563 U.S. 816, 817-18 (2011); United States v. Faust, 853 F.3d 39, 57 (1st Cir. 2017); United States v. Seabrooks, 839 F.3d 1326, 1347 (11th Cir. 2016); Rivera v. United States, 716 F.3d 685, 688-89 (2d Cir. 2013).

[191] United States v. Trent, 767 F.3d 1046, 1057 (10th Cir. 2014) (citing United States v. Bynum, 669 F.3d 880, 887 (8th Cir. 2012); United States v. Williams, 488 F.3d 1004, 1009 (D.C. Cir. 2007); and United States v. McKinney, 450 F.3d 39, 44 (1st Cir. 2006)).

[192] United States v. Smith, 775 F.3d 1262, 1266-67 (11th Cir. 2014).

serious potential risk of physical injury to another.").[193] The decision raises no question as to the validity of the mandatory minimum sentences imposed under the serious drug offense prong of Section 924(e).[194]

SAFETY VALVE

Low-level drug offenders can escape some of the mandatory minimum sentences for which they qualify under the safety valve found in 18 U.S.C. § 3553(f). Congress created the safety valve after it became concerned that the mandatory minimum sentencing provisions could have resulted in equally severe penalties for both the more and the less culpable offenders.[195] The safety valve is available to qualified offenders convicted of violations of the possession-with-intent, simple possession, attempt, or conspiracy provisions of the Controlled Substances or Controlled Substances Import and Export Acts.[196]

The safety valve is not available to avoid the mandatory minimum sentences that attend other offenses, even those closely related to the covered offenses. Section 860 (21 U.S.C. § 860), which outlaws violations of Section 841 near schools, playgrounds, or public housing facilities and sets the penalties for violation at twice what they would be under Section 841, is not covered. Those charged with a violation of Section 860 are not

---

[193] Johnson v. United States, 135 S. Ct. 2551, 2563 (2015) (construing 18 U.S.C. § 924(e)(2)(B)(ii)).

[194] *Cf. In re* Davis, 929 F.3d 1297, 1298 (11th Cir. 2016).

[195] H. R. REP. NO. 103-460, at 4 (1994); United States v. Carillo-Ayala, 713 F.3d 82, 88 (11th Cir. 2013).

[196] 18 U.S.C. § 3553(f) ("Notwithstanding any other provision of law, in the case of an offense under section 401, 404, or 406 of the Controlled Substances Act (21 U.S.C. 841, 844, 846) or section 1010 or 1013 of the Controlled Substances Import and Export Act (21 U.S.C. 960, 963), the court shall impose a sentence pursuant to guidelines promulgated by the United States Sentencing Commission under section 994 of title 28 without regard to any statutory minimum sentence, if the court finds at sentencing ... ").

eligible for relief under the safety valve provisions.[197] In addition, safety valve relief is not available to those convicted under the Maritime Drug Law Enforcement Act, even though the act proscribes conduct closely related to the smuggling and trafficking activities punished under Sections 960 and 963 (21 U.S.C. §§ 960, 963).[198]

For the convictions to which the safety valve does apply, the defendant must convince the sentencing court by a preponderance of the evidence that he satisfies each of the safety valve's five requirements.[199] He may not have more than one criminal history point.[200] He may not have used violence or a dangerous weapon in connection with the offense.[201] He may not have been an organizer or leader of the drug enterprise.[202] He must have provided the government with all the information and evidence at his disposal.[203] Finally, the offense may not have resulted in serious injury or death.[204]

---

[197] United States v. Phillips, 382 F.3d 489, 499-500 (5th Cir. 2004); United States v. Koons, 300 F.3d 985, 993 (8th Cir. 2002); United States v. Kakatin, 214 F.3d 1049, 1050-51 (9th Cir. 2000); United States v. Anderson, 200 F.3d 1344, 1346-348 (11th Cir. 2000); United States v. McQuilkin, 78 F.3d 105, 108 (3d Cir. 1996).

[198] United States v. Gamboa-Cardenas, 508 F.3d 491, 496-503 (9th Cir. 2007).

[199] United States v. Syms, 846 F.3d 230, 235 (7th Cir. 2017); United States v. Claxton, 766 F.3d 280, 305 (3d Cir. 2014); United States v. Schmitt, 765 F.3d 841, 842 (8th Cir. 2014); United States v. Rodriguez, 676 F.3d 183, 191 (D.C. Cir. 2012); United States v. Aidoo, 670 F.3d 600, 606-607 (4th Cir. 2012); United States v. Pena, 598 F.3d 289, 292 (6th Cir. 2010); United States v. Larios, 593 F.3d 82, 89 (1st Cir. 2010); United States v. Altamirano-Quintero, 511 F.3d 1087, 1098 (10th Cir. 2007); United States v. Mejia-Pimental, 477 F.3d 1100, 1104 (9th Cir. 2007).

[200] 18 U.S.C. § 3553(f)(1) ("[T]he defendant does not have more than 1 criminal history point, as determined under the sentencing guidelines.").

[201] *Id.* § 3553(f)(2) ("[T]he defendant did not use violence or credible threats of violence or possess a firearm or other dangerous weapon (or induce another participant to do so) in connection with the offense.").

[202] *Id.* § 3553(f)(4) ("[T]he defendant was not an organizer, leader, manager, or supervisor of others in the offense, as determined under the sentencing guidelines and was not engaged in a continuing criminal enterprise, as defined in section 408 of the Controlled Substances Act").

[203] *Id.* § 3553(f)(5) ("[N]ot later than the time of the sentencing hearing, the defendant has truthfully provided to the Government all information and evidence the defendant has concerning the offense or offenses that were part of the same course of conduct or of a common scheme or plan, but the fact that the defendant has no relevant or useful other information to provide or that the Government is already aware of the information shall not preclude a determination by the court that the defendant has complied with this requirement.").

[204] *Id.* § 3553(f)(3) ("[T]he offense did not result in death or serious bodily injury to any person.").

One Criminal History Point

More than one "criminal history point" is safety valve disqualifying.[205] The criminal history point qualification refers to the defendant's criminal record. The Sentencing Guidelines assign criminal history points based on a defendant's past criminal record. Two or more points are assigned for every prior sentence of imprisonment or juvenile confinement of 60 days or more, or for offenses committed while the defendant was in prison, was an escaped prisoner, or was on probation, parole, or supervised release.[206] A single point is assigned for every other federal or state prior sentence of conviction, subject to certain exceptions.[207]

Foreign sentences of imprisonment are not counted;[208] nor are sentences imposed by tribal courts;[209] nor summary court martial sentences;[210] nor sentences imposed for expunged, reversed, vacated, or invalidated convictions;[211] nor sentences for certain petty offenses or minor misdemeanors.[212] The Sentencing Guidelines list two classes of these minor misdemeanor or petty offenses that are not counted for criminal history purposes and thus for safety valve purposes. One class consists of eight types of minor offenses, like hunting and fishing violations or juvenile truancy that are not counted regardless of the sentence imposed.[213] The other class consists of arguably more serious offenses, such as gambling or prostitution, that are excused only if the offender was sentenced no more severely than to imprisonment for 30 days or less or to

---

[205] *Id.* § 3553(f)(2); United States v. Monzo, 852 F.3d 1343, 1351 (11th Cir. 2017).

[206] U.S.S.G. §§ 4A1.1(a), (b), (d); 4A1.2(d). United States v. Yepez, 704 F.3d 1087, 1089-90 (9th Cir. 2012) (a federal crime committed while the offender is on state probation is no less so because a state court subsequently terminates the probationary term as of the time it was originally ordered (*i.e.*, before the federal crime was committed)).

[207] U.S.C.G. §§ 4A1.1(c); 4A1.2.

[208] *Id.* § 4A1.2(h).

[209] *Id.* § 4A1.2(i).

[210] *Id.* § 4A1.2(g). Sentences imposed by general and special courts martial are counted, *id.*

[211] *Id.* §§ 4A1.2(j); 4A1.2, cmt. n.6.

[212] *Id.* § 4A1.2(c).

[213] The full list includes: "fish and game violations, hitchhiking, juvenile status offenses and truancy, local ordinance violations (except those violations that are also violations under state criminal law), loitering, minor traffic infractions (e.g., speeding), public intoxication, [and] vagrancy." *Id.* § 4A1.2(c)(2).

probation for less than a year.[214] Both classes also include similar offenses to those listed "by whatever name they are known."[215]

Only the Nonviolent

The safety valve has two disqualifications designed to reserve its benefits to the nonviolent. One involves instances in which the offense resulted in death or serious bodily injury. The other involves the use of violence, threats, or the possession of weapons. The weapon or threat of violence disqualification turns upon the defendant's conduct or the conduct of those he "aided or abetted, counseled, commanded, induced, procured, or willfully caused."[216] It is not triggered by the conduct of a co-conspirator unless the defendant "aided, abetted, [or] counsel ..." the co-

---

[214] Again, the full list consists of: "careless or reckless driving, contempt of court, disorderly conduct or disturbing the peace, driving without a license or with a revoked or suspended license, false information to a police officer, gambling, hindering or failure to obey a police officer, insufficient funds check, leaving the scene of an accident, non-support, prostitution, resisting arrest, [and] trespassing." *Id.* § 4A1.2(c)(1).

[215] *Id.* §§ 4A1.2(c)(1), (c)(2). The Sentencing Guidelines suggest a number of factors to assist in the determination of whether an unlisted offense may be consider "similar" for purposes of Section 4A1.2(c): " (i) a comparison of punishments imposed for the listed and unlisted offenses; (ii) the perceived seriousness of the offense as indicated by the level of punishment; (iii) the elements of the offense; (iv) the level of culpability involved; and (v) the degree to which the commission of the offense indicates a likelihood of recurring criminal conduct." *Id.* § 4A1.2, cmt. n.12(A). *See, e.g.*, United States v. Foote, 705 F.3d 305, 307-308 (8th Cir. 2013) (possession of small amount of marijuana punishable by a small fine is not a similar offense to a similarly fined traffic offense); United States v. Burge, 683 F.3d 829, (7th Cir. 2012) (abandonment of a llama in violation of state wildlife code is sufficient similar to fish and game violations); United States v. DeJesus-Concepcion, 607 F.3d 303, 305-306 (2d Cir. 2010) (third degree unauthorized use of a vehicle is not a similar offense to careless or reckless driving); United States v. Calderon Espinosa, 569 F.3d 1005, 1008 (9th Cir. 2009)(offense of loitering for drug activities is loitering "by whatever name it is known"); United States v. Russell, 564 F.3d 200, 206 (3d Cir. 2009) (misdemeanor marijuana possession is not similar to public intoxication); United States v. Pando, 545 F.3d 682, 684 (8th Cir. 2008) (driving while intoxicated is not similar to careless or reckless driving, citing U.S.S.G. § 4A1.2, cmt. n.5); United States v. McKenzie, 539 F.3d 15, 17-18 (1st Cir. 2008) (shoplifting is not similar to "insufficient funds check"); United States v. Garrett, 528 F.3d 525, 527-29 (7th Cir. 2008) (bail jumping is similar to contempt of court); United States v. Sanchez-Cortez, 530 F.3d 357, 359-60 (5th Cir. 2008) (military AWOL offense was not similar to truancy); United States v. Cole, 418 F.3d 592, 599-600 (6th Cir. 2005) (underage (over 18 but under 21) possession of alcohol was similar to a juvenile status offense).

[216] U.S.S.G. § 5C1.2, cmt., n.4.

conspirator's violence or possession.[217] Disqualifying firearm possession may be either actual or constructive.[218] Constructive possession is the dominion or control over a firearm or the place where one is located.[219] Disqualification requires that the threat of violence or possession of a firearm be "in connection with the offense,"[220] and may include threats against witnesses.[221] In many instances, possession of a firearm in a location where drugs are stored or transported, or where transactions occur, will be enough to support an inference of possession in connection with the drug offense of conviction.[222]

The Sentencing Guidelines define "serious bodily injury" for purposes of Section 3553(f)(3) as an "injury involving extreme physical pain or the protracted impairment of a function of a bodily member, organ, or mental faculty; or requiring medical intervention such as surgery, hospitalization, or physical rehabilitation."[223] On its face, the definition would include

---

217 United States v. Denis, 560 F.3d 872, 873 (8th Cir. 2009); United States v. Figueroa-Encarnacion, 343 F.3d 23, 34 (1st Cir. 2003); United States v. Sarabia, 297 F.3d 983, 989 (10th Cir. 2002).

218 United States v. Leanos, 827 F.3d 1167, 1170 (8th Cir. 2016); United States v. Jackson, 552 F.3d 908, 909-10 (8th Cir. 2009) (citing United States v. Matias, 465 F.3d 169, 173-74 (5th Cir. 2006); United States v. Herrera, 446 F.3d 283, 287 (2d Cir. 2006); United States v. McLean, 409 F.3d 492, 501 (1st Cir. 2005); United States v. Gomez, 431 F.3d 818, 820-22 (D.C. Cir. 2005); United States v. Stewart, 306 F.3d 295, 327 n.19 (6th Cir. 2002), but noting in apparent disagreement United States v. Zavalza-Rodriguez, 379 F.3d 1182, 1186-187 (10th Cir. 2004)).

219 United States v. Stewart, 306 F.3d 295, 326 (6th Cir. 2002).

220 18 U.S.C. 3553(f)(2). United States v. Sandoval-Sianuqui, 632 F.3d 438, 443 (8th Cir. 2011) (the disqualifying violence or threat of violence extends to efforts to avoid detection or conviction). *But see* United States v. CarilloAyala, 713 F.3d 82, 91 (11th Cir. 2013) ("At least one of our sister circuits appears to hold that imposition of the enhancement under [U.S.S.G] § 2D1.1(b)(1) [(enhancement under the drug conviction guideline for *possession* of a dangerous weapon without explicitly requiring that it be *possessed in connection* with the offense)] necessarily precludes safety valve relief ... See United States v. Ruiz, 621 F.3d 390, 397 (5th Cir. 2010).... We hold that not all defendants who receive the enhancement under § 2D1.1(b)(1) are precluded from relief under subsection (a)(2) of the safety valve. Where 'a firearm was possessed' by the defendant personally, and yet the defendant also seeks the protection of the safety valve, the district court must determine whether the facts of the case show that a 'connection' between the firearm and the offense, though possible, is not probable.").

221 United States v. Ortiz, 775 F.3d 964, 968-69 (7th Cir. 2015).

222 United States v. Carillo-Ayala, 713 F.3d at 92; United States v. Jackson, 552 F.3d 908, 910 (8th Cir. 2009); United States v. Stark, 499 F.3d 72, 80 (1st Cir. 2007); United States v. Stewart, 306 F.3d 295, 327 (6th Cir. 2002).

223 U.S.S.G. § 5C1.2, cmt. n.2; § 1B1.1, cmt. n.1(L).

serious bodily injuries, such as one that requires hospitalization, suffered by the defendant as a result of the offense.[224] Unlike the gun and violence disqualification in Section 3553(f)(2), the serious injury disqualification in Section 3553(f)(3) may be triggered by the conduct of a coconspirator.[225]

Only Single or Low Level Offenders

The Guidelines disqualify anyone who acted as a manager of the criminal enterprise or who receives a Guideline level increase for his aggravated role in the offense.[226] Thus, by implication, it does not disqualify a defendant to have received a Guideline decrease based on his minimal or minor participation in a group offense or a defendant who acted alone.[227]

Tell All

The most heavily litigated safety valve criterion requires full disclosure on the part of the defendant. The requirement extends not only to information concerning the crimes of conviction, but also to information concerning other crimes that "were part of the same course of conduct or of a common scheme or plan," including uncharged related conduct.[228]

---

[224] The Eleventh Circuit in a nonbinding opinion seems to have come to same conclusion. United States v. ValenciaVergara, 264 F.App'x. 832, 836 (11th Cir. 2008) ("The district court did not clearly err in denying Valencia-Vergara a reduction under the safety valve provisions. The evidence shows that both he and one of his codefendants sustained second and third degree burns on their bodies, for which they had to be treated at a hospital.").

[225] *Cf.* United States v. Grimmett, 150 F.3d 958, 960-61(8th Cir. 1998).

[226] U.S.S.G. §§ 5C1.2(a)(4), cmt. n.5; United States v. Syms, 846 F.3d 230, 235-36 (7th Cir. 2017); ("'Organizer ... supervisor of others in the offense, as determined under the sentencing guidelines' as used in subsection (a)(4), means a defendant who receives an adjustment for an aggravating role under § 3B1.1 (Aggravating Role*)"). E.g.,* United States v. Gonzalez-Mendoza, 584 F.3d 726, 729 (7th Cir. 2009); United States v. Bonilla-Filomeno, 579 F.3d 852, 858 (8th Cir. 2009); United States v. Nobari, 574 F.3d 1065, 1083-84 (9th Cir. 2009); United States v. Rendon, 354 F.3d 1320, 1333 (11th Cir. 2003).

[227] The Sentencing Guidelines recommend a sentencing increase for offenders who acted as organizers, leaders, managers, or supervisors of a criminal enterprise with multiple participants and a sentencing reduction for offenders who acted as minimal or minor participants in such an enterprise. U.S.S.G. §§ 3B1.1, 3B1.2.

[228] United States v. Ceballos, 605 F.3d 468, 472 (8th Cir. 2010); United States v. Altamirano-Quintero, 511 F.3d 1087, 1096 (10th Cir. 2007) (citing United States v. Montes, 381 F.3d

Neither Section 3553(f) nor the Sentencing Guidelines explains what form the defendant's full disclosure must take. At least one court has held that under rare circumstances disclosure through the defendant's testimony at trial may suffice.[229] The stipulation of facts in a plea bargain without more ordinarily will not qualify.[230] Most often, the defendant provides the information during an interview with prosecutors or by a proffer.[231] The defendant must disclose the information to the prosecutor, however. Disclosure to the probation officer during preparation of the presentence report is not sufficient.[232] Moreover, a defendant does not necessarily qualify for relief merely because he has proffered a statement and invited the prosecution to identify any additional information it seeks; for "the government is under no obligation to solicit information from a defendant."[233] A defendant's proffer must be "truthful."[234] On the other hand, past lies do not render a defendant ineligible for relief under the

---

631, 635-36 (7th Cir. 2004); United States v. Johnson, 375 F.3d 1300, 1302-303 (11th Cir. 2004); United States v. Salgado, 250 F.3d 438, 459 (6th Cir. 2001); United States v. Cruz, 156 F.3d 366, 371 (2d Cir. 1998); United States v. Miller, 151 F.3d 957, 958 (9th Cir. 1998); and United States v. Sabir, 117 F.3d 750, 753 (3d Cir. 1997)).

229 United States v. DeLaTorre, 599 F.3d 1198, 1206 (10th Cir. 2010); United States v. Delgrosso, 852 F.3d 821, 829 (8th Cir. 2017) (citing and contrasting United States v. Hinojosa, 728 F.3d 787, 790 (8th Cir. 2013) where the trial court granted safety valve relief for a defendant who argued ignorance of co-defendant's misconduct but admitted he unreasonably failed to take the steps to investigate).

230 *E.g.*, United States v. Cruz-Romero, 848 F.3d 399, 402 (5th Cir. 2017).

231 *E.g.*, United States v. Rebolledo-Delgadillo, 820 F.3d 870, 879 (7th Cir. 2016).

232 United States v. Cervantes, 519 F.3d 1254, 1257 (10thCir. 2008) ("In making this determination, we join the First, Second, Fourth, Fifth, Seventh, and Ninth Circuits in ruling that a probation officer is not the government for the purposes of the safety valve.") (citing United States v. Wood, 378 F.3d 342, 351 (4th Cir. 2004); Emezuo v. United States, 357 F.3d 703, 706 n.2 (7th Cir. 2004); United States v. Contreras, 136 F.3d 1245, 1246 (9th Cir. 1998); United States v. Jimenez Martinez, 83 F.3d 488, 495-66 (1st Cir. 1996); United States v. Rodriguez, 60 F.3d 193, 195-96 (5th Cir. 1995); and United States v. Smith, 174 F.3d 52, 56 (2d Cir. 1999)).

233 United States v. Milkintas, 470 F.3d. 1339, 1345 (11th Cir. 2006) (citing United States v. O'Dell, 247 F.3d 655, 675 (6th Cir. 2001); United States v. Ortiz, 136 F.3d 882, 884 (2d Cir. 1997); United States v. Flanagan, 80 F.3d 143, 146- 47 (5th Cir. 1996); and United States v. Ivester, 75 F.3d 182, 185-86 (4th Cir. 1996)); United States v. Cruz-Romero, 848 F.3d 399, 402 (5th Cir. 2017) (plea bargain fact stipulation standing alone is insufficient); United States v. Claxton, 766 F.3d 280, 306 (3d Cir. 2014) ("The mere fact that the investigators did not ask the 'right' questions for purposes of Claxton's safety valve claim did not relieve him of his burden under the safety valve provision.").

234 18 U.S.C. § 3553(f)(5); *Rebolledo-Delgadillo*, 820 F.3d at 879-80.

truthful disclosure criterion of the safety valve, although they may undermine his credibility.[235]

SUBSTANTIAL ASSISTANCE

> Upon motion of the Government, the court shall have the authority to impose a sentence below a level established by statute as a minimum sentence so as to reflect a defendant's substantial assistance in the investigation or prosecution of another person who has committed an offense. Such sentence shall be imposed in accordance with the guidelines and policy statements issued by the Sentencing Commission pursuant to section 994 of title 28, United States Code.[236]

The substantial assistance provision was enacted with little fanfare in the twilight of the 99th Congress as part of the wide-ranging Anti-Drug Abuse Act of 1986, legislation that established or increased a number of mandatory minimum sentencing provisions.[237] The section passed between

---

[235] United States v. Rodriguez, 676 F.3d 183, 190-91 (D.C. Cir. 2012) ("The provision does not distinguish between defendants who provide the authorities only with truthful information and those who provide false information before finally telling the truth."); United States v. Wu, 668 F.3d 882, 888 (7th Cir. 2011) ("Here, in contrast, the district court denied the reduction. It believed that Wu's credibility had been undermined by inconsistencies in his statements and his ultimate retraction."); United States v. Padilla-Colon, 578 F.3d 23, 31-2 (1st Cir. 2009) ("Inconsistencies between statements made during the proffer and statements made to the authorities on other occasions are not necessarily disqualifying. But the court may legitimately consider such inconsistencies in deciding on the truthfulness of the proffer."); United States v. Mejia-Pimental, 477 F.3d 1100, 1108 (9th Cir. 2007) ("The district court therefore erred, as a matter of law, in finding Mejia-Pimental ineligible for safety valve relief on the basis of the lies and delays that preceded his final proffer."); United States v. Jeffers, 329 F.3d 94, 99-100 (2d Cir. 2003) ("[A] sentencing court may not disqualify a defendant at the threshold from eligibility for safety valve relief based solely on his commission of perjury at trial, where the defendant otherwise fulfills the statutory criteria under 18 U.S.C. § 3553(f)(1)-(5). To do so would contradict the plain language of the statute and contravene the statutory deadline for full compliance with its criteria at the time of the commencement of the sentencing hearing. A court may, of course, consider the relevance of the prior perjury or other obstructive behavior in making a factual finding as to whether the defendant has made a complete and truthful proffer in compliance with 18 U.S.C. § 3553(f)(5).").

[236] 18 U.S.C. § 3553(e).

[237] Section 1007(a) of P.L. 99-570, 100 Stat. 32-07-7 (1986).

the date authorizing the Sentencing Guidelines and the date the Guidelines became effective. Rather than replicate the language of Section 3553(e), the Guidelines contain an overlapping section which authorizes a sentencing court to depart from the minimum sentence called for by the Guidelines.[238] A motion asking the court to sentence a defendant beneath the statutory mandatory minimum must be filed under Section 3553(e); a motion under Section 5K1.1 of the Guidelines alone is insufficient.[239] The government has at least a year to file its motion for substantial assistance.[240]

---

[238] U.S.S.G. § 5K1.1 ("Upon motion of the government stating that the defendant has provided substantial assistance in the investigation or prosecution of another person who has committed an offense, the court may depart from the guidelines. (a) The appropriate reduction shall be determined by the court for reasons stated that may include, but are not limited to, consideration of the following: (1) the court's evaluation of the significance and usefulness of the defendant's assistance, taking into consideration the government's evaluation of the assistance rendered; (2) the truthfulness, completeness, and reliability of any information or testimony provided by the defendant; (3) the nature and extent of the defendant's assistance; (4) any injury suffered, or any danger or risk of injury to the defendant or his family resulting from his assistance; (5) the timeliness of the defendant's assistance."); *see also* FED. R. CRIM. P. 35(b) (quoted below).

[239] Melendez v. United States, 518 U.S. 120, 123-24 (1996) ("[T]he Courts of Appeals disagree as to whether a Government motion attesting to the defendant's substantial assistance and requesting that the district court depart below the minimum of the applicable sentencing range under the Guidelines also permits the district court to depart below any statutory minimum ... We now hold that such a motion does not authorize a departure below a lower statutory minimum.").

[240] FED. R. CRIM. 35(b) (captions omitted) ("(1) Upon the government's motion made within one year of sentencing, the court may reduce a sentence if the defendant, after sentencing, provided substantial assistance in investigating or prosecuting another person. (2) Upon the government's motion made more than one year after sentencing, the court may reduce a sentence if the defendant's substantial assistance involved: (A) information not known to the defendant until one year or more after sentencing; (B) information provided by the defendant to the government within one year of sentencing, but which did not become useful to the government until more than one year after sentencing; or (C) information the usefulness of which could not reasonably have been anticipated by the defendant until more than one year after sentencing and which was promptly provided to the government after its usefulness was reasonably apparent to the defendant. (3) In evaluating whether the defendant has provided substantial assistance, the court may consider the defendant's presentence assistance. (4) When acting under Rule 35(b), the court may reduce the sentence to a level below the minimum sentence established by statute.").

Upon the Motion of the Government

As a general rule, a defendant is entitled to a sentence below an otherwise applicable statutory minimum under the provisions of § 3553(e) only if the government agrees.[241] The courts have acknowledged that due process, equal protection, or other constitutional guarantees may provide a narrow exception.[242] For instance, a defendant is entitled to relief if the government's refusal constitutes a breach of its plea agreement.[243] A defendant is also "entitled to relief if the prosecutor's refusal to move was not rationally related to any legitimate Government end."[244] Some courts have suggested that a defendant is entitled to relief if the prosecution refuses to move under circumstances that "shock the conscience of the court," or that demonstrate bad faith, or for reasons unrelated to substantial assistance.[245]

The court is under no obligation to grant the government's substantial assistance motion and the defendant is not entitled to be heard on the issue.[246]

---

[241] *Melendez*, 518 U.S. at 125-26 ("We believe that § 3553(e) requires a government motion requesting or authorizing the district court to impose a sentence below a level established by statute as a[a] minimum sentence before the court may impose such a sentence."); United States v. Massey, 663 F.3d 852, 860 (6th Cir. 2011).

[242] Wade v. United States, 504 U.S. 181, 185-86 (1992); United States v. Patton, 847 F.3d 883, 885 (7th Cir. 2017); United States v. Gomez, 705 F.3d 68, 79 (2d Cir. 2013).

[243] United States v. Doe, 741 F.3d 359, 362-63 (2d Cir. 2013); United States v. Barnes, 730 F.3d 456, 457 (4th Cir. 2013); United States v. Motley, 587 F.3d 1153, 1159 (D.C. Cir. 2009); United States v. Smith, 574 F.3d 521, 525 (8th Cir. 2009).

[244] *Wade*, 504 U.S. at 186; *Patton*, 847 F.3d at 885.

[245] United States v. Freemont, 513 F.3d 884, 889 (8th Cir. 2008) ("The district court may review the government's refusal to make a motion in limited circumstances. First, the district court may review the government's decision for an unconstitutional motive ... Second, a district court can compel a § 3553(e) motion if the government acknowledges the defendant provided substantial assistance, but refuses to make a motion expressly because the defendant engaged in unrelated misconduct – a reason unrelated to the quality of the defendant's assistance ... Third, the district court may be able to compel a motion if the government acted in bad faith by refusing to make a motion."); *but see* United States v. Perez, 526 F.3d 1135, 1138 (8th Cir. 2008) (citing cases evidencing a split within the circuit over whether bad faith provides a sufficient based to compel a government motion); United States v. Doe, 865 F.3d 1295 (10th Cir. 2017) (noting a split between the circuits and within the circuit on the question).

[246] United States v. McMahan, 872 F.3d 717, 719-21 (5th Cir. 2017) (declining to be guided by a contrary conclusion in United States v. Gangi, 45 F.3d 28 (2d Cir. 1995), announced before Rule 35(b) was amended).

To Reflect a Defendant's Substantial Assistance

Any sentence imposed below the statutory minimum by virtue of Section 3553(e) must be based on the extent of the defendant's assistance; it may not reflect considerations unrelated to such assistance.[247] It has been suggested that a court may use the factors found in Section 5K1.1 of the Sentencing Guidelines for that determination.[248] District courts appear to have some latitude as to the method used to calculate the reduction for substantial assistance e.g., "offense-level-based reductions, month-based reductions, and percentage-based reductions."[249]

The substantial assistance exception makes possible convictions that might otherwise be unattainable. Yet, it may also lead to "inverted sentencing," that is, a situation in which "the more serious the defendant's crimes, the lower the sentence – because the greater his wrongs, the more information and assistance he had to offer to a prosecutor"; while in

---

[247] United States v. Spinks, 770 F. 3d 285, 287 (4th Cir. 2014); United States v. Lee, 725 F.3d 1159, 1168 (9th Cir. 2013); United States v. Williams, 687 F.3d 283, 286 (6th Cir. 2012); United States v. Span, 682 F.3d 565, 566 (7th Cir. 2012); United States v. Winebarger, 664 F.3d 388, 392-93 (3d Cir. 2011) ("Congress's chosen language explicitly indicates that the reduction below the statutory minimum is to 'reflect' a defendant's assistance to the government in investigating and prosecuting other offenders. This language does not give a court carte blanche to sentence a defendant below a statutory minimum sentence based on non-assistance-related factors once it is established that the defendant provided assistance to the government"); United States v. Burns, 577 F.3d 887, 894 (8th Cir. 2009) (en banc) ("Where a court has authority to sentence below a statutory minimum only by virtue of a government motion under § 3553(e), the reduction below the statutory minimum must be based exclusively on assistance-related considerations"); United States v. Jackson, 577 F.3d 1032, 1036 (9th Cir. 2009); United States v. Hood, 556 F.3d 226, 234 n.2 (4th Cir. 2009) (citing United States v. Richardson, 521 F.3d 149, 159 (2d Cir. 2008) and United States v. Desselle, 450 F.3d 179, 182 (5th Cir. 2006)).

[248] United States v. Gabbard, 586 F.3d 1046, 1051 (6th Cir. 2009) (citing United States v. Richardson, 521 F.3d at 159). U.S.S.G. § 5K1.1(a) ("The appropriate reduction shall be determined by the court for reasons stated that may include, but are not limited to, consideration of the following: (1) the court's evaluation of the significance and usefulness of the defendant's assistance, taking into consideration the government's evaluation of the assistance rendered; (2) the truthfulness, completeness, and reliability of any information or testimony provided by the defendant; (3) the nature and extent of the defendant's assistance; (4) any injury suffered, or any danger or risk of injury to the defendant or his family resulting from his assistance; [and] (5) the timeliness of the defendant's assistance.").

[249] United States v. Marroquin-Medina, 817 F. 3d 1285, 1289 (11th Cir. 2016).

contrast the exception is of no avail to the peripheral offender who can provide far less substantial assistance.[250]

CONSTITUTIONAL CONSIDERATIONS

Defendants sentenced to mandatory minimum terms of imprisonment have challenged their sentences on a number of constitutional grounds beginning with Congress's legislative authority and ranging from cruel and unusual punishment through ex post facto and double jeopardy to equal protection and due process. Each constitutional provision defines outer boundaries that a mandatory minimum sentence and the substantive offense to which it is attached must be crafted to honor.

Legislative Authority

The federal government is a creature of the Constitution; it enjoys only such powers as can be traced to the Constitution.[251] Among the powers which the Constitution bestows upon Congress are the powers to define and punish felonies committed upon the high seas, to exercise exclusive legislative authority over certain federal territories and facilities, to make rules governing the Armed Forces, to regulate interstate and foreign commerce, and to enact legislation necessary and proper for the execution of those and Congress's other constitutionally granted powers.[252] It also grants Congress authority to enact legislation necessary and proper to the

---

[250] United States v. Brigham, 977 F.2d 317, 318 (7th Cir. 1992) ("Mandatory minimum penalties, combined with a power to grant exceptions, create a prospect of inverted sentencing. The more serious the defendant's crimes, the lower the sentence – because the greater is wrongs, the more information and assistance he has to offer to the prosecutor. Discounts for the top dogs have the virtue of necessity, because rewards for assistance are essential to the business of detecting and punishing crime. But what makes the post-discount sentencing structure topsy-turvy is the mandatory minimum, binding only for the hangers one.").

[251] U.S. CONST. amend. X.

[252] *Id.* art. I, § 8, cls.10, 17, 14, 3, and 18, respectively.

execution of those powers which it vests in any officer or department of the federal government.[253]

Many of the federal laws with mandatory minimum sentencing requirements were enacted pursuant to Congress's legislative authority over crimes occurring on the high seas or within federal enclaves,[254] or to its power to regulate commerce.[255] When a statute falls for want of legislative authority, the penalties it would impose fall with it. This has yet to occur in the area of mandatory minimum sentences relating to controlled substances.

Commerce Clause

"The Congress shall have Power ... To regulate Commerce with Foreign Nations, and among the several States, and with Indian Tribes."[256] This clause vests Congress with authority to regulate three broad categories of interstate commerce. In the words of *United States v. Lopez*, "[f]irst, Congress may regulate the use of the channels of interstate commerce.... Second, Congress is empowered to regulate and protect the instrumentalities of interstate commerce, or persons or things in interstate commerce, even though the threat may come only from intrastate activities.... Finally, Congress's commerce authority includes the power to regulate those activities having a substantial relation to interstate commerce."[257]

Applying these standards, the *Lopez* Court concluded that the Commerce Clause did not authorize Congress to enact a particular statute which purported to outlaw possession of a firearm on school property. Because the statute addressed neither the channels nor instrumentalities of interstate commerce, its survival turned upon whether it came within Congress's power to regulate activities that have a substantial impact on

---

[253] *Id.* art. I, § 8, cl.18; *see generally* United States v. Comstock, 560 U.S. 126 (2010).

[254] *E.g.,* 18 U.S.C. § 2241(a) ("Whoever, in the special maritime and territorial jurisdiction of the United States ... knowing causes another person to engage in a sexual act – (1) by using force against that other person ... shall be ... imprisoned for any term of years or life ... ").

[255] *E.g., Id.* § 2251(a), (e) ("(a) Any person ... who transports any minor in or affecting interstate or foreign commerce ... with the intent that such minor engage in any sexually explicit conduct for the purpose of producing any visual depiction of such conduct.... (e) Any individual who violates ... this section shall be ... imprisoned not less than 15 years.... ").

[256] U.S. CONST. art. I, § 8, cl. 3.

[257] United States v. Lopez, 514 U.S. 549, 558-59 (1995).

interstate commerce.[258] Here, the statute was found wanting. "[B]y its terms" it had "nothing to do with commerce or any sort of economic enterprise."[259] It "contain[ed] no jurisdictional element which would ensure, through case-by-case inquiry, that the firearm possession in question affect[ed] interstate commerce."[260] Its impact on commerce was so remote that to credit it would envision a virtually boundless power and one reserved to the states, the Court explained.[261]

A few years later, the Court in *United States v. Morrison*[262] reiterated "that Congress may [not] regulate noneconomic, violent criminal conduct based solely on that conduct's aggregate effect on interstate commerce. The Constitution requires a distinction between what is truly national and what is truly local."[263] Yet purely intrastate activities may have a sufficient impact on interstate commerce to bring them within the reach of Congress's Commerce Clause power. So it is in the case of the Controlled Substances Act. The Court concluded in *Gonzales v. Raich* that:

> Given the enforcement difficulties that attend distinguishing between marijuana cultivated locally and marijuana grown elsewhere and concerns about diversion into illicit channels, we have no difficulty concluding that Congress had a rational basis for believing that failure to regulate the intrastate manufacture and possession of marijuana would leave a gaping

---

[258] *Id.* at 559.
[259] *Id.* at 561.
[260] *Id.*
[261] *Id.* at 563-64 ("The Government argues that possession of a firearm in a school zone may result in violent crime and that violent crime can be expected to affect the functioning of the national economy in two ways. First, the costs of violent crime are substantial, and, through the mechanism of insurance, those costs are spread throughout the population. Second, violent crime reduces the willingness of individuals to travel to areas within the country that are perceived to be unsafe. The Government also argues that the presence of guns in schools poses a substantial threat to the educational process by threatening the learning environment. A handicapped educational process, in turn, will result in a less productive citizenry. That, in turn, would have an adverse effect on the Nation's economic well-being.... Thus, if we were to accept the Government's arguments, we are hard pressed to posit any activity by an individual that Congress is without power to regulate. "); *id.* at 567 ("To uphold the Government's contentions here, we would have to pile inference on inference in a manner that would bid fair to convert congressional authority under the Commerce Clause to a general police power of the sort retained by the States.").
[262] 529 U.S. 598 (2000).
[263] *Id.* 617-18.

> hole in the CSA [Controlled Substances Act]. Thus ... when it enacted comprehensive legislation to regulate the interstate market in a fungible commodity, Congress was acting well within its authority to 'make all Laws which shall be necessary and proper' to 'regulate Commerce ... among the several States.' That the regulation ensnares some purely intrastate activity is of no moment." [264]

Treaty Power

The Constitution grants the President authority to negotiate treaties and the Senate the authority to approve them in the exercise of its advice and consent prerogatives.[265] Almost a century ago, the Court observed that "[i]f the treaty is valid there can be no dispute about the validity of the statute under Article I, § 8, as a necessary and proper means to execute the powers of the Government."[266] The Controlled Substances Act might be considered implementation of various treaties of the United States relating to controlled substances.[267] In fact, the Controlled Substances Act begins with the congressional finding and declaration that "[t]he United States is a party to the Single Convention on Narcotic Drugs, 1961, and other international conventions designed to establish effective control over international and domestic traffic in controlled substances."[268] Congress was even more explicit in the Psychotropic Substances Act of 1978 when it declared, "[i]n implementing the Convention on Psychotropic Substances, the Congress intends that, consistent with the obligations of the United States under the Convention, control of psychotropic substances in the United States should be accomplished within the framework of the procedures and criteria for classification of substances provided in the Comprehensive Drug Abuse Prevention and Control Act of 1970."[269]

---

[264] 545 U.S. 1, 22 (2005) (internal citations omitted).

[265] U.S. CONST. art. II, § 2, cl. 2.

[266] Missouri v. Holland, 252 U.S. 416, 432 (1920).

[267] *E.g.*, SINGLE CONVENTION ON NARCOTIC DRUGS, Mar. 30, 1961, 18 U.S.T. 1407, 520 U.N.T.S. 204; CONVENTION ON PSYCHOTROPIC SUBSTANCES, Feb. 21, 1971, 32 U.S.T. 543, 1019 U.N.T.S. 175.

[268] 21 U.S.C. § 801(7).

[269] *Id.* § 801a(3). At least one court has held that extraterritorial application of the Controlled Substances Export and Import Act's prohibitions, and by implication its mandatory minimum penalties, constitute a permissible exercise of "Congress' treaty-making power

Territorial and Maritime Jurisdiction

The Constitution empowers Congress "to define and punish Piracies and Felonies committed on the high Seas, and Offenses against the Law of Nations."[270] The courts have held that the Maritime Drug Law Enforcement Act (MDLEA), which includes mandatory minimum sentencing requirements, constitutes a valid exercise of Congress's authority under the High Seas Felonies Clause.[271]

Necessary and Proper

"The Congress shall have Power ... To make all Laws which shall be necessary and proper for carrying into Execution the foregoing Powers, and all other Powers vested by this Constitution in the Government of the United States, or in any Department or Officer thereof."[272] It has never been thought that the Necessary and Proper Clause empowers only those laws that are absolutely necessary. Instead, "[l]et the end be legitimate, let it be within the scope of the constitution, and all means which are appropriate, which are plainly adapted to that end, which are not prohibited, but consist[ent] with the letter and spirit of the constitution, are constitutional."[273] Thus, the Necessary and Proper Clause makes possible those statutes that are rationally related to the implementation of another constitutional power.[274]

The Court in *United States v. Comstock* provided a hint of the scope of Necessary and Proper Clause.[275] The statute there authorized the Attorney General to continue to hold a federal inmate, pending a civil commitment

---

under the Necessary and Proper Clause." United States v. Lawrence, 727 F.3d 386, 397 (5th Cir. 2013).

270 U.S. CONST. art. I, § 8, cl. 10.

271 United States v. Hernandez, 864 F.3d 1292, 1303 (11th Cir. 2017) (citing United States v. Campbell, 743 F.3d 802, 809-12 (11th Cir. 2014)); United States v. Ballestas, 795 F.3d 138, 146-47 (D.C. Cir. 2015). The Eleventh Circuit had previous held, however, that the MDLEA rests beyond the reach of the *Law of Nations Clause*. United States v. Bellaizac-Hurtado, 700 F.3d 1245, 1253-58 (11th Cir. 2012).

272 U.S. CONST. art. I, § 8, cl. 18.

273 McCulloch v. Maryland, 4 Wheat. (17 U.S.) 316, 421 (1819).

274 Sabri v. United States, 541 U.S. 600, 605 (2004) ("*McCulloch v. Maryland* ... establish[es] review for means-ends rationality under the Necessary and Proper Clause.").

275 United States v. Comstock, 560 U.S. 126 (2010).

determination, after his scheduled date of release.[276] The Court analyzed the breadth of the power without any explicit reference to any other constitutional power, deciding that:

> [T]he statute is a "necessary and proper" means of exercising the federal authority that permits Congress to create federal criminal laws, to punish their violation, to imprison violators, to provide appropriately for those imprisoned, and to maintain the security of those who are not imprisoned but who may be affected by the imprisonment of others.[277]

Justice Scalia, in his *Raich* concurrence, saw the Necessary and Proper Clause as a necessary Commerce Clause supplement for legislation like the Controlled Substances Act that purports to regulate purely in-state activity.[278] Moreover, as noted above, at least one lower federal appellate court considers the Necessary and Proper Clause the implementing vehicle for enactment of the Maritime Drug Law Enforcement Act under Congress's treaty-making powers.[279]

Limits on Legislative Authority

The Constitution both grants and limits Congress's legislative authority. In the area of mandatory minimum sentences for controlled substance violations, the constitutional challenges have arisen largely under the Eighth Amendment's Cruel and Unusual Punishment Clause; the equal protection element of the Fifth Amendment; the Fifth and Sixth Amendment components awakened by *Apprendi v. New Jersey* and its progeny; and the separation-of- powers doctrine.

---

[276] 18 U.S.C. § 4248.

[277] *Comstock*, 560 U.S. at 149.

[278] Gonzales v. Raich, 545 U.S. 1, 34 (Scalia, J., concurring in the judgment) ("Congress's regulatory authority over intrastate activities that are not themselves part of interstate commerce (including activities that have a substantial effect on interstate commerce) derives from the Necessary and Proper Clause.").

[279] United States v. Lawrence, 727 F.3d 386, 397 (5th Cir. 2013).

Cruel and Unusual Punishment

Mandatory minimums implicate considerations under the Eighth Amendment's Cruel and Unusual Punishment Clause.[280] The clause bars mandatory capital punishment statutes[281] and mandatory imposition on a juvenile of life imprisonment without the possibility of parole.[282] Although the case law is somewhat uncertain, it seems to condemn punishment that is "grossly disproportionate" to the misconduct for which it is imposed,[283] a standard which a sentence imposed under a mandatory minimum statute might breach only under extreme circumstances.

The Supreme Court decision in *Harmelin v. Michigan*[284] seems to make a defendant's Eighth Amendment arguments in a controlled substances case more difficult. The defendant in *Harmelin* was a first-time offender convicted of possession of 672 grams of cocaine, enough for possibly as many as 65,000 individual doses. Under the laws of the State of Michigan, the conviction carried with it a mandatory sentence of life imprisonment without the possibility of parole. The Court splintered over the question of whether Harmelin's mandatory sentence offended the Eighth Amendment because it was grossly disproportionate to his offense.

Five members of the Court concluded that it did not. Two members, Justice Scalia and Chief Justice Rehnquist, simply refused to recognize an Eighth Amendment proportionality requirement, at least in noncapital cases.[285] Justices Kennedy, O'Connor, and Souter concluded the Eighth Amendment does in fact forbid "extreme sentences that are grossly

---

[280] The Eighth Amendment to the United States Constitution states in its entirety, "[e]xcessive bail shall not be required, nor excessive fines imposed, nor cruel and unusual punishments inflicted."

[281] Woodson v. North Carolina, 428 U.S. 280, 305-306 (1976).

[282] Miller v. Alabama, 567 U.S. 460, 489 (2012). Virtual all contemporary convictions for federal offenses are convictions without the possibility of parole, because Congress abolished parole in the case of federal crimes over three decades ago. Section 212(a), P.L. 98-473, 98 Stat. 1987 (1984).

[283] Ewing v. California, 538 U.S. 11, 31-32 (2003).

[284] 501 U.S. 957 (1991).

[285] *Id.* at 994 (Scalia, J., with Rehnquist, Ch.J.) (citations omitted) ("Proportionality review is one of several respects in which we have held that 'death is different', and have imposed protections that the Constitution nowhere else provides. We would leave it there, but will not extend it further.").

disproportionate to the crime."[286] They explained, however, that Harmelin's sentence was not grossly disproportionate to the severity of his crime – that is, a crime whose "pernicious effects ... demonstrate that the ... legislature could with reason conclude that the threat posed to the individual and society by possession of this large an amount of cocaine—in terms of violence, crime, and social displacement—is momentous enough to warrant the deterrence and retribution of a life sentence without parole."[287]

Decisions of the lower federal courts seem to confirm that the Eighth Amendment precludes a mandatory term of imprisonment in drug trafficking cases only in those exceptionally rare cases when the punishment is grossly disproportionate to the offense.[288]

---

[286] *Id.* at 1001 (Kennedy, J., with O'Connor & Souter, JJ., concurring in part and concurring the judgment).

[287] *Id.* at 1003.

[288] *See, e.g.*, United States v. Syms, 846 F.3d 230, 236 (7th Cir. 2017) (151-month sentence for conspiracy to distribute cocaine) (citations omitted) ("Only extreme sentences that are 'grossly disproportionate' to the crime will be deemed cruel and unusual. Additionally, 'eighth amendment challenges to sentences that are both prescribed by the [sentencing] guidelines, and within the statutory maximums established by Congress, are not looked on with disfavor.'"); United States v. Camberos-Villapuda, 832 F.3d 948, 953 (8th Cir. 2016) ("This court has ruled on numerous occasions that the imposition of a mandatory life sentence under that statute [21 U.S.C. § 841(b)(1)(A)] does not violate the Eighth Amendment's prohibition on cruel and unusual punishment."); United States v. Law, 806 F.3d1103, 1107 (D.C. Cir. 2015) (quoting Miller v. Alabama, 567 U.S. 460, 481 (2012)) ("Law also contends ... that the life sentence the court imposed ... violates the Eight Amendment because it constitutes cruel and unusual punishment. This contention is foreclosed by precedent. The Supreme Court rejected it in *Harmelin v. Michigan* ... In its recent opinion in *Miller v. Alabama*, the Supreme Court left *Harmelin* undisturbed ... '[L]ife without parole is permissible for nonhomicide offenses – except ... for children ... Our reading thus neither overrules nor undermines nor conflicts with *Harmelin*.'"); United States v. Flores-Alvarado, 779 F.3d 250, 257 n.3 (4th Cir. 2015) (life sentence for recidivist trafficker); United States v. Gay, 771 F.3d 681, 686-87 (10th Cir. 2014) (262-month sentence for crack trafficker) (citing *Harmelin*); United States v. Adams, 768 F.3d 219, 224-25 (2d Cir. 2014) (210-month sentence for marijuana trafficker) ("Lengthy prison sentences, moreover, even those that exceed any conceivable life expectancy of a convicted defendant, do not violate the Eighth Amendment's prohibition against cruel and unusual punishment when based on a proper application of the Sentencing Guidelines or statutory mandated consecutive terms. We have also recognized that in a noncapital case it is exceedingly rare to uphold a claim that a sentence within the statutory limits is disproportionately severe.").

Equal Protection

The Equal Protection Clause of the Fourteenth Amendment condemns statutory classifications invidiously based on race, or constitutionally suspect factors. Moreover, "[d]iscrimination on the basis of race odious in all aspects is especially pernicious in the administration of justice."[289] These prohibitions apply with equal force under the equal protection component of the Fifth Amendment's Due Process Clause.[290] An explicit racial classification scheme can survive only under the most exceptional circumstances.[291] A statute, racially neutral on its face but discriminatory in its impact, cannot survive if racially motivated.[292] The circumstances surrounding the passage of a legislative measure with discriminatory impact may provide evidence of improper racial motivation.[293]

At one time, possession with intent to distribute crack cocaine (cocaine base) was punished 100 times more severely than possession with intent to distribute cocaine in powdered form.[294] Defendants claimed the distinction had a racially disparate impact. The claim was almost universally rejected.[295]

---

[289] *Pena-Rodriquez*, 137 S. Ct. 855, 868 (2017).

[290] Buckley v. Valeo, 424 U.S. 1, 93 (1976).

[291] Personnel Administrator v. Feeney, 442 U.S. 256, 272 (1979).

[292] Arlington Heights v. Metropolitan Housing Corp., 429 U.S. 252, 264-66 (1977).

[293] *Id.* at 267-68.

[294] At one time, for example, the same mandatory minimum sentence applied to 5000 grams of powder cocaine as applied to 50 grams of crack cocaine. 21 U.S.C. § 841(b)(1)(A) (2006 ed.).

[295] *E.g.*, United States v. Dumas, 64 F.3d 1427, 1429 (9th Cir. 1995) (citing United States v. Harding, 971 F.2d 410 (9th Cir. 1992)) ("We have previously considered and rejected 'as enacted' equal protection challenges to 21 U.S.C. § 841(b) and USSG § 2D1.1... [W]e refused to apply a strict level of scrutiny to the sentencing distinction between crack and powder cocaine. We noted that, on its fact, section 841(b) implicates neither a suspect class nor a fundamental right. Therefore, we reviewed the distinction only under the rational basis test, the lowest level of scrutiny applicable to equal protection challenges. We held that the crack/powder cocaine distinction survived rationality review because, although crack and powder cocaine are different forms of the same drug, Congress reasonably could have considered that crack's differing physiological and psychological effects, and its greater marketability, made crack a greater societal problem meriting more severe punishment."); United States v. Fenner, 600 F.3d 1014, 1024-25 (8th Cir. 2010); United States v. Wimbley, 553 F.3d 455, 463 (6th Cir. 2009); United States v. Eirby, 262 F.3d 31, 41 (1st Cir. 2001); United States v . Matthews, 168 F.3d 1234, 1250-51 (11th Cir. 1999); United States v. Holton, 116 F.3d 1536, 1548 (D.C. Cir. 1997); United States v. Perkins, 108 F.3d 512, 518 (4th Cir. 1997); United States v. Teague, 93 F.3d 81, 84-5 (2d Cir. 1996); United States v. Reddrick, 90 F.3d 1276, 1282 (7th Cir. 1996); United States v.

Juries, Grand Juries, and Due Process

The Constitution demands that no person "be held to answer for a capital or otherwise infamous crime, unless on a presentment or indictment of a grand jury" and that "[i]n all criminal prosecutions, the accused shall enjoy the right to a speedy and public trial, by an impartial jury."[296] Moreover the Supreme Court's In re Winship decision explained that due process requires that the prosecution prove beyond a reasonable doubt "every fact necessary to constitute the crime" with which an accused is charged.[297] After Winship, the question arose whether a statute might authorize or require a more severe penalty for a particular crime based on a fact— not included in the indictment, not found by the jury, and not proven beyond a reasonable doubt. Pennsylvania passed a law under which various serious crimes (rape, robbery, kidnapping, and the like) were subject to a mandatory minimum penalty of imprisonment for five years, if the judge after conviction found by a preponderance of the evidence that the defendant had been in visible possession of a firearm during the commission of the offense.[298] Had the Pennsylvania statute created a new series of crimes? For example, had it supplemented its crime of rape with a new crime of rape while in visible possession of a firearm? And if so, did the fact of visible possession have to be proven to the jury beyond a reasonable doubt?[299]

The Supreme Court concluded that visible possession of a firearm under the statute was not an element of a new series of crimes, but was instead a sentencing consideration that had been given a legislatively

---

McKinney, 53 F.3d 664, 678 (5th Cir. 1995); United States v. Williamson, 1500, 1503 (10th Cir. 1995); United States v. Frazier, 981 F.3d 92, 95 (3d Cir. 1992); *contra* United States v. Clary, 846 F. Supp. 768, 796-97 (E.D. Mo. 1994) (holding that the 100 to 1 sentencing ratio found in the 21 U.S.C. § 841(b) and the implementing U.S. Sentencing Commission Sentencing Guidelines constitute a violation of the Constitution's equal protection guarantees), rev'd, 34 F.3d 710 (8th Cir. 1994).

296 U.S. CONST. amends. V, VI.

297 *In re* Winship, 397 U.S. 358, 364 (1970).

298 42 Pa.Cons.Stat. 9712 (1982), reprinted in McMillan v. Pennsylvania, 477 U.S. 79, 81-2 n.1 (1986).

299 The right to grand jury indictment was not implicated since the Sixth Amendment right to grand jury indictment applies only to federal prosecutions, Alexander v. Louisiana, 405 U.S. 625, 633 (1972).

prescribed weight.[300] As such, the Pennsylvania statutory scheme neither offended due process nor triggered any right to a separate jury finding.[301]

There followed a number of state and federal statutes under which facts that might earlier have been treated as elements of a new crime were simply classified as sentencing factors. In some instances, the new sentencing factor permitted imposition of a penalty far in excess of that otherwise available for the underlying offense. For instance, the Supreme Court found no constitutional defect in a statute which punished a deported alien for returning to the United States by imprisonment for not more than 2 years, but which permitted the alien to be sentenced to imprisonment for not more than 20 years upon a post-trial, judicial determination that the alien had been convicted of a serious crime following deportation.[302]

Perhaps uneasy with the implications, the Court soon made it clear in *Apprendi* that, "under the Due Process Clause of the Fifth Amendment and the notice and jury trial guarantees of the Sixth Amendment, any fact (other than prior conviction) that increases the *maximum* penalty for a crime must be charged in an indictment, submitted to a jury, and proven beyond a reasonable doubt."[303] Side opinions questioned the continued vitality of *McMillan*'s mandatory minimum determination in light of the *Apprendi*.[304]

Initially unwilling to extend *Apprendi* to mandatory minimums in *Harris v. United States*,[305] the Court did so in *Alleyne v. United States*.[306]

---

300 McMillan v. Pennsylvania, 477 U.S. 79 (1986).

301 *Id.* at 84, 93.

302 Almendarez-Torres v. United States, 523 U.S. 224, 247 (1998).

303 Apprendi v. New Jersey, 530 U.S. 466, 476 (2000) (emphasis added).

304 "Thus, the Court appears to hold that any fact that increases or alters the range of penalties to which a defendant is exposed – which, by definition, must include increases or alterations to either the minimum or maximum penalties – must be proved to a jury beyond a reasonable doubt. In *McMillan*, however, we rejected such a rule to the extent it concerned those facts that increase or alter the minimum penalty to which a defendant is exposed. Accordingly, it is incumbent on the Court not only to admit that it is overruling *McMillan*, but also to explain why such a course of action is appropriate under normal principles of *stare decisis*." *Id.* at 533 (O'Connor, with Kennedy, Breyer, JJ., and Rehnquist, Ch.J., dissenting) (referring to *McMillan v. Pennsylvania*, 477 U.S. 79 (1986). *See also id.* at 518, 521-22 (Thomas, J., concurring); *Rethinking Mandatory Minimums After Apprendi*, 96 NW. U. L. REV. 811 (2002); Levine, *The Confounding Boundaries of "Apprendi-land": Statutory Minimums and the Federal Sentencing Guidelines*, 29 AMER. J. CRIM. L. 377 (2002).

305 Harris v. United States, 536 U.S. 545, 568 (2002).

Alleyne was convicted under the statute that imposes a series of mandatory minimum penalties upon defendants who carry a firearm during and in furtherance of a crime of violence (5 years for carrying; 7 years for brandishing; 10 years for discharging).[307] The jury found him guilty of carrying; the trial court judge concluded the gun had been brandished.[308] The Sixth Amendment requires that the question of brandishing had to be found by the jury, the Court declared:

> *Harris* drew a distinction between facts that increase the statutory maximum and facts that increase only the mandatory minimum. We conclude that this distinction is inconsistent with our decision in *Apprendi* and with the original meaning of the Sixth Amendment. Any fact that, by law, increases the penalty for a crime is an element that must be submitted to the jury and found beyond a reasonable doubt. Mandatory minimum sentences increase the penalty for a crime. It follows, then, that any fact that increases the mandatory minimum is an element that must be submitted to the jury.[309]

Neither *Apprendi* nor *Alleyne* limits Congress's authority to establish mandatory minimum sentences or limits the authority of the courts to impose them. They simply dictate the procedural safeguards that must accompany the exercise of that authority. Thus, the lower federal appellate courts have held that the neither the Fifth nor Sixth Amendment requires that "facts that determine whether a defendant is eligible under the safety valve for a sentence below the statutory minimum" need be found by the jury beyond a reasonable doubt.[310]

---

[306] 133 S. Ct. 2151 (2013).

[307] 18 U.S.C. § 924(c).

[308] *Alleyne*, 133 S. Ct. at 2156.

[309] *Id.* at 2155.

[310] United States v. Leanos, 827 F.3d 1167, 1169-70 (8th Cir. 2016) (citing United States v. King, 773 F.3d 48, 55 (5th Cir. 2014); United States v. Lizarraga-Carrizales, 757 F.3d 955, 997-99 (9th Cir. 2014); and United States v. Harakaly, 734 F.3d 88, 97 (1st Cir. 2013)).

Separation of Powers

While "it remains a basic principle of our constitutional scheme that one branch of the Government may not intrude upon the central prerogatives of another,"[311] the Supreme Court has observed that "Congress has the power to define criminal punishments without giving the courts any sentencing discretion."[312] Thus, the lower federal courts have regularly upheld mandatory minimum statutes when challenged on separation-of-powers grounds,[313] and the Supreme Court has denied any separation-of-powers infirmity in the federal sentencing guideline system, which at the time might have been thought to produce its own form of mandatory minimums.[314]

---

[311] Loving v. United States, 517 U.S. 748, 757 (1996).

[312] United States v. Chapman, 500 U.S. 453, 467 (1991).

[313] United States v. Carpenter, 819 F.3d 880, 892 (6th Cir. 2016); United States v. Major, 676 F.3d 803, 811 (9th Cir. 2012); United States v. Nigg, 667 F.3d 929, 934-35 (7th Cir. 2012); United States v. Page, 604 F.3d 1268, 1274 (11th Cir. 2010); United States v. Walker, 473 F.3d 71,76 (3d Cir. 2007); United States v. Rasco, 123 F.3d 222, 226-27 (5th Cir. 1997); United States v. Prior, 107 F.3d 654, 660 (8th Cir. 1997).

[314] Mistretta v. United States, 488 U.S. 361 (1989). Mistretta, sentenced under the guidelines to 18 months' imprisonment for conspiracy to distribute cocaine, argued that the guidelines constituted an unconstitutional delegation of Congress's legislative authority and that the service of judges upon the Commission constituted extrajudicial service at odds with the separation of powers doctrine. The Court rejected both arguments concluding "that in creating the Sentencing Commission ... Congress neither delegated excessive legislative power nor upset the constitutionally mandated balance of powers among the coordinate Branches," *Id.* at 412.

INDEX

D

G

H

I

J

K

L

O

P

R

S

T

U

V

W

Y